THE INDIAN CONCEPT OF VALUES

The Indian Concept of Values

Shanti Nath Gupta

MANOHAR
1978

First Published 1978

Published by
Ramesh C. Jain
for Manohar Book Service
2 Ansari Road, Darya Ganj
New Delhi-110002

Composed by
Sunil Composing Co.
C-241, Mayapuri Phase II,
New Delhi-110064

Printed at
Ruby Offset Works
C-241, Mayapuri Phase II,
New Delhi-110064

The biological are only the ontological presupposition of the spiritual, that is to say, their actuality is a condition for the realization of the latter. . . . But their value-quality is not a material condition for spiritual qualities. . . . Between the two, there is a relation of *conditio sine qua non.* But as regards the former, the condition is merely external and ontological and for the latter, the condition is a structural, an internally axiological organic relation of value-entities as such.

Nicolai Hartmann

Preface

Ancient Indian thought, which has come down to us through the centuries of its development in the form of a cultural heritage, has always been the source of inspiration. Eminent writers like S.N. Dasgupta, S. Radhakrishnan, P.T. Raju and others have systematically endeavoured to interpret and communicate the spirit of Indian philosophical tradition to the Western world. On account of its unique spiritualistic cultural pattern it holds a special charm for scholars who try to bring it within the focus of the scientific tradition of the West. A new branch of philosophical thinking—comparative philosophy—has been developed to make intelligible the concepts and methods of both parts of the world to each other.

Particular systems and sections of Indian philosophy have been subjected to careful research and critical study by scholars from various angles, but there has hardly been any attempt to study value in its comparative significance. The concept of value is important, not only because it is one of the leading trends of recent philosophical thinking, but also because it forms the basis of the cultural pattern of a nation. Intensive empirical research in some values or their aspects is available in the form of books and monographs, but the uniqueness of the Indian way of life and its spiritualistic outlook as a part of a philosophical heritage cannot be brought to light clearly unless the entire system of values in Indian thought is studied sensitively. That alone would reveal the integral unity of the various values of life and the true rationale behind the whole scheme.

It seems to be both interesting and worthwhile to note that Indian genius has been keenly conscious of the economic, political, hedonistic and moral values of life besides the spiritual and religious values which dominate the entire cultural scheme.

The traditional concept of the trinity of values (trivarga) points to the non-spiritual values of life while the spiritual end of human life as the fourth value has always been presupposed and foregone. Hence, the fourfold-value concept (catuṣpuruṣārtha) consisting of artha as the politico-economic values, kāma as the hedonistic values, dharma as the moral values and mokṣa as the religious and spiritual goal of life, precisely and neatly represents the Indian concept of values in its true and comprehensive character.

These four values are found to form the basis of the division of ancient philosophical literature on values in Sanskrit, because each particular value of life has been treated as a separate field of investigation and constitutes the thematic essence of a special branch of literature. The phenomenon of value and valuation takes place in almost every field of human life and activity, and in studies of the various sciences like economics, political science, ethics, psychology, aesthetics, religion and metaphysics. They not only enrich the philosophical concept of value but also constitute its significance.

The uniqueness of the Indian concept of values lies in the fact that the material and mental values have been integrated with moral and spiritual values of life, so that each value has been accorded its respective place in a system in which an exact scale of values had been visualized and a transition from the non-spiritual to the spiritual values is sought to be established. Hence, it is of central importance to investigate, with regard to the Indian concept of values, how certain values are preferred to others and what the principle of such gradation is.

It is maintained that Indian thought has been working towards demonstrating a philosophical monism of values by postulating a supreme value in the form of a spiritualistic end of life (liberation). It is, therefore, believed that in view of Mokṣa as the highest and most supreme value, other values of life including moral values pale into insignificance; values are distinguished as higher and lower, and lower values are condemned in face of the higher. As a result of this interpretation, artha and kāma are condemned as stumbling block in the way of spiritual regeneration. This may be due to a misunderstanding of the proper value-perspective implied in the Indian concept of values. At a superficial glance it seems to favour repudiation of the lower and the baser, but a closer examination reveals how difficult it is to believe in it.

The present work is an attempt to demonstrate that Indian thinkers have been working upon a system of values in which all values, higher or lower, are values in their own right—they are absolute, independent and underivable and as such are autonomous; the higher is higher axiologically, but depends upon the lower for its ontological basis and the lower is independent of the higher only ontologically but derives its axiological significance from the higher. Thus artha, kāma, dharma and mokṣa are distinct and underivable. They form a system or group which as a whole provides the value-perspective for the proper ordering of human life. Values like artha and kāma refuse to be derived from mokṣa; so there is, in fact, a pluralism of values which is not inconsistent with the concept of a system of values. As a matter of fact, only independent and underivable values can form a real system; but if values can be derived from one supreme value, there is a monism of values, not a system, which points to the fact of harmony and gradation of values. The faith in transcendental values does not clash with values of empirical existence; for mokṣa is a matter of realization which can be achieved in this very life. Śaṅkara's conception of Brahma-realization in this life (jīvan-mukti) and Buddhistic ideal of Bodhisattva is a reflection of this view.

The fact of value preference and the problem of value-gradation are the most important questions which modern theory of value has to face, for unless the otherwise universal, absolute, independent and autonomous values are systematized into a coordinated picture, a philosophy of values will not be in a position to provide human race with a comprehensive and correct value-perspective, which is essential for a balanced growth and progress of humanity. The present study may, it is hoped, prove quite helpful in this regard in as much as Indian concept of values, which epitomizes and blends both material and moral, mental and spiritual values to form a unified perspective, indicates the manner and direction in which the contemporary civilization may have to solve its problems.

I am fully aware of the magnitude of the difficulties which beset this task. First, the study of the Indian concept of values means going through the entire gamut of ancient Indian thought which is surely enormous and unwieldy. The responsibility for the necessary condensation becomes more onerous. The study, therefore, is confined to the five fundamental concepts, viz., artha, kāma, dharma, mokṣa and Brahman which have been found to be quite exhaustive of the Indian concept of values. Secondly, the problem of value-gradation has been of crucial importance for various thinkers of value. I have, therefore, concentrated on it with a view to approaching the subject from a precise angle. The study of this problem will not only give us a deep insight into the Indian way of thinking about various values, but also help to bring to light the true character and import of each value. It is proposed to study select authors and representative texts in order to make this task more precise. Lastly, the study of various values will have to be conducted in all those specialized fields in which they occur, and the diversity of the subject-matter of such fields poses a serious difficulty here. The study will have to be confined to the universal and philosophical aspects of various values, leaving out those details and aspects which have no philosophical significance. It is not difficult to sift the relevant from the irrelevant. The study has been reinforced throughout by making some important and necessary comparisons with similar ideas of other Indian and Western thinkers before arriving at final observations.

I take this opportunity to pay a tribute of deep and heartfelt gratitude to Dr. N.S.S. Raman, Reader in Philosophy, Panjab University, Chandigarh, under whose able guidance the present project is completed. He has been a source of inspiration for me from the beginning till the end of this work and his clear judgment, mature understanding and critical sense have been my unfailing help in almost all that I have written in this thesis. I am also indebted to Mr. S.P. Kanal, formerly Reader in Philosophy, University of Delhi, for his guidance. I owe a deep debt of gratitude to Dr. P.T. Raju who has been a source of inspiration to me through his scholarly writings and original ideas enshrined in them.

Thanks are due to late Prof. Prem Nath, head of the Department of Philosophy, Panjab University, Chandigarh, for giving me facilities to work.

Bhatinda
2 October 1977

S.N. Gupta

List of Abbreviations

AS. : *Arthaśāstra* of Kautilya

BG. : *Bhagavad-Gītā*

KS. : *Kāmasūtra* of Vātsyāyana

MS. : *Manusmṛti*

RB. : Rāmānuja-Bhāṣya on the *Brahma-sūtra*

SB. : *Śaṅkara-Bhāṣya* on the *Brahma-sūtra*

SK. : *Sāṅkhya-Kārikā* of Īsvarakṛṣṇa

Contents

CHAPTER ONE

Introduction

What is unique and fundamental about the cultural pattern which intrinsically represents the characteristic outlook and way of Indian people, is the Indian concept of values and the manner in which values of life should be ordered to forge a unity of purpose. It is undoubtedly spiritualistic in so far as it allows a marked precedence of spiritual values over material and hedonistic values, but it, nevertheless, provides a comprehensive perspective in which an entire spectrum of values ranging from socio-economic and hedonistic to moral, religious and spiritual has been revealed.

The Indian concept of values is represented in the concept of fourfold aim of human life (catuṣpuruṣārtha) which consists of politico-economic values (artha), hedonistic values (kāma), moral values (dharma) and religio-spiritual values (mokṣa). The traditional triumvirate of values (trivarga) refers to the threefold aim of human life consisting of dharma, artha and kāma, which are considered to be mundane and empirical; it presupposes mokṣa as the fourth and transcendental ideal of human life. The special consideration for mokṣa not only dominates the philosophical activity in India, but also prepares a ground for a conception of the absolute value in the form of the absolute reality (Brahman) at the hands of the vedāntins. Thus, the five concepts of dharma, artha, kāma, mokṣa and Brahman form the bases of the Indian concept of values. These five concepts also provide the basis of the division of ancient philosophical literature in Sanskrit, because each concept refers to a particular value which constitutes the thematic import of a particular branch of study called Śāstra and also becomes its motive-force. Thus, the division of literature into arthaśāstras, kāmaśāstras, dharmaśāstras, mokṣaśāstras and brahmanśāstras is valid on the five concepts of values.

The tendency to make each concept as the sole object of philosophical study and to confine it within the bounds of a particular field alone which seems to be a result of simple division of labour, has consciously and unconsciously led to two problems. Firstly, the Indian thinkers who found themselves preoccupied with the study of a particular value, not only neglected other values thus distorting the true value-perspective implied in the Indian concept of values, but also failed to develop a systematic theory of value as such, and as a result of this there was a woeful lack of a proper and intensive enquiry into the nature, problem and definition of value in general in Indian philosophy with the exceptions of Mīmāṁsā-Sūtras and Vedānta-Paribhāṣā wherein after an initial attempt to define the fundamental notion of value, the subject is lifted up into a discussion of scriptural text or metaphysical issues which has hardly anything to do with it. Thus, the Indian genius has failed to isolate the abstract and philosophical aspect of the problem of value from its concrete and specific setting of human values as such.

Secondly, the process of compartmentalization of the subject-matter of specific values culminates in the tendency to view all values from the point of view of a particular value which is erroneously conceived to provide in itself a wholesome aim of human life. Thus four values look like four different cultures. This has resulted in a lop-sided development of the value-theory and a distortion of the original conception implied in Indian culture. The fallacious approach of scholars (Śāstrins) to the problem has thrown the entire scheme of values into chaos, leaving the students of Indian philosophy and culture guessing about the true rationale behind the scheme of values and the principle of unity implied in it. It is abundantly clear that the Indian concept of values is systematically worked out on the basis of a simple pluralism of values, but the fact has been cleverly misinterpreted to prove a valuational monism by postulating a principle of derivation or subsumption of values under one supreme value which is believed to encompass all other values of human life.

A principle of gradation of values is intrinsically bound up with the notion of values, because preference of values is itself valuational. Accordingly, the Indian concept of values seeks to integrate the material and biological with the moral and spiritual values so that each value is accorded a rightful place in a system which as a whole is the true aim of human life. The idea of harmony of values (anubandha) as maintained by Kautilya, Vātsyāyana and *Mahābhārata* provides a ground of value preference, but it fails in a practical situation in which the realization of one is opposed to that of another. Such attempts to conceive harmony in values illustrate the pluralistic approach of these thinkers which was found to be unsavoury by dharmaśāstrins and mokṣaśāstrins. The latter, therefore, seeks to establish a monism on the basis of a supreme value in the form of moral value (dharma) and religio-spiritual value (mokṣa, Brahman) respectively. Values are distinguished as higher and lower, but if the lower is ruled out of court in face of the higher, it is sure to disturb the very principle on which the distinction between higher and lower values is made. Now if the Cārvākas contend that pleasure is the end of life (Kāmohi eka paramodharma) or Kautilya thinks that material gain (artha) is supreme as an instrument of both pleasure and maintenance of law and order in society (sukhasya mūlam dharmaḥ, dharmasya mūlamarthaḥ), it will be as fallacious as the view according to which artha and kāma should pale into insignificance in face of the moral and spiritual ends of life (dharma, mokṣa), unless the true principle of such gradations is brought to light.

The controversies of pluralism versus monism, activistic versus non-activistic moralities, woredly versus other-woredly values, empirical versus transcendental, non-spiritual versus spiritual values, and metaphysical versus valuational with regard to the Indian concept of values, can be set at rest on the ground that values form an hierarchical system in which all values, higher or lower, are values in their own right. The depth of satisfaction is the true measure of axiological richness of a value, and strength is purely an ontological consideration. Such methodological notions have been developed by Nicolai Hartmann in his book, *Ethics*.

Artha, which is purely economic and biological values, must form the ontological basis of all other values, and kāma which means pleasure of sexual and artistic pursuits, adds to life its qualitative richness and thus will be graded higher than artha. Dharma, which refers to moral values, must constitute the regulative norms for both artha and kāma; it is, therefore, higher than both. Mokṣa as the spiritual fulfilment of man must come at the top of all other values, and the Brahman as a value is not different from mokṣa. Thus artha, kāma, dharma and mokṣa or brahman together form an hierarchical system which is the comprehensive aim of human life and to single out any of them and consider it alone as the ideal of man will not be in consonance with the true spirit of the Indian concept of values.

This thesis according to which values form a system seems to be vulnerable on the ground that mokṣa or Brahman, which is a value of transcendental state, refuses to be harmonized with the so-called empirical values like artha, kāma and dharma, because it is sometimes believed that on the attainment of the highest state of mokṣa or Brahman, nothing else (empirical) stays as valuable. The contention that highest freedom is inconsistent with values of empirical existence, is fallacious, because the ideal of Jīvan-mukti of Śaṅkara and Bodhisattva of the Mahāyāna Buddhists imply realization of the Brahman or enlightenment in this very life, and a living person will need all that is necessary for the maintenance of life, society and morality. Life itself is the ontological basis of the highest achievement. It is true that on the attainment of the top, the person (sidhapuruṣah) looks upon life, society and morality differently from one whose sole aim is material gain (artha) or pursuit of pleasure (kāma), but to condemn them in the face of the higher is to cut off the very roots of value-realization which would also be repugnant to the idea of value-system. Śaṅkara himself accepts that mokṣa or the Brahman is a supreme value, the highest of all values (paramapuruṣārthaḥ); now 'highest' is a relative term which necessarily entails a reference to the lower values. Thus, the concept of mokṣa or the Brahman implies the essential recognition of other values.

The view that the transcendental state (mokṣa) is in continuation with the values of the empirical existence, runs into another difficulty—that of demonstrating the transition from the lower to the higher on some principle, for otherwise values will refuse to be graded as higher or lower axiologically. This difficulty can be circumvented on the basis of Śaṅkara's principle of sublation. It is a metaphysical principle which has been adapted to explain the manifestations of the lower values on the basis of the reflection theory as developed by the Śāṅkarites in Vedānta-Paribhāṣā. According to it, the transcendental is not the negation of empirical but in a sense its consummation and culmination so that empirical values are the reflections or the imperfect and limited expressions of the fullness of the transcendental, e.g., empirical pleasure (kāma) is nothing but a limited and partial manifestation of the infinite bliss (ānanda). The limitations here are due to the defects and inadequate psychic modes which the lower manifestations have to pass through. Hence, there is no antagonism between the higher and the lower values; they can be interrelated and integrated into one system in which the distinctions on axiological and ontological grounds remain valid for their hierarchical gradation into the higher and lower.

CHAPTER TWO

The Notion of Value

The science of value (axiology) although it owes its origin to the Western philosophical tradition can provide us with a point of view from which we can examine ancient Indian philosophy. It has made available certain concepts, notions and principles which are not only found central to all philosophical thinking, but can also become the basis for a reinterpretation of ancient moral systems. Since we propose to study the Indian concept of values, it becomes necessary that certain basic problems and methodological notions regarding value are explained in the beginning.

The word "value" is used in many different senses and carries with it such divergent implications that the task of formulation of a definite idea of value is necessary. Our task is not merely analytical like E. Hall's or like that of many other recent ethical and social thinkers who try to base their entire approach to value on scientific method; our intention is not to dismiss traditional approaches to morality as emotive or non-sensical as some of the positivists do, but to study the idea of value as a part and parcel of Indian tradition. Nevertheless, certain tendencies of modern European theory of value are useful for us to arrive at a precise understanding of the notion of value and its application to the interpretation of Indian thought.

The main concern of a modern scientific theory of value is to define value exactly and to find out its nature and significance. The problem of the relations between value and existence and between value and reality is of great relevance on metaphysical grounds. While subjective theories are concerned with finding out the psychological import of valuation, other theories maintain value as a quality inherent in objects. This in short, is a revival of the familiar old controversy as to whether values are subjective or objective. From the idealistic angle, values are self-existent entities. Implied or otherwise, connected with these problems, there is the problem of preference of some values to others. The principle of such preference or gradation must be central to a theory of value, especially when any historical system of values like the Indian concept of values is studied.

Definitions of Value

According to the Oxford English Dictionary, 'value is worth, utility, desirability and qualities on which these depend'. Although the word "worth" is of Anglo-Saxon or Germanic origin (cf. "wert" in German) and value is of Latin origin (cf. "valere" in Latin and "valeur" in French), yet "worth" can be regarded as an equivalent of value. Utility and desirability do imply some philosophical significance in as much as the former suggests the economic origin of the concept of value and the latter points to a psychological definition of the word, viz., the valuable is desirable. In general, value has been defined in terms of many concepts, e.g., (1) value as utility, (2) value as pleasure, (3) value as interest, and (4) value as an intrinsic good.

In economics, the notion of value is used in two senses, viz., (1) value in use and (2) value in exchange. The purchasing power of a commodity is certainly to be distinguished from its capacity to satisfy human needs. The second definition of value is not applicable when we deal with moral, aesthetic and religious values, but utility in the sense of capacity to satisfy human needs and wants is quite significant here. The modern doctrine of utilitarianism is not so much concerned with utility in the economic sense as it is with the universal pleasure or happiness, although the word 'utilitarianism' is derived from the word 'utility'. Utilitarianism of Bentham, Mill and Sidgwick is a belief in universalistic ethical hedonism based on the principle of determining the moral worth of an action according to the standards of pleasurable consequences. C.D. Broad who represents the common view, relates utilitarianism with hedonism; but hedonism is based on the psychological feeling of pleasure whereas utility cannot be called a psychological feeling. The pragmatic principle of determining truth-value on the basis of the utility or workability of an idea or proposition brings it closer to the thesis that utility is value. The notion of utility implies a reference to something for which a thing is useful. For instance, a commodity possesses value because it satisfies some human desire, but the question at once arises: Why should desires be satisfied at all? The answer being, 'for the purpose of life'. This would lead to the question: Is life worth living? Such an infinite regress can only be resolved when an absolute end is reached and that end will be what is valuable in itself. It is true that this absolute end is never reached by this process, nevertheless, it serves as a standard or an ultimate criterion of valuation.

This analysis leads to an important distinction between instrumental and absolute values. The value of means towards an end is an instrumental one, and the value of an end which is an end in itself and never a means towards an end, is, therefore, an absolute value. There is another similar distinction between intrinsic and extrinsic values. The value of a part which is a part of a whole is an extrinsic value, but a thing which if it were to exist by itself and did not need anything else for its existence, would have a value which would be intrinsic.[1] It is around this fundamental concept of value as absolute or intrinsic that a great deal of philosophical controversy is centred.

One of the ways of defining the notion of value is in terms of "approval" which is meant to be an emotional attitude in favour of the object or course of action. Apart from the difficulty in defining exactly what is "worthy" or "approved", for worth is the same as value, there remains the problem of whose approval should count. "Approval" can mean at least three things: (i) approval by an individual, (ii) approval by majority of individuals, and (iii) approval by convention. The first by itself cannot constitute moral "value". The second is problematic as moral 'worth' cannot be established by counting of heads. The third would remove altogether any halo attached to moral value for it would merely be what is practised by a group for a considerable course of time; thus, the element of choice which is so essential to the validity of approval theory is eliminated defeating the very purpose of the latter.

Similarly a circular argument is involved in all those attempts which define value in terms of psychological concepts like desire or interest. The Mīmāṁsakas have tried to define value (artha) as worthy of being desired; the satisfaction of desire, resulting in pleasure or pain, constitutes the essence of value (artha) which is positive or negative depending upon whether the pleasure or pain is greater.[2] J.S. Mill in his book *Utilitarianism* maintains that 'that which is itself valuable is itself desirable'. He believes that the fact that a thing is desired makes it desirable. Mill commits here a gross linguistic fallacy by taking 'desired' to mean "desirable", which is not really what is desired but what ought to be desired. R.B. Perry defines value[3] in terms of "interest". According to him, value is 'an object of interest to someone', for it emanates from 'the peculiar relation between the interest and its object'. Perry, therefore, states that value is 'the special character of an object which consists in the fact that interest is taken in it'.[4] Similarly, Vātsyāyana refers value (kāma) to desire and the state of its satisfaction which commits him to a sort of hedonism. All these definitions which define value in terms of some psychological state, desire, liking, approval, interest or pleasure presuppose the fact that fulfilment of desire or interest is good. They are circular definitions.

A biological definition of value was propounded in the nineteenth century by Herbert Spencer in terms of adaptation of organism to environment. The principle of conformity to evolutionary development inevitably implies an absolute standard, for otherwise better or worse adjustments have no meaning. Nothing can be termed as good according to evolutionary development unless it is defined as change for the better and this involves us in a vicious circle. 'The Good', writes A.C. Ewing, 'cannot be defined as what is in conformity with good development'.

All such definitions explain value in terms of something which is a non-value—psychological, biological or sociological. They somehow presuppose the notion of value, though they fail to account for the notion in precise terms.[5] G.E. Moore repudiates these definitions on the ground of what he calls naturalistic fallacy, which consists in defining value in terms of a naturalistic object like desire, interest, etc., for according to him the universal predicate of value is applicable to these naturalistic objects and the definition would take us into an infinite regress. Moore, therefore, concludes that the notion of 'good' is indefinable. Hence it follows that 'value' is also an indefinable predicate.

If definition is to be given strictly according to logical rules, i.e., *per genus et differentiam*, the idea of value perhaps cannot be defined, for it is a simple notion, the genus of which does not exist. It is in this sense that a strict logical definition of value is impossible. But G.E. Moore holds that whatever is analysable is definable, and according to him, only complex things can be defined in terms of the parts of which they are composed. The "good" is held to be indefinable in so far as it is a simple object of thought like "yellow".[6] It is on account of Moore's own view of definition that "good" seems to be indefinable, for otherwise, even a simple notion like "yellow" has been defined by referring to its place in the colour spectrum. Similarly "good" has been defined in terms of "ought to exist". But Moore does not accept this since "ought" itself implies a relation to action, i.e., on this definition "good" comes to mean that 'it is such as it is somebody's duty to realize it' and simple notions cannot imply relations. In order to define the uniqueness of this "quality" called good, Moore makes out that it is that to which all ethical judgments refer to.[8] But ethical judgments presuppose the "good". Moore will say that ' good" can only be immediately apprehended.

It may, therefore, be said, that when Moore thinks "good" is indefinable, he does not mean that it is unknowable. A knowledge of the notion of "good" or "value" is possible in terms of metaphysical definitions. A.C. Ewing holds out this possibility when he writes, 'I have a word to say about a quite different way of defining ethical concepts, that is, in terms of metaphysics. A metaphysical definition is a definition by reference to the ultimate nature of the real as distinguished from the less ultimate aspect in which reality is conceived as appearing for natural sciences.' And he suggests that ethical concepts can be understood with reference to God. According to him, 'To say something is good or right is to say that it is commanded by God.'[8] Here again, goodness of one who commands is presupposed, for unless he is good, it will not be good to obey him. Thus Ewing's attempt makes no headway in breaking through the vicious circle.

It is, therefore, clear that the notion of value cannot be defined in terms of non-value notions, for all such definitions refute themselves.[9] Value is an unique, ultimate and underivable concept, which has its own essence and being. It belongs to "the being" which Plato first discovered, the realm which we can spiritually discern, but cannot see or grasp. Nicolai Hartmann subscribes to this view when he maintains that 'values are essences'. "Essence" according to him, 'is the kind of Being of that "through which" everything participating in it is just as it is.'[10] He writes, "values emanate neither from the things nor from the percipient. . . they are not even capable of being directly grasped by thought; rather are they immediately discerned only by an inner vision like Plato's "Ideas". . . . Man's sensing of values is the annunciation of their Being. . . in their peculiar idealistic kind of existence.[11] According to him, values are the prerequisites of valuable things (goods). The experience of value is apriori. He writes, 'what is evident is that values possess the character of absoluteness, of principles and that the knowledge which we have of them can be no other than aprioristic knowledge.'[12] The whole legitimacy and objectivity of values is made to fall on the sense of value inherent in us. The essence of values always remains transcendent to the existential reality.

Nicolai Hartmann further maintains that the essentiality of values lies in its self-existence. 'Values subsist independently of the consciousness of them. Consciousness can grasp or miss them, but cannot make them or spontaneously decree them.'[13] Knowledge of values is genuine knowledge of Being. The mode of Being peculiar to values is "Ideal Self-existence". In this respect, values resemble the concepts of Mathematics and Logic. Hartmann observes, 'The values are originally patterns of an ethical ideal sphere, of a realm of its own structures, its own laws and order.'[14] It exists beyond reality just as much as beyond consciousness, an ethical ideal sphere, not manufactured, invented or dreamed, but actually existing and capable of being grasped through the feeling for values.[15] Hartmann characterizes this Being of values by identifying it with "ought-to-be".[16] In other words they have their own rights to exist. Hartmann's "ought-to-be" is not dependent upon any "ought-to do", the latter is attached with the former, i.e., values should exist although it is nobody's duty to make them exist. Hartmann identifies values with the principles of existence and as such they are conditions of possibilities, they determine the real.[17]

Hartmann's axiology can be related to the theory of stratification of being which appears in his important works.[18] His definition of values as essences having ideal self-existence or Being of an ethical ideal sphere is another case of metaphysical definition which reduce "ought" to "is". If values are a Being or existence, they will lose their unique and fundamental character for axiology and become a part of metaphysical reality. Their reference to human reality is what gives the concept of values a unique significance. Hartmann, however, makes them real in a platonic world of supersensible essences cut off from the empirical world.

However, Hartmann seems to be quite careful in making a distinction between metaphysical Being and a purely ethical ideal sphere. The realm of values is grasped in "the feeling for values". There is no doubt that he uses the metaphysical jargon to elucidate his position, but even so he does not fail to distinguish between the two spheres. But if the realm of values is to be characterized only in terms of "ethical", he is obviously caught up in a circle. His distinction between the two spheres of the ontological and the ethical is not clear. Further, Hartmann's position is open to certain serious doubts regarding the absolute character of values. These doubts occur in the face of the subjective and relativistic theories of values on the one hand and theories which plead for a purely objectivistic approach to values on the other. The latter treat value as a unique quality belonging to the external objects. A detailed examination of these views is now necessary.

Subjective and Relativistic Theories

Since values can only be grasped in consciousness, it is a natural inference that values exist only for human consciousness. Two deductions can be made from this inference, viz., (i) value is a function of valuational process and is thus always subjective, and (ii) values are relative because they are relative to the person who evaluates. Both of them cast a serious doubt on the objectivity and absoluteness of values. These propositions are not exactly identical, but one draws support and cogency from the other.

If the meaning and significance of value is to be understood in terms of the act of valuation with which it is connected, the subjective theory must define a specific and invariable subjective state in which the entire value-content is given. Hence, many efforts have been made in this direction and desire, liking, interest, striving, volition, act and satisfaction have been suggested so that value has been conceived as a function of these subjective states. But valuational experience comprehends varied situations and a vast variety of objects, as it is hard to point to any one subjective state with which value may be inalienably identified. The greatest drawback from which these attempts suffer is the inadequate character of such mental states to cover up the entire gamut of valuation and value-situation.

The state of satisfaction is the most significant of all other mental states in so far as almost all of them, including desire, striving and liking, lead to pleasurable feelings. This fact may commit this position to hedonism which is the point of culmination of subjective theories. Mill defines value in terms of desire and discovers that pleasure is the only thing which we desire. He bases his ethical hedonism on psychological facts. But his argument that, since we as a matter of fact desire pleasure, or pleasure is the only object of desire, therefore pleasure is desirable is not tenable. Perhaps pleasure needs some different principle in order to justify it. The Mīmāṁsakas suggest a principle consisting of (a) apūrva, and (b) scriptural injunction as the moral authority in order to make pleasure desirable.[19] Pleasure, as a matter of fact, exercises a reinforcing influence on desire for the continued pleasure of the value-object, but it cannot be considered as the necessary concomitant of all valuational experience, for it is present even when the situation is judged as disvaluational.

Sometimes the source of value is traced to the striving and desiring which covers up both pleasure and the effect, it has on the person.[20] Valuation, however, may have no effect on the present subject when the object of values, e.g., some historical event, lies remotely in the past. It may then be asserted that such a value-judgment on a past event is not valuable; but even this is a value-judgment, because here as elsewhere value is determined by desires and inclinations of the present subject in the same manner as they determine the original judgment. The analysis of volition and states of satisfaction would demonstrate the fact that values are related to the subject.

The main contention of subjective accounts of value is that if the whole character of valuational experience is not delivered in any one psychic state, it cannot be found beyond the subject as a whole. Value, according to this view, intimately depends upon a multiplicity of factors in the personal life of the subject, and is intrinsically bound up with his existence. The Nyāya-vaiśeṣikas, for example, consider virtue (dharma) as the subjective category of the self, as the condition or inner disposition of the mind.[21] The Sāṁkhya shares this view.[22] It is clear, therefore, that either virtue (dharma) is taken to mean differently from its ordinary sense here or value is made to depend upon the subjective life of the person.

There is still another sense of subjectivity of values which is peculiar to the position of the logical positivists. They accord a differential treatment to values than the objects of spatio-temporal world. Value-statements, according to them, are mere pseudo-propositions which express emotional attitudes of persons without any empirical evidence on which they can be validated. This view of subjectivity is only tenable on the logical positivist's own ground, for desires, emotions, sentiments and purposes of human beings are hard facts studied by positive sciences like psychology and they occur in positive conditions and according to natural laws.

Though subjective theories of value may not exclude the possibility of considering value as objective or valid, yet they may logically attribute a character to values which binds them to the subject in another way, viz., it is always found to be relative to the subject. This is the second of the twin propositions under study. For instance Sreenivasa Iyenger writes,

'There is not even a shade of a shadow of doubt . . . that value cannot exist apart from the desires of the conscious subject . . .' and proceeds to give his own formula of value, 'Given such and such a desire, the corresponding value of the object arises.'[23] His aim lies in proving that value is relative to the subject. Undoubtedly, value-judgment changes according to the desire-situation, but this variability in valuation cannot prove value to be ultimately relative. In the absence of hunger, for example, even the best of dishes may look worthless, unless eating is a matter of habit; but the dish has a determinate structure and a human subject also has a determinate constitution of his own, hence, the dish does retain its value for another subject.

Thus, value depends on the relations between goods and subjects, and variability of value-estimation in accordance with the variations of desire-situation is no sign of the relativity of values, but of their relationality, which is universal and objective. Such a view seems to have confused relationality with relativity. Nicolai Hartmann maintains a clear distinction between the relativity and relationality of values. Values, according to him, possess relational structures which do not make them relative to subjects. He observes, 'The relational structure of contents is not relativity as regards values . . . . The difference between relationality and relativity which is often effaced, is as essential for a clear understanding in Ethics as in theoretical philosophy. The opposite of relationality is sub-strata, that of relativity is the absolute . . . the relation of the value of goods to the subject is an absolute relation which is comprised in the content of their values. The thing and the subject are here objectively drawn into the structure of the valuational materials . . . . The binding relation is purely objective and absolute.'[24]

Hartmann further elucidates the point of relation between values and subjects by distinguishing between three kinds of such relations, viz., (i) subject as subject, (ii) subject as object, and (iii) subject as the bearer of values.[25] But these relations do not affect the absolute ontological character of values; they only constitute the inner structure of value-contents. And surprisingly enough, he confines this account of relationality of values only to concrete values, while values as standards remain totally unaffected by relations.[26]

It is clear, therefore, that subjective theories as well as relativistic theories have failed to exhaust value-contents by subjective states and conditions. Values cannot be considered as mere functions of subject-object relations, for even the act of valuation implies the reference to a third entity, i.e., the standard or ideal norm which by itself becomes the ground of rejecting purely a relative and subjective account of values.

Value as a Quality of Objects

If objectivity is to have any meaning, it cannot be denied of the spatio-temporal objects. This suggests yet another way of establishing the objectivity of values—by regarding them as qualities inherent in objects. Dewey's conception of value, for example, lies in seeking value as a quality embodied or actually present in the cognitive objects. The epistemological evidence for the objectivity of value cannot be different from that of objects.

According to Dewey's naturalism, whatever is immediately given in our sensory experience is real. Concrete objects of the world possess such immediacy and are, therefore, real. But this immediate experience also reports that qualities like "blue", "hot", etc., are abstractions from things. What is perceptible to immediate experience is a blue flower or a hot stove, and never blueness or hotness. Here Dewey makes a distinction between sensory qualities (in the Lockean sense) and other emotional qualities like "beautiful", "ugly", "adorable" or "awful" by terming them as a tertiary qualities.[27] According to Dewey, all valuations are properties of things at par with other secondary qualities and it is foolish to separate them from the real cognitive properties of concrete objects of our immediate experience.

Immediate experience obviously does not guarantee the objective reality of qualities at par with objects, for qualities are mere abstractions. The only way to demonstrate the objectivity of qualities on this thesis is to regard them as trans-subjective. Even that is not possible, for the colour-blind man may fail to appreciate the otherwise visible difference between red and green. If immediate experience is the only doorway to reality, the tertiary as well as secondary qualities depend upon the observer and his sensory apparatus. They can be regarded as objective if the reality of relations between the subject and object, both having determinate structures, be recognized; but in this case, qualities will no more be inherent in objects, they will be functions of subject-object relations.

Dewey succeeds in giving an objective account of values and demonstrating the compulsory nature of value-judgments on the same footing as judgments of facts, but the original pragmatic motivation of his philosophy seems to be defeated; for judgments of facts do not exercise upon us an obligatory influence as value-judgments are supposed to do. Perhaps Dewey wants to emphasize the objectivity of value at the cost of its utility for human action and social progress to which Dewey seems to be wedded.[28] John Dewey has shown an original urge to establish objective ethics and aesthetics,[29] but it has taken him round in a vicious circle in which he can either have objectivity of values or a pragmatic motivation of his value-theory.

The account of value as a unique quality inherent in objects will not be complete unless the powerful influence of G.E. Moore's conception of "intrinsic value" is considered. The uniqueness of Moore's theory lies in the fact that he takes "the good" in the sense of "good-in-itself" which is independent of all alleged relations with the subject and his states.[30] He maintains a distinction between "good" and "the good". The former is a universal predicate of all things good and the latter means "intrinsic value".[31] "Good" is a simple, unanalysable and undefinable notion and as such, is a unique object of thought.[32] If "good" is indefinable, it will be difficult for Moore to characterize the uniqueness of value-notion.

Moore may refer the simple notion of "good" to his notion of "intrinsic value", which is absolute, i.e., if it exists all alone, it is a value or it is an end in itself.[33] Intrinsic value, according to him, is an absolute whole, having the internal relations of the parts of which it consists. The uniqueness of such a whole is that it is an expression of "Organic Unity" of parts,[34] that is, 'the value of such a whole bears no regular proportion to the sum of the values of its parts'.[35]

When we ask Moore to give us an example of intrinsic

value, he pushes us ahead to his conception of "ideal" which is the notion of absolute human good, and cites "pleasure of aesthetic enjoyment" and "pleasure of human intercourse" as examples of such an "ideal".[36] Do these conceptions imply no reference to other objects or states of the subject? To quote C.D. Broad here, 'No state of affairs can be good or bad unless it is or contains as constituent some conscious mental state'.[37] Moore will say that the whole is not the same as its parts and value is a "totally resultant" property of the various constituents, and it shall not make it dependent or less absolute in any way.

There is no doubt that Moore has succeeded in giving us a complete account of value in all its senses, including "goodness", "intrinsic value" and "the absolute ideal", but he has not been able to define exactly the uniqueness of value-essence. To say that it is an organic unity does not amount to a definition of intrinsic value. The uniqueness of value-essence can be explained with reference to values as ideal norms in the form of principles or laws. This leads us to the question of the ideality of values.

Value and Existence

Whenever an attempt is made to regard value as an objective entity or a quality inherent in objects so that values are considered as much real as facts themselves, we are at once faced with the question whether values behave like facts. If values are treated at par with facts they fail to exercise normative influence on us and "ought" becomes meaningless, and if they are not they could be condemned as mere shadows of reality or figments of our imagination. This stems from the undefinable basic relationship between value and existence. Value-essences are said to have their own existence and if value is even equated with existence, it would be committing a grave fallacy identifying "ought" with "is". The ideal is no more an ideal if it exists; an actualized value becomes a fact. But do ideals exist? Do values have existence?

The confusion over this basic issue of the exact relationship between values and existence has much vitiated our understanding of the Indian attitude of attributing both ontological and axiological status to ṛta, dharma and Buddhistic dharma in the sense of elements of existence. The word "sat" happens to mean existence, truth and goodness. Existence (sat), consciousness (cit) and bliss (ānanda) constitute the essence of the absolute reality of Brahman which is both value and existence.[38] Prof. Urban also uses such expressions as would convey the impression that values have existence.[39] He writes, 'values are part of the nature of things', and 'constitute the key to the nature of the real'. He uses three words, namely, "exist", "real" and "valid". In a more systematic thesis, *The Intelligible World*, he is opposed to the identification of value with existence, and favours the identification of value with reality. He criticizes Rickert for identifying existence with reality and conceiving of values as unreal.[40]

P.T. Raju identifies reality with true existence. 'True existence is, again, existence of which we are certain,'[41] he observes, 'Reality is the same as existence or being. . . . Even science is a theory of value. . . .' But surely logic is not opposed to the "ought". Its real "is" is also an "ought".[42] But he distinguishes between true existence and seeming existence. He says, 'It (logic) has also to differentiate between the true "Is" which is ideal and the seeming "Is" which is what we call the actual.' It is clear, therefore, that these idealist philosophers do not differ much on this point except in using certain terms in definite connotations. The true existence of Raju, the reality of Urban and the ideality of Rickert mean the same and "seeming existence" of Raju, "existence" or "being" of Urban and "existence" or "reality" of Rickert are the same. Hence, Rickert's "reality" or "existence" is the same as Raju's "seeming existence". The confusion is perhaps because of the use of these words in definite senses. But this will not be so if the existence of what is here called true existence or reality is denied, for it is believed that if existence means anything, it is predicated to only the spatio-temporal world. Then there is a real difference in points of view.

The two terms "value" and "fact" belong to two different universes of discourse. Fact is essentially a notion used to describe the spatio-temporal world or phenomenon, and existence is believed to belong to such facts. In this sense the concept of existence seems to exclude all reference to ideals or values which are considered to have a reality of their own. Now if "real" is used both for "existence" and "value", it has been used with two different meanings. Hence, here the distinction between existence, reality and value is linguistic only.

The question remains as to whether existence as a description of the actual world-order is opposed to or harmonious with the concept of values. It is a matter of common existence that values, more so human values, are realized in the actual world, but the fact remains that the fullest realization and fulfilment of values or ideals lies beyond the scope of the actual world. This leads to an essential gap between actual existence and value. Nicolai Hartmann regards this relation between the actual and the ideal as essentially that of opposition, tension and strain which is felt by the moral consciouseness in the form of an "ought-to-be". He writes, 'the self-existence of values subsists independently of their own actualization. But this independence does not signify indifference to actuality or non-actuality'.[43] This tension and tendency produces an impulsion towards actualization of values.

The examination of the relation between existence and value has led to a dichotomy between "value" and "existence". If values are regarded as real yet as opposed to the actual world, it is on account of their ideal nature, and due to this ideal reality, they are sometimes condemned as superfluous addenda to facts by some, while other consider them as principles of reality and conditions of the actual on the same account. The word "real" is used in the realistic sense in the former and in the idealistic sense in the latter. If "existence" is reserved for the actual world, the question remains as to what the exact nature of ideal reality of values is.

Ideal Reality and Value

In posing the question of the reality of values, we are at once reminded of the classic contention of the idealists. We have seen that values, in the form of ideals, are implied in both the act of valuation and the conception of value as a unique quality in the cognitive objects. If such ideals do not exist in the same sense as objects of the actual world, can they be conceived as real in any other way? Idealism is a belief in the reality of ideals. The following propositions are found to constitute this contention of idealism in this regard:

(1) Value is identified with reality; the real is the valuational.
(2) The essential contrast between 'the real' and 'the unreal' is also the means of distinction between value and disvalue.
(3) The degrees of reality are the same as the degrees of value. The doctrine of value-constitution of reality entails a valuational ordering of reality.
(4) The highest reality is the supreme value at the same time. Lower orders of reality are determined according to their approximation to the highest reality which is the principle and source of all other values.

All these four propositions seem to be implied in the Platonic doctrine of "Ideas". "Ideas" are essences. Essence is 'that through which everything participating in it is just as it is'. These "Ideas" of Plato belong to a realm which is distinct from the realm of actual objects. They are the principles of reality. The highest among those "Ideas" is the idea of "the Good". The idea of "the Good" becomes the supreme principle of reality. Thus according to this metaphysics of conceptual realism, values are reality and existence of the highest order, they are the conditions of the determination of the real.

Platonic idealism has been the source of inspiration for idealists throughout the ages, till the doctrine of ideal reality emerged as the stronger of the two in the form of "absolute idealism" of Hegel, who makes reason the sole arbiter of reality. But contrary to Platonic tradition, where value is the key to the understanding of reality and itself constitutes the highest reality above the valuational categories, the Absolute is neither good nor bad. Bradley follows the same line when he holds that value is a relational concept and is, therefore, not applicable to the Absolute which is above all relations. It seems that Śaṅkara, like Hegel and Bradley, conceives of the supreme reality of the Absolute (Brahman) above the value-categories which implies subject and object. But it is hard to believe that the Absolute of Śaṅkara is devoid of value-contents, for, a positive characterization of it as a pragmatic measure, has been given by Śaṅkara himself as sat-chit and ānanda which means existence, consciousness and bliss.[44] These constitute not only the essence of the Absolute, but also the definition of absolute value.[45] But Śaṅkara maintains that beyond this positive description of the Absolute, it is truly indescribable (tattvānyatvābhyāmanirvacanīya.)

The logical outcome of absolute idealism caused the greatest disappointment to value-philosophers who wanted to make value the condition of reality. They had to follow the lead of Immanuel Kant rather than that of Hegel and Bradley, in abandoning pure reason in favour of practical reason or value as the ground of reality. Rāmānuja also found Śaṅkara's Absolute as empty, void and ineffective in inspiring an ethico-religious life. He was, therefore, led to believe that the Absolute is the embodiment of all values such as knowledge, goodness and beauty.[46]

The idealistic argument, therefore, succeeds in demonstrating the ideal reality of values. But in trying to define absolute reality, we face the danger of raising it too high thus losing the necessary normative impact on human beings. Ideals are reality, they are absolute, ultimate and universal, but that should not come in the way of their being a source of moral inspiration for men. There is need for a doctrine of conceptual realism which is able to maintain the ideal reality of values true to their absolute character and provide for an intermediate agency as well which may bring the realm of values to bear on the world of individuals. Nicolai Hartmann's thesis of values as ideal self-existences fulfils this need by providing an active entity in the form of a human agency which can bridge the gulf between the axiological realities of ideals and the ontological world order (existence). Man is the metaphysical connection between the world of values and existence, conscious of the former and embedded in the latter. He is, therefore, the *prius* of values. This connection is established through the experience of "ought" which 'issues from the value and is not attached directly to its carrier, but to a mediating element in the real, to the subject to whose judgment it leaves the decision as to whether the realization of values is to be carried out or not'.[147]

The attitude of the subject is the central point in all value-actualization.[48]

According to Hartmann, "values are also principles". They are conditions of possibilities in the ethical sphere.[49] In this sense values are "ought-to-be" which further determines "ought-to-do" which is not attached to every "ought-to-be".[50] We say that universal peace ought to "be", but it does not mean that it is someone's duty to bring it about. Hartmann then distinguishes between "ideal ought-to-be" which is the formal condition of value and "positive ought-to-be" which presupposes the real self-existent-world.[51] The distance between the "ought-to-be" from the existent is the axiological dimension between value and disvalue. Good and bad are directional opposites on the ethical dimension of "ought-to-be".[52] He further maintains that plurality of dimensions and variety of values belong only to the contents or materials of value whereas "ought-to-be" is always singular as the formal validity of its contents. There is, therefore, concrete unity of a principle.[53]

The metaphysical weakness of such a principle of ideal reality of values lies in the weakness of the human subject who is the intersecting point between the two heterogenous determinations of "ideal ought-to-be" and the "existent". 'He is the administrator of the ought in the world of real existence. He is not an absolutely faithful administrator of this metaphysical good; he can betray it.'[54] Whether he recognizes this "ought" and commits himself to it or not, depends upon man and his constitution. But Hartmann admits that 'this weakness of the principle is at the same time the strength of the subject; it is his qualitative greatness, his position of power in the world . . . . He is not only a mirroring surface but . . . he forms, moulds, transforms and builds up; he is a world-creator in little'.[55] Hence the gap between values and facts, reality and existence (in the sense of actual world order) will have to be recognized, leaving scope for moral effort to bridge it, which makes the task of value-realization real and meaningful.

It is, therefore, on conceptual realism that values can be conceived as real and effective. Values as qualities of objects and the relationship of subjects and objects appear as concrete values, which refer to ideals as their standards and principles. Ideals are reality, objective, absolute and ultimate. They are ideal self-existences,[56] both as essences and principles of the actual world of values. The opposition between value and existence, reality and world is the condition of value-realization through the human agency, which maintains a status in both the realms.

Gradation of Values

The ability to grade values is presupposed in the realm of values. Without this presupposition, it is not possible to inter-relate them. The principle of gradation must itself be valuational, for it is implied in the very consciousness of values. Preference, choice, decision and conflict implicitly presuppose a ranking of values on a scale. But this order of rank cannot be arbitrarily fixed. Values have to be properly analysed and elaborated.

The problem of gradation leads to certain fine distinctions between values, and such distinctions cannot be imposed unless values themselves admit them. For instance, it is a common tendency to distinguish between the instrumental values of a means and the absolute value of an end in itself. Similarly, there is the distinction between extrinsic and intrinsic values, the former belonging to the parts or means and the latter belonging to the whole in itself. In such distinctions, as we have seen, there is a tendency to derive one value from another; for example the instrumental value is deducible from the absolute value and the extrinsic from the intrinsic. It means that instrumental and extrinsic values are not values in their own right. It may be said, therefore, that they have no right to be called values, for values are self-existent. The belief in the self-existence of values implies that they are complex.[57]

There is another distinction between higher and lower values. The tendency to prefer one value to another is implied in the sense of values, which means that values are graded as "higher" or "lower", the order of precedence presupposes the height in a scale. But it does not follow from this that lower values are derivable from the higher. We have already admitted that values are absolute and self-existent, and hence they are axiologically irreducible. According to Hartmann, the "height" of values is only a dimension of values *sui genris*. He introduces another dimension of values along with the "height" of values, viz., "strength" of values[58] to safeguard the lower values from the higher. Higher values are higher so far as their "height" is concerned and lower are lower on the same basis, but for their "strength", higher values depend upon the lower values. In other words, higher values depend upon the lower for their material.

The two dimensions of "height" and "strength" are in a way opposed to each other. Hartmann makes the position clear when he writes, 'The higher value may be precisely the weaker, the lower the stronger within certain limits; this indirect proportionality may well agree; the higher values are generally more complex structures, the lower are the more elemental . . . . The lower categories are the stronger and more independent, while the weaker and more conditioned are the higher and more complex . . . . One may easily be convinced that in general, the reverse relation holds between height and strength'.[59] Values are values whether they are higher or lower. The order of preference of the higher or the lower, according to their rank on the basis of their height and strength, comes only when they are placed in a scale. Hence values always form a system in which they are interrelated according to their height and strength.

Hastings Rashdall talks of such a system of values when he says, '. . .the true criterion of morality is the tendency of an act to promote a well-being which includes many other good things besides pleasure among which virtue is the greatest. The value of these elements in human life is determined by the practical reason intuitively, immediately or apriori.'[60] He leaves the task of preference of one good to another entirely to the dictates of practical prudence; but as to how it functions or whether there is any criterion behind this intuitive faculty, is a question left unanswered by Rashdall except that he provides an indirect criteria on the basis of justice, the interpretation of which again depends upon prudence. He admits, 'The ideal end or good for man is not a number of goods lying side by side and having no relation to one another but a particular kind of life in which various elements are harmoniously combined.'[61] Rashdall here comes round to the idea of values forming a system. He has also accepted the principle of commensurability of goods (values); but how we can prefer one good to another, is a question which will have to be answered for an intelligible account of the system of values.

In fact, we need a principle or principles which can serve as the criterion or criteria of value-preference. In other words we want to know how a value can be ranked in a system. The distinction between higher and lower on the basis of height and strength is only a dimension and does not constitute a criterion. W.M. Urban, on an analysis of value-consciousness, discovered three criteria on which values could be preferred. He found that (i) intrinsic values are superior to instrumental values, (ii) permanent values are preferred to transitory values and (iii) productive values are preferred to unproductive ones.[62] But we have already seen that such distinctions between values are not tenable on the view that values are always absolute, autonomous, self-existent and permanent. Instrumental, transitory and unproductive values are not values at all in so far as they are derivative.

Nicolai Hartmann advocates five distinguishing marks in this context, viz., (i) durability, (ii) non-divisibility, (iii) axiological dependence, (iv) depth of satisfaction and (v) absoluteness. He observes, 'Each one of these criteria is enough to show that moral values are higher than biological values . . . Supertemporality, indivisibility, dependence and absoluteness are one and the same; these form features which evidently constitute marks common to the whole class.'[63] There is only one characteristic left, i.e., depth of satisfaction, which does not belong to all values in the same sense as other features. It is, according to him, the true test of the height of a value, for the kind of satisfaction varies qualitatively with each value-fulfilment. But even here the task of comparison will have to be left ultimately to value-consciousness, because depth of satisfaction is more or less a dimension rather than a criterion of measurement. He declares in the end that it is impossible to find any unifying principle of values and the tendency towards monism in values is only philosophical. He writes, 'In this search of unity, the ideal system of values must always hover before us as the task of possible and historical systems and that regardless of how near or how far we may be from the goal.'[64]

There is only one way out of this difficult situation and that is the conception of a supreme value which is regarded as the highest so that other values are declared higher or lower with reference to it on the basis of subsumption to the highest. We find this concept in the system of historical moralities. For example, we find such a conception of supreme value in the form of the Absolute (Brahman), mokṣa, or the nirvāṇa in the Indian system of values.[65] But the acceptance of such a unifying principle for values, in the form of a supreme value, will be open to the following objections:

(1) The supreme value is only postulated and as such, it may not always be held valid in as much as any other value may also be supposed to be supreme without any common ground. It cannot be ultimately validated.

(2) In a system, wherein a supreme value is postulated, other values are subsumed under it; other values will, therefore, be derived from it. This violates the autonomy and self-existence of values.

(3) The supreme value can only be supreme in fórm and not in content, because for content, it shall depend upon the lower values. The idea of a supreme value will, therefore, remain empty as in the case of the Platonic "Idea of the Good". To say that the 'Good' is supreme is to say that the idea of value is supreme and nothing more. The Indian conception of the Absolute (Brahman) which possesses existence, consciousness and bliss as constituting the essence of the supreme value, is a promising lead which merits serious consideration and discussion.

A system of values may be conceived without a supreme value, wherein values exist in their own right and status and are graded accordingly.

Pluralism of Values

No account of values can be considered complete unless we face the question as to what the various values are. The task of preparing an exhaustive list of human values seems to be beset with difficulties both epistemological as well as methodological, because the phenomenon of value occurs in various and diverse fields, and with respect to numerous objects, experience and states of persons. One point, however, stands out clear, that there is a pluralism of values. We have seen that an attempt to evolve a unifying principle of values, as is found in the historical systems of values, is not tenable. The belief in the multiplicity of values is not inconsistent with the concept of a system of values wherein values are graded as "higher" or "lower". Values present themselves in groups clustering around one fundamental value—nucleus, so to say. These groups are interconnected and may form a system in which each is graded according to its height and strength. This depends upon the cultural pattern of the society or nation or a person. The list of values prepared speculatively and deontologically, apart from any cultural background is bound to remain formal and theoretical.

Urban, in his book *Fundamentals of Ethics*, has given us a list of human values in which he includes biological, material, mental, aesthetic, moral, religious and spiritual values.[66] These are broad spheres wherein values are located, but they do not refer to values as such. Archie J. Bahm keeping this point in mind attempts at a classification of ultimate values. According to him, there are four ultimate values, pleasure, satisfaction, enthusiasm and contentment. They are arrived at respectively in accordance with four theories—those of hedonism, voluntarism, romanticism and ānandism.[67] Similarly, Edward Spranger investigates into these concrete values in his book *Lebensformen.*[68] He is of the opinion that the psychical structure of the individual subject is of no consequence in determining the validity and order of values. Thus rejecting subjectivism, Spranger puts forth an ideal system of values which itself approaches the meaning of the normative spirit determining how value should be carried out. Spranger's analysis of the content of value-experience, by their metaphysical character, reminds us of the Indian concept of dharma. Further, like the Indian concept of varṇāśrama-dharma, Spranger's idea of the forms of life involves an investigation into the various basic human types, for instance the rational man, the economic man, the aesthetic man, the social man, the religious man, etc. Besides this his formulations of the ends of life, in sense of the achievement of the basic goals of man, like the theoretical goal, the economic goal, the power goal, the aesthetic goal and the religious goal correspond closely to the ancient Indian structure of values expressed in the four puruṣārt as.

G.E. Moore's list of two intrinsic values—of aesthetic enjoyment and pleasure of human and social intercourse seems to be given only to illustrate his conception of intrinsic value. Perhaps he does not intend to put forward a list of values.[69]

Nicolai Hartmann has given us a fairly comprehensive list of values as such, as he devotes one full volume (Vol. II) of his book *Ethics* to it. The list consists of two main types, viz., (i) values as goods which condition the content of values and (ii) values as such. The former are subdivided into two groups according as they belong to the subject or situation. Values relating to the subject are life, consciousness, activity, etc., and situation-values are existence, power, happiness, etc. The second category of values can also be sub-divided into two groups, viz., (i) fundamental moral values such as the good, the noble, richness of experience, purity, etc., and (ii) specific values such as justice, wisdom, courage, fidelity, faith, modesty and values of social intercourse, etc. He includes in his list of specific values the values of love of the remote, personal love, personality and radiant virtue. We find that Hartmann by virtue of his great concern for ethics, worked upon a comprehensive list of moral values. There is no doubt that the distinction between moral values and other values is hard to make, but in an axiological scheme, a scheme of values in keeping with their status and sphere will have to be worked out. Moral values will take their place in the system as one of the groups.

In Indian philosophy there is a notion of the trinity of values (trivarga) which has caught the imagination of Indian thinkers through the ages. The three values consist of bio-economic values (artha), hedonistic values (kāma) and moral values (dharma). The concept of the trinity of values (trivarga) obviously does not include the fourth value which is undoubtedly accepted as the ultimate and supreme value pertaining to the spiritual and religious value (mokṣa or nirvāṇa). The concept of the four values of life is known as catuṣpuruṣārtha, i.e., the four-fold aim of human life. The four values here merely indicate the various spheres wherein values of each type are located, and it will be quite fruitful to investigate into this conception for further details. This study shall not only reveal the cultural pattern evolved and acknowledged in the life of the Indian nation, but also bring to light the range of human values. It will be quite interesting to find out how the Indian mind has endeavoured to unify the diverse human values into a system, for the criterion of gradation of values in a scale intimately reveals the underlying principle of values.

CHAPTER THREE

Problem of Values in Indian Thought

The notion of value has been found to imply a number of problems, such as defining the concept of value and characterizing its metaphyisical nature, of gradation and classification. The Indian genius, owing to its excessive preoccupation with metaphysical problems, seems to have neglected them. At least, the keenness and vigour with which the Indian thinker analyses and investigates metaphysical problems, is missing in the field of the theory of value. This may have been due to the overwhelming influence of the vedānta. One thing will, however, have to be acknowledged that the very concept of value owes its origin to recent times and it is possible to study ancient systems of thought in its light. The task of rediscovering values does not amount to merely reinterpreting them but also demonstrating the fact that there has been an unbroken continuity of contemporary value-philosophy with ancient morality found in the Indian systems of thought.

THEORETICAL PHILOSOPHY AND INDIAN TRADITION

Indian tradition favours a close relationship between theory and practice. It seeks to combine in a subtle manner doctrine and life, thought and religion. It is sometimes asserted that there has been no pure philosophy in India.[1]

Two distinct functions of knowledge have been acknowledged

in Indian thought; one which is theoretical, viz., revealing the existence of some object (artha-praricchitti) and the other which is practical, viz., helping in the attainment of some purpose in life (phalaprāpti). This does tell facts apart from values, but the Indian tendency is to subordinate the former function to the latter. Theory is for practice and doctrine for life is the consistent trend of Indian thinkers.[2] The Indian approach is, therefore, sufficiently value-oriented.

This does not mean that desire to know has not, on its own, prompted Indian genius so that knowledge for its own sake has not been an ideal worthy of pursuit. Naciketa's spirit of enquiry[3] about the ultimate nature of reality marks a distinct approach to knowledge for its own sake—a knowledge which begins from wonder and mystery and gets consummated in realization (darśana). The Upanisadic seer asks, 'what is that by knowing which everything can be known?'[4] Here the thirst for knowledge is pure and simple not motivated by extraneous consideration. In the *Bhagavad-Gītā* Lord Krishna speaks of a type of knowledge 'attaining which nothing else remains to be known'.[5]

Epistemology and methodology are the chief concerns of the Nyāya philosophers. But knowledge for its own sake as the ideal of philosophy, has not much attraction to the Indian mind. Purely theoretical knowledge is put at a disadvantage if it is not validated on the basis of experience as the necessary proof of its validity. For gaining such an experience, some course of practical discipline is always prescribed.[6] Thus for an Indian philosopher, knowledge (jñāna) is not a mere intellectual understanding but a realization (darśana). Nothing short of the vision (darśana) of the real is the ultimate motive of philosophy in India. In this sense of the term knowledge (jñāna), it is an end in itself.

Value as the Motive-Force

If knowledge is not to be kept aloof from the problems of life, its pursuit must be purposively directed towards human achievement. Knowledge is made meaningful in terms of its ability to investigate and promote the attainment of some end of human life. Value and its study acts as the motive-force of the entire philosophical activity which is divided according to the field in which it is carried on. In Indian thought, there have been four such distinct spheres of human achievement, called puruṣārthas or ends of life—dharma, artha, kāma and mokṣa to which a fifth one may be added, namely, that of quest after the absolute reality (Brahman).[7] These five concepts divide ancient philosophical literature in India into five categories. Each is directed to the study of that specific value which constitutes its motivational force. Such a study is commonly known in India as science or systematic study (śāstra). The five-fold division of philosophical literature of ancient India is as follows:

(1) Brahmaśāstras are the scientific study of the nature of absolute reality. The Absolute (Brahman) is the subject-matter of this branch of knowledge (Brahmavidyā). The Absolute (Brahman) which is the highest and ultimate reality, presents itself as the expression of the supreme value of life.[8] Its motive-force is expressed in the first of the famous aphorism (Sūtra)[9], 'Then therefore enquiry into the Absolute.'[10]

(2) Mokṣaśātras are the systematic study of the highest spiritual state of liberation (mokṣa).[11] The philosophical systems which undertake this study, take their start from the problem of the self (ātman) and investigate into the nature of the self and the means of the highest attainment of spiritual freedom (mokṣa-sādhana). If the highest state of self (mokṣa) is regarded as identical with the Absolute (Brahman), mokṣaśāstra is the same as Brahmaśāstra.

(3) There is another type of literature in Sanskrit called Dharmaśāstras which are originally concerned with the nature and exposition of moral values (dharma) in the form of virtue, duty, moral standard, social norm and law.[12] The entire sphere of moral values becomes the central theme of these moral treatises (dharmaśāstras).

(4) Kāmaśāstras are a type of literature which concentrate on the pursuit of one of the important values of life, pleasure (Kāma). It is mainly concerned with sex and other pursuits of the sensual and hedonistic culture. This aspect of human life is subjected to scientific study with a view to the attainment

of the fullest and healthiest satisfaction, which is acknowledged as one of the values.

(5) Arthaśāstras concern themselves with material gain and maintenance of life.[13] Artha is an expression for politico-economic values, which constitute the thematic import of such a type of literature. Kautilya's *Arthaśāstra* is a systematic account of political economy (artha) and social organization.

It is clear, therefore, that the various problems with which various systems of Indian thought are concerned, are basically problems of human values. This five-fold division of systems on the basis of their motive-force can be considered to be exhaustive of the whole of ancient philosophical literature in Sanskrit. Every category of literature undertakes to study the nature and importance of one specific value of life, in a thorough and systematic manner. The Absolute (Brahman), ultimate salvation (mokṣa), moral values (dharma) hedonistic culture (kāma) and political economy (artha) are the basic problems of Indian thought.

The Problem of the Absolute

In a sense, the problem of absolute reality is implied in all philosophy. There is one conception of knowledge which makes it not only instrumental in the realization of the 'Real', but an end in itself, when knowledge is regarded as reality. Knowing is not a way to Being; it is itself Being. Knowledge is identical with reality; to know means to be.[14] Now the question remains as to what is that knowledge? What is the ultimate reality? This has been the basic problem of the vedāntins. It was originally initiated by the Upaniṣadic sages whose mystic utterances express more of a mystery than a solution of this fundamental problem of ultimate reality. It became the exclusive concern of the vedāntins who called themselves the true interpreters of the vedic tradition. They displayed vigour and freedom of thought in building their own systems, in which we find an expression of the highest order of Indian idealism.

The Brahmaśāstra pertains to a type of literature which originates from the *Vedānta-sūtras*, *Upaniṣads* and the *Bhagavad-*

Gītā in the form of commentaries and interpretations. The *Vedānta-sūtra* is also called *Brahma-sūtra*, because it is an exposition of the doctrine of the Absolute (Brahman). Literally the *Vedānta* means the end of veda which further may mean the final portions of the vedas or *Upaniṣads* or the ultimate aim of veda (knowledge). These aphorisms (*Sūtras*) have been subjected to interpretations on the basis of preconceived points of view at the hands of commentators of whom the chief are Śaṅkara, Rāmānuja, Mādhva, Vallabha, Nimbārka and Bhāskara. Each of them develops his distinct system of thought with regard to the nature of ultimate reality (Brahman) and man's relation to it. The classical standpoints of Śaṅkara and Rāmānuja give us an insight into the nature of the Absolute which is not only regarded as the metaphysical ultimate but also the highest value.

The metaphysical nature of the Absolute is sometimes believed to be the ground of absolute values. The doctrine of the Absolute implies an inevitable relation of value and reality so that absolute reality is absolute value at the same time. The metaphysical characterization of the Absolute must, therefore, determine the nature and content of absolute and ultimate values. What is the exact relation of value and the Absolute depends itself on whether or not, or how far, the concept of value is allowed to determine the Real. Absolute values such as Truth, Beauty, Goodness and Holiness are believed to inhere in the Absolute as Rāmānuja holds,[15] but sometimes the Absolute is made to rise above all valuational considerations. And if the essence of the Absolute is constituted by existence (sat), consciousness (cit) and bliss (ānanda),[16] the problem of relation between value on the one hand and existence, reality and consciousness on the other will crop up. A discussion of such implications of the Absolute shall reveal the Indian way of thinking about absolute values, their metaphysical standing and their relation to concepts like essence, reality, existence, etc. The problem of the relation of value with the Absolute ultimately depends upon the metaphysical notion of unity and diversity, identity and difference (bhedābheda).

On this ground, there is a real difference of approach between the various vedāntins of whom Śaṅkara and Rāmānuja are conspicuous. Śaṅkara believes in absolute unity of the Absolute so that absolute values are the essence of the Absolute, while

Rāmānuja believes in identity-in-difference so that absolute values are related to the Absolute as qualities to the substance. The conception of absolute unity, according to Śaṅkara's advaita, seems to be logically higher than that of Rāmānuja's viśiṣṭādvaita. It remains to be seen whether or not the logically higher is also higher from the valuational point of view. However, a discussion of the nature of Brahman must be based on an account of the absolute and ultimate values obtainable from the Indian absolutistic systems (i.e., advaita and viśiṣṭādvaita).

Human Suffering and the Self

The fact of evil and human suffering in the form of grief, frustration, bereavement, disease and death has deeply impressed the Indian mind. It has been provoked to think about the causes of suffering and the way of deliverance from it. The existence of the self is affirmed through suffering and it is the self which is ultimately delivered. Two distinct states of the self are recognized, viz., (i) self in the state of suffering and (ii) self in the state of freedom. The former is a state of bondage (bandhana) and the latter is a state of freedom (mokṣa). The former state is metaphysically interpreted as due to the false self while freedom is the essence of the true self. Thus the realization of the true self by breaking through the bonds of the false self is regarded by Indian thinkers as the final destiny of man which is characterized as freedom. It is variously viewed and designated as mukti, mokṣa or nirvāṇa.

Once the Indian mind is set thinking about the self and its ultimate reality, the problem is discussed thread-bare from all angles. There are two chief approaches, viz., the theory of the self (ātmavāda) and the (ii) Buddhistic theory of negation of the self (anātmavāda). The theory of the self (ātmavāda) is further divided into two, viz., the theory of one universal self (ekātmavāda) and the theory of multiplicity of selves (anekātmavāda).

The main concern of the Buddhists is the problem of suffering (duḥkha), the causes of suffering (duhkha-samudāya), the possibility of ending suffering (nirodha) and finally, the way (mārga).[17] Suffering is the commotion of elements (dharma) with which man identifies falsely as the self; but when the elements come to a final rest (nirvāṇa), a mere blank is substituted in its place. It is sometimes believed that this negativistic view of the final destiny of man (nirvāṇa) is due to beginning from the false premise of the negation of self (anātmavāda). Śaṅkara emphasizes the impossibility of the denial of the self (ātman), it is self established existence as conscious essence.[18]

Starting from the theory of multiplicity of selves (anekātmavāda) which forms the bedrock of many systems of Indian thought like the Nyāya-vaiśeṣika, Sāṅkhya-Yoga and Jainism, we arrive at both positive and negative views of the final destiny of man (mokṣa). The most positive account of liberation in the form of affirmation of the soul is available in Jainism[19] and the Nyāya-vaiśeṣika stops just short of the negative state of utter materiality in mokṣa. Sāṅkhya which is a systematic account of the nature of suffering and means of liberation (mokṣa),[20] arrives at isolation (kaivalya) as the centre of pure consciousness. But if pure-consciousness is posited as the essence of the self, then the multiplicity of selves becomes untenable in the absence of any principle.

The Indian mind is logically led to accept the premise of one universal self (ekātmavāda) which has been the contention of the vedāntins. "All this is not-self" (sarvamanātmam) of the Buddhists becomes "all this is self" (ātmaivedaṃ sarvaṃ) of the Advaita-Vedānta. Now if the essence of this self is regarded as pure consciousness,[21] then all selves are the same essence which is the Absolute self (paramātma) as well as the Absolute Reality (Brahman).[22] The Absolute (Brahman) is identified with the final state (mokṣa).[23] Hence starting from either point, viz., objective or subjective, we arrive at the same absolute and ultimate. The brahmaśāstra becomes mokṣaśāstra.

THE MORAL PROBLEM

Once the destiny of man is defined, the question as to how it can be attained, arises. Hence the problem of finding out ways and means to achieve liberation (mokṣasādhana) in the form of moral training or spiritual discipline or good life occupies the Indian mind next. What is duty? What is virtue? What is the nature of the law which operates in all spheres including life, society and nature? The responsibility to abide by social laws is as much moral as the inner obligation. The whole problem can be viewed as nothing but moral to the core, as indicated by the Indian concept of 'dharma'. The good life is undoubtedly a sure way to the final goal of life but it can also be viewed as a goal in itself. The concept of dharma, therefore, shall afford us an insight into Indian thinking about the full realm of moral and cultural values.

The dharmaśāstras give us an exposition of the concept of dharma in all its implications. Of them, the *Manusmṛti*, *Yajña-valkyasmṛti* and the *Bhagavad-Gītā* are philosophically significant. Manu and Yajñavalkya give us an account of the ancient Indian concept of law, taken both in the sense of moral standards as well as prevailing social norms.[24] It is based on social order, obtainable from the four-fold ordering of society (varṇadharma).[25] Both are concerned with giving an elaborate application, in minute codified detail and with proper analysis of the ancient Indian concept of dharma. Both of them are more or less similar in outline except for those details which crept in due to the historical conditions prevailing in that period and are not philosophically relevant.

The *Bhagavad-Gītā* which is regarded as the central book of the Hindus, centres around the problem of duty.[26] It comprehends almost all metaphysical trends in a sweeping synthesis which makes it a compendium of all traditional Indian metaphysics. But one does not fail to form one's own conclusions as to one's duty and the ultimate values of moral life. Thus the *Bhagavad-Gītā* presents a new and forceful view of ethics and the moral regeneration of man. Dharma is one word which for Indians connotes duty, virtue, norm, culture and the highest moral value.

Sex and Pleasure as Value

The importance of mental health and a satisfied life must be implied in any conception of human values. The good life, which is a sure way towards the final, spiritual achievement, is based on a preparation and discipline at the lower levels. The training in self-regulation comes across formidable resistance in the form of passion, desire, sex, etc., which is likely to throw orderly life into confusion and turmoil. But at the same time, such psychic forces cannot be repressed or negated in the interest of a higher culture, because they do not thus cease to exist, and may lead to guilt, remorse and frustration. Sex and other psychic inclinations towards satisfaction enrich our emotional life and become an essential ingredient of happiness and health. It is, therefore, imperative, according to Indian thinkers that the potential of psychic force in the form of sex be subjected to an intensive study to assess its depth and the content of satisfaction which it can afford. This is exactly the task which is undertaken by the type of literature in Sanskrit known as kāma-sūtras. The concept of kāma comes to stand for sexual and sensual pleasure or a life of hedonistic culture.

The concept of kāma refers to a hedonistic account of human life and its values. The argument for a life of pleasure must be based on the value of the this-worldly life and its affirmation. For a hedonistic tone of culture, a proper climate of opinion had to be built on a purely naturalistic account of human life and the world. The Cārvākas prepared the ground by demolishing the supernaturalistic systems of thought and recommended a materialistic and hedonistic view of life. But their impact on the Indian way of thinking and the values of life was more negative than positive. A more systematic exposition of the hedonistic thesis was needed to create the actual conditions for such a culture. And it had to be in keeping with the higher values of life recognized by Indian culture. Vātsyāyana's treatise on the subject gives us a systematic philosophy based upon a scientific study of sex and the art of love. He puts forth a consistent hedonistic thesis, according to which pleasure alone is the intrinsic value (kāmohi eka paramodharmaḥ). He develops it through his interpretation of some older authoritative texts available in the form of sex-aphorisms (Kāmasūtras). He tackles the problem more from the practical rather than the philosophical point of view. Undoubtedly, it does yield certain norms and principles for the regulation of the sex life for the maximization of pleasure-value (kāma). Some of his observations at the beginning of his treatise are philosophically significant. But the hedonistic thesis within the domain of moral culture maintains a force which cannot be refuted at any higher level.

The Problem of Politico-Economic Values

The value of life will have to be acknowledged in all schemes of values, for it is the essential condition of moral and spiritual culture. It conditions the content of all higher values. The hedonistic tone of life presupposes it and also the socio-economic means for its maintenance. The problems of life and politico-economic affairs of man are comprehended by the Indian term 'artha' which connotes values of a well-ordered society and economic welfare. If life is to be valued, economic means will have to be managed for its sustenance and a well-ordered society and a good government are to be provided for peaceful social living. Thus, the problem of political economy works itself out in the full range of economic and socio-political values (artha) which are essential for life and mankind.

Deriving inspiration from the glorious past, as is customary with the Indian thinkers there have been many aphorisms on material wealth (arthasūtras) which might have served as a source of inspiration for later thinkers on the subject, but no such work is extant, except that the vedas have always shown a deep concern for material prosperity and social order. Gods and Goddesses are prayed to for wealth and strength.[27] The four-fold classification of society is contained in the famous hymn to Puruṣa. It later became the basis of the caste-system in India.

Of all the sources in Sanskrit literature which deal with the subject of material gain (artha), Kautilya's *Arthasāstra* is the most systematic. He discusses the topic in comprehensive detail including the science of politics, the form of government, the rule of law and other values of worldly life. Besides this, we have a few more references to this topic in the *Mahābārata* (śāntiparva) known as the moral teachings of Vidura (Viduranīti). The law books of Manu and Yajñavalkya also show deep concern for political and social norms. But Kautilya's work is quite representative of all arthaśāstras for its systematic and exclusive treatment of the politico-economic values of life.

Nature and Definition of Values

It is clear by now that Indian thinkers have been pre-occupied with specific fields or departments such as the Absolute, liberation, morality, sex and material gain. Every value belongs to a specific department of life. The guiding principle in every treatise is the nature and importance of that specific value with which it shows an original concern. The jurisdiction of the subject is delimited by value-consideration. Because of such a compartmentalized approach to the study of values, an exclusive concern for defining the very notion of value and characterizing its nature has not been shown. This problem is undoubtedly fundamental and merits discussion at the initial stages of every work, as is done in the contemporary West, but there is a woeful gap in the Indian treatment of values in this respect. Every treatment on the subject of values is either lifted into a higher metaphysical discussion or allowed to sink down into practical details. The former is true of works on moral and spiritual values and the latter is true of mental and material values (kāma to artha). Every study of a value presupposes value as such.

There is a tendency amongst Indian thinkers to push the topic to its higher principles and locate the entire values in terms of the highest without caring to define the fundamentals. For example, every treatment of the problem of the Absolute aims at defining value in terms of the highest metaphysical reality. Similarly, liberation (mokṣa) is the essential value for "mokṣa-śāstrins". The theory of duty as discussed in the *Bhagavad-Gītā* again belongs to the category of the morally highest. There have been some minor attempts both in *Kāmasūtra* as well as in *Arthaśāstra* to discuss value as such. They happen to use the word "artha" for the notion of value (puruṣārtha). Value (artha) is divided into two, (i) positive value (artha) and (ii) negative value (anartha). But here again, value (artha) is defined in terms of the specific value treated in the respective treatises.

Let us take up the attempt of Jaimini to define the nature of value in the *Pūrva-Mimāṁsa* which is chiefly concerned with the problem of duty.[28] He refers it to the notion of good (artha) and defines good as that which is worthy of being aimed at or desired. The desirable is made an object of desire. What is the essence of this good or value (artha)? It is asserted that the principle of pleasure and pain is the constitutive criterion of value. In other words, values are of two kinds: positive and negative. Positive value (artha) is that which produces a surplus of pleasure over pain while negative value (anartha) produces the opposite.[29] Values are further divided into empirical (dṛṣṭārthas) and non-empirical (adṛṣṭārthas). Duty, being of the second kind, should not only produce pleasure in excess of pain, but also be sanctioned by the authority of the scriptures.[30] Hence, the whole account again lapses into a discussion not intimately concerned with the fundamental nature of value. *Jaimini-sūtras* suffer on account of a lack of detailed ethical study and independent thinking on the subject, because they are mainly concerned with dharma as ritual.

Hence, the basic problem of value as such has been neglected in Indian thought. It is in the context of general philosophy and metaphysical thought that higher values are located and in the context of special sciences like arthaśāstra and kāmaśāstra that other values are found. The axiological problems are made to depend upon some fundamental notions like the Absolute, self, moral law, sex and polity and a thorough study of such concepts will have to be made in order to arrive at a correct conception of values in Indian thought.

The Problem of Gradation of Values

The multiplicity of values as obtainable from the Indian concept of values leads to a problem of values which is implied in any pluralism of values. In the absence of a valid ground of preference or a principle of value-gradation, the values will not form a coherent system essential for human activity and progress. Indian thought has arrived at all sorts of values, ranging from the economic to the spiritual, but the question how are we to grade them still remains. Indian writers seem to be seriously concerned with this problem.

The concept of the "trinity of values" (trivarga) figures in Kautilya who recommends a life of enjoyment and pleasure (kāma), because a life without pleasure is good for nothing, but at the same time it should not be opposed to the considerations of virtue (dharma) and wealth (artha).[31] He further maintains that it be achieved in a balanced manner with all the three values in a harmony, for an imbalanced enjoyment of them leads to misery.[32] But he declares finally that economic values are to be preferred, because virtue and pleasure depend upon them.[33] And in the end, he leaves the whole matter of preference of values to the teacher (ācārya) and ministers (āmātya) who set the conventions.[34] Perhaps he makes practical prudence the sole arbiter of values or it is his practical wisdom which leaves such matters to human choice.

Similarly Vātsyāyana recognizes three ends of life (trivarga) consisting of wealth, pleasure and virtue and makes their study the subject-matter of his treatise.[35] He subjects wealth and pleasure to the regulation of law.[36] Wherever there is a clash of interests the cārvākas and even Vātsyāyana are forced to downgrade virtue in face of pleasure and wealth, but other systems of thought will do just the opposite. This transvaluation of values is really interesting. Vātsyāyana declares in unequivocal terms that pleasure is the only intrinsic value which should be preferred to both wealth and virtue which are its means.[37]

The concept of 'trinity of value' also occurs in the law book of Manu who observes, 'Some say their good lies in dharma and artha and some, in dharma alone while the rest contend that artha is the main good, but the correct position is that human good lies in the harmony of the three.'[38] He writes that wealth and pleasure which transgress the limits of virtue are not worthwhile.[39] An exactly similar gradation of the three values is available in the *Mahābhārata* in which a person called Vidura declares, 'It is by the help of virtue that sages have been able to cross the world. The stability of the world depends on virtue, which is the foremost of all values. Wealth is said to be the middling and pleasure is the lowest of the three. Hence we must live with controlled soul paying our best attention to virtue'.[40] Lord Krishna in the *Bhagavad-Gītā* identifies himself with that pleasure which is not at strife with virtue.[41]

The principle of gradation of their values has been suggested on the basis of the idea of harmony of values (anubandha). But how can this harmony be valued? Vātsyāyana, while advocating the concept of harmony of values, lays down the rule, viz., 'if by realization of one, the other values get realized, it is harmony'.[42] But this formula will not hold when there is a real conflict in the realization of values. It is, therefore, necessary that a valid ground of harmony be provided to solve the problem. In this connection, T.R. Gharpure writes, 'A common scholastic exercise was to compare the relative importance of the three values (*trivarga*). There was unanimity in the view that each be preferred in union with the other two, the preceding factor in the order of enumeration being given preference over the succeeding. . . . A comparative study of this character is necessary.'[43]

A comparative study of this problem of valuational gradation reveals that every writer prefers the value with which he chiefly deals; arthaśāstrins preferring wealth, kāmaśāstrins preferring pleasure and dharmaśāstrins preferring virtue. Their grounds are totally different. Kautilya makes instrumentality the ground of preference so that economic values become the basis of pleasure and virtue, while Vātsyāyana prefers pleasure to wealth and virtue on the basis of its intrinsicality. Virtue is considered to be superior to the other two on account of its higher and moral nature. Now if values are to form a coherent system as is implied in the Indian concept of values, the controversy of value-gradation will have to be settled.

There is another concept, viz., the four-fold aim of human life (catuṣpuruṣārtha) which includes liberation (mokṣa) besides the three values (trivarga). The fourth value of mokṣa is not usually mentioned on account of its non-empirical and other worldly nature, but it is always acknowledged in the Indian scheme of values. But by adding a new spiritual value, the problem of gradation will not get solved except that the spiritual value (mokṣa) will have to be preferred to the other three, and for this, a principle which validates the superiority of the spiritual to the worldly and also demonstrates the transition from the empirical to transcendental values, will have to be evolved. Indian theory of value will have to face this problem of gradation of values ultimately. It is exactly this problem with which the present dissertation is intimately concerned.

Preference of values on the avowed ground of the distinction between intrinsic and extrinsic values is not tenable, because all values are absolute and intrinsic. Similarly, the distinction between empirical and transcendental values is also not valid, because all values are essences and, as such, they are transcendental and apriori. The values of the Absolute (Brahman) and liberation (mokṣa) cannot maintain their superiority on account of their transcendental nature, but because they are spiritual values, and the spiritual is higher than the moral which in turn must be superior to whatever is mental and material and even mental values will have to be rated higher than physical existence. The criterion of preference here will not be any other than the depth of satisfaction, which differs in case of every value, increasing qualitatively as we go from artha to kāma, from kāma to dharma and from dharma to mokṣa or Brahman. This thesis is strictly in keeping with the concept of higher and lower values arrived at in the previous chapter. Artha as the value of physical existence and mokṣa or Brahman as the spiritual values stand at the extremities; the former is extreme in "strength" and the latter in "height" while other values lie in between them. But this scheme is not complete unless each specific value is studied in its true character and such a study will, it is hoped, reveal the entire concept of values in Indian thought.

Division of the Subject

The Indian concept of values refers to five specific values of human life which are indicated by the terms Brahman, mokṣa, dharma, kāma and artha. The connotation of each seems to be nebulous in as much as each pertains to a domain of its own in which many values of the same type are located; they centre around one fundamental value which forms their nucleus. These five values not only form the motive-force of philosophical systems, but also divide ancient Sanskrit literature on philosophy accordingly.

A thorough study of the five-fold values comprising the whole of Indian philosophical literature (since almost all Indian philosophy is practical in its end), means an enormous task which must be limited and made precise to be made possible. Hence, it is intended to narrow down the textual references only to representative literature, so that the task of interpreting the original text becomes manageable without disturbing the total perspective of values. The whole scheme is carried out into five chapters. Each is devoted to the study of one value. The study of material values is confined to Kautilya's *Artha-śāstra*, hedonistic values, to Vātsyāyana's *Kāmasūtra*. Since both of these treatises contain details on the subjects of political economy and sex respectively, it is not difficult to find references which are philosophically relevant. Similarly, for an insight into the Indian concept of dharma, it will be necessary to study the *Bhagavad-Gītā* and *Manusmṛti* which characterize it as duty or virtue, but the Buddhistic account of dharma cannot be ignored because of its different approach to the concept of dharma. The study of mokṣa comprises the discussion of the Buddhistic view of nirvāṇa from the point of view of a theory negating the reality of the self and of the Sāṅkhya system from the point of view of a metaphysics of the plurality of selves. The study of mokṣa, however, is not exhausted unless Śaṅkara's and Rāmānuja's doctrines of the Absolute are studied. Hence the study of Kautilya, Vātsyāyana, *Bhagavad-Gītā*, Manu, Buddhism, Sāṅkhya, Śaṅkara and Rāmānuja from the point of view their value-philosophy will be adequate to help form conclusions regarding the Indian concept of values. Necessary comparisons with similar points of view of some Western thinkers have been made to make the whole treatment intelligible.

The problem of gradation of values continues to be the main concern in the study of each value till final observations in this respect are arrived at which are reserved for the conclusion which forms a separate chapter at the end.

CHAPTER FOUR

Artha as Politico-Economic Value

KAUTILYA'S THOUGHT

A study of Kautilya's "science of polity" (*Arthaśāstra*)[1] is undertaken here, for it provides an intimate understanding of the Indian attitude towards the economic and political values of life. The discussion of the subject is bound to relate to the conditions regarding the socio-political order and the economic set-up obtainable in these times when the work was written.[2] On a philosophical analysis of it, we find certain concepts which are fundamental to the Indian concept of values and represent Indian thinking, irrespective of the historical perspective. Let us approach him for answers to two of our questions, viz., (i) What is the exact nature of artha-values? and (ii) How can it be related to the other values of life?

Kautilya, like other orthodox Indian writers, upholds the authority of the vedas (trayīsthāpanā),[3] but derives inspiration from one of them (*Atharvaveda*) which relates to his subject.[4] He refers to four sciences, namely (i) science of logic, (ii) the three vedas, (iii) agriculture and commerce and (iv) science of government or punishment.[5] Although the first is important, maintenance of the first three depends upon the science of government (daṇḍanīti),[6] because it helps in the achievement of what is not achieved and protects that which is already achieved and leads towards progress and prosperity,[7] and if it fails, anarchy (law of the jungle) shall prevail wherein the stronger shall exploit the weaker, like the bigger fishes eating away the smaller ones.[8] Arthaśāstra or the science of polity pertains to it. Kautilya defines political science as that which comprises a discussion of the views of ancient teachers regarding the acquisition and maintenance of the earth.[9] The word "earth" is specially significant and refers both to the source of income as well as the human society supported by it. Both meanings pertain to the word "artha" also, which has wider connotations otherwise, but Kautilya limits them to two, viz., money and social organization or state.[10] In Sanskrit, the word, "artha" happens to be used in a variety of senses, which refers to human activity, its psychic motivations, means and ends.[11] Kautilya distinguishes between three kinds of results of human actions, viz., (i) progress, (ii) retrogress and (iii) status quo,[12] and between two types of actions for their attainment, (i) human and (ii) providential[13] and regards them as the two wheels of this life.[14] Events due to unknown factors are due to Providence and those, by known factors, are human.[15] He leaves out the former and confines his discussion to the latter.[16] Hence, the connotation of artha should be limited to an endeavour within the ambit of human and known factors.[17] Kautilya likes to use the word for ends achievable through human effort, and reserves it for desirable ends or positive value, and anartha means a negative value. He leaves it to human prudence to decide between the two types of values. As a matter of fact, he thinks that the science of polity (arthaśāstra) is basically concerned with methods or devices by which this value can be achieved, and enumerates thirty-two of them (tantrayuktayaḥ).[18]

He distinguishes between the two aspects of value-achievement, viz., means and ends (Śaktsidhiśca); means constitute the power by which valuational activity is performed (balamśaktiḥ) and belong to three categories, viz., knowledge and advice are of the first type; money, power and punishment of the second and prowess, initiative and courage belong to the third.[19] Ends constitute happiness (sukham sidhiḥ) which are also of three types corresponding to the respective three types of means. Thus, Kautilya thinks that knowledge, money and power are fundamental to the achievement of value (artha). Means are not only conducive to other means but are also blended with ends,[20] because without proper means like money, no value can be achieved despite tremendous efforts. Hence, the importance of the study of the science of polity.

Kautilya maintains that the science of polity is concerned with the maintenance of people in their proper stations and duties as laid down in the Vedas, according to the scheme of the four-fold social order and the four stages of life.[21] He states the specific duties, accordingly, which do not differ from those prescribed in other law books (dharmaśāstra). Over and above these, there are universal duties for all persons irrespective of their station and stage of life, viz., non-violence, truth, purity, non-jealousness, compassion and forgiveness.[22] The secret of heaven and freedom (mokṣa) lies in doing one's own duties (dharma) and its opposite leads to disintegration and destruction.[23] According to him, maintenance of the four-fold social order and the four stages of human life (varṇāśrama-dharma) is the basis of social organization and public welfare, which he accepts an authority of the Vedas.[24] He does not dare think of any other scheme of social organization but his originality lies in his independent mode of implementation of the same.

Kautilya's Concept of a King

Kautilya makes the king as the sole protector of the social order. He keeps the people in their proper stations.[25] He was familiar with different forms of government such as a republic, a democracy, a federation, etc., but he thinks that a monarchy with a powerful king is the best form of government. Throughout his great work, he points in minute details the functions and the duties of the king.

Kautilya divides the whole society (nature) into two parts, namely (i) king and (ii) subjects.[26] At one place he also seems to imply that the king is the society, i.e., the welfare or illfare of the state is inevitably bound up with the king so that he is state personified; but nothing in the rest of his work warrants such an interpretation. Rather, he dwells upon the systematic distinction between a king and his subjects. He enumerates seven elements constitutive of the sovereignty of states, viz., (i) the king, (ii) the minister, (iii) the country, (iv) the fort, (v) the treasury, (vi) the army and (vii) the friends.[27] He designates the king as owner or sovereign (svāmin), because he holds the pivotal position in the whole social set-up. He describes the king as a person who is well versed in the sciences,[28] has controlled his senses (indrijita),[29] keeps company with the old (vṛadhasaṁyoga)[30] and possesses other natural qualities (Ātma-sampadā). Of his natural equipment, he lists hundreds of qualities both of the head and the heart under four heads (i) hereditary qualities (abhigami-kaguṇa), (ii) intellectual endowments (prajñāguṇa), (iii) conative aptitudes (utsāhaguṇa) and (iv) moral capacities (ātmasampanna).[31] Regarding the duties and functions of the king, he wants him to be always energetic, wakeful and ambitious,[32] since he is to exercise vigilance over officers and affairs. He then chalks out a daily time-table for the king which he should follow strictly, in order to discharge all his duties carefully. It is he who is to appoint all officers according to their qualities and duties. The officers fall into the following categories: (i) ministers (amātya),[33] (ii) ambassadors (rājadūta),[34] (iii) presidents of various departments (vibhāgādhyakṣa)[35] and (iv) spies of the secret police (guptacara).[36]

Despite absolute and sovereign powers enjoyed by the king, he is subjected to heavy responsibilities according to Kautilya. He is responsible for the maintenance of law and order, both from inside and outside disturbances through punishment and good government.[37] He is responsible for the welfare, good behaviour and progress of the public. He is to identify himself with public welfare. If the public is happy, he is so, and in their good lies his good; because he is not to do good which is dear to himself but that which is dear to the public.[38] He is undoubtedly made the instrument of public welfare. The king is supposed to attend to public welfare comprising: (i) agrarian reforms,[39] (ii) good maintenance of forests and pastures,[40] (iii) check over brothel houses[41] and (iv) management in cases of natural calamities.[42] The king is also to see to the moral and spiritual advancement of his subjects which is the primary function of the state.[43]

The king is also to see to the demands of justice. Kautilya enumerates four forms of justice, based on eternal truth (dharma), evidence (vyavahāra), history (carita) and order of the king (śāsana). The order of the king is held superior to history and history to evidence and evidence to eternal truth in case of a dispute.[44] At the same time, Kautilya upholds the dignity of eternal law (dharma),[45] for in the next lines he idealizes the king who administers justice always in accordance with law, evidence and conventions.[46] Law or eternal truth (dharma) may be superior to evidence and conventions or ethos of the people but it is not superior to the royal order, which is the final authority; for if this fails, dharma cannot exist.[47] It is, therefore, clear that Kautilya believes that the institution of kingship is the mainstay of the entire social organization, law and order, justice and progress.

Power as a Value

Kautilya systematically brings out the most important implication of artha, i.e., the ideal of power. The seizure of power is the central principle in his concept of administration. He seems to idealize the king who is rather ambitious and exerts to expand his kingdom (vijīgiṣu).[48] Kautilya provides special guidance to the king desirous of carrying out his campaign against his neighbouring states.[49] He lays down the traditional four ways for realizing the ideal of power, viz., (i) peace (sāma), (ii) appeasement through gifts (dāna), (iii) division (bheda) and (iv) punishment (daṇḍa),[50] but with an obvious difference he sanctions all sorts of means (fair or foul, moral or immoral) for gaining power. He acknowledges the wisdom of using other dirty methods, such as deceit (māyā), neglect and insult (upekṣā) and magic (inderjala). He takes great care to regulate the appointment and functions of the secret police,[51] which seems to be central to his whole scheme, and he recommends all sorts of methods including arson, sabotage, deceit, murder, poisoning, debauchery, pollution of drinking water, destruction, etc., for coping with enemies.[52] For this, according to him, spies (dūta), prostitutes (veśyā), sycophants (thugs), sham ascetics and professional prisoners (viṣakanyā) should be employed. Kautilya's logic is very plain; he says, a king should aim at seizure of power and should not bother about fairness of means. If the ends are good, the means by which they are achieved, can never be bad, for it is the ends which justify the means.[53] On this ground, he subordinates morality (dharma) and happiness (kāma) to power (artha), for the former cannot survive without the latter. Power is the highest goal of life.

Throughout his treatise, his earnest endeavour is to demonstrate how to establish a unified pattern of social control under the single centralized authority of the king. He believes in unfettered and absolute power of the king. The only restraining factors stem from his own sense of fairness, responsibility and wisdom. He is responsible for public welfare, because otherwise he is likely to fall. The check of wisdom is also subordinated to the attainment of power-ideal which is enhanced by wise means alone. He shows scant regard for the fundamental rights of the public, against the vast powers sanctioned to the king. But this charge pales away into insignificance in the face of his concept of an ideal king in whose personality, the demands of social welfare, justice, social order and of moral and spiritual uplift are harmonized in a purposive unity directed towards the maximization of power (artha). An ideal king is conceived as a psychosis in which all elements of value (artha) are combined, and directed towards itself.

COMPARISONS

Other Indian writers on polity, who have preceded or succeeded Kautilya have, by and large, subscribed to the same outline which has been advocated by him. Manu, Yājñavalkya, Vyāsa and Sukra have accepted the same pattern of social organization, on the basis of four classes or castes and the four stages of human life (varṇāśramadharma).[54] Yājñavalkya omits the fourth caste from his system and confines himself to the twice-born or the educated (dvija)[55] and bases caste on birth or purity of blood (sajāti).[56] The institution of kingship is recommended for the maintenance of social order. They believe in the divine origin of kings.[57] In the *Mahābhārata*, the evolution of the institution of kingship is traced from the state of righteousness to a state of decadence and from it to the birth of kingship which is a perpetual remedy against disorder and degradation.[58] But these authorities do not favour the doctrine of absolute power of king as Kautilya has advocated. They agree that dharma is superior to the king's authority. The authority of interpreting the sacred law or truth (dharma) vests in the learned (brahmin) and it alone is the source of the sovereign power of the king (kshātra). Dharma is superior to power (artha) and a king will have to look to the sacred law for justifying his actions. The king's chaplain (purohita) is the embodiment of moral and spiritual power (Brahman) which acts as the restraining condition on the otherwise absolute power of the king. Yājñavalkya agrees that the authority of the king is limited by the sacred law (dharma) for the interpretation of which he should appoint his scholarly chaplain or mentor (purohita) but reserves the right of the king with a trained intellect to override his counsel.[59] Kautilya is unique in denying the Brahmins the privilege of being above all temporal laws of kings.

Indian political thinking oscillates between the two extremes of the king's absolute power as advocated by Kautilya and authority of the king restricted by law (dharma) as contended in the *Mahābhārata* and *Manusmṛti*. But much depends upon the actual working of a government. Theoretically, even Kautilya's ideal king will not be less responsible to eternal law or public well-being than otherwise. Wisdom, justice, law and a sense of responsibility should rule as they actually do in the life of men and nations. The matter depends upon the quality of leadership available for public administration. Kautilya conceives of his ideal king as the best vehicle of wisdom, justice and law; while the others want to divide leadership into two distinct entities—law in the person of the scholarly chaplain and power in the person of a king.

Plato and Kautilya

It is exactly at this point that Plato's ideas about justice, state and social order prove to be immensely useful. Plato's discussion of justice which is the theme of one of his greatest works *The Republic*, seems to have a close resemblance to the Indian concept of dharma. Both mean the same as virtue or goodness (the greek word *areti* is translated as such). Plato makes it a quality of proper functioning of an organ or part of a personality or society in the beginning of his discussion[60] and goes on to develop a systematic account of justice which is made to depend on the harmonious functioning of the various capacities of an individual and of classes in a society.[61] Society is organized on the same pattern as one individual; man writ large is society.[62] This conception of society is comparable to the Indian idea of the eternal person (puruṣa)[63] which is found in the *Ṛgveda* and forms the basis of Indian social organization in terms of the four classes. But one thing must be noted in this connection, viz., the Indian concept of the eternal person (puruṣa) is that of a cosmic Being embodying the totality of the cosmos, both world and society, but Plato will not subscribe to this, for he wants to build his ideas on society on a possible analogy between the individual personality and society.[64]

The division of Indian society into four classes owes itself to the cosmic puruṣa; the learned and wise (brahmins) are his mouth, the warriors (rājanya) are his arms, the traders and agriculturists are his thighs and the servile class (śūdra) constitute his feet.[65] Perhaps this division is as much on the basis of labour and function as on analogy. Similarly, Plato first defines the virtues[66] of the individual and bases them on the three distinct elements found in the human personality (soul), namely (i) physical needs or desires, (ii) the spirited part and (iii) the rational element, and grades them in an hierarchical order placing reason at the top. Satisfaction of physical needs is necessary for life but often they may have to be held in check, which means that temperance is the characteristic virtue of the first element. The rational element in us guides us to the right path and goal, its virtue lies in wisdom or knowledge; and the spirited part is the natural ally of the reason in so far as it helps us to face the hazards and difficulties of the path shown by the 'kindly light' of reason. Its virtue is courage. The virtue of temperance wards off the temptations of pleasure and indulgence. Hence all these elements should work in harmony in an ideal character which is characterised by justice which is the fourth virtue.[67]

On the pattern of the individual personality, Plato develops a tripartite division of society comprising: (i) rulers or "guardians", (ii) warriors or soldiers and (iii) merchants. This is altogether a vocational break-down of society, strictly based on systematic training, education and selection.[68] 'The only people who can be safely entrusted with absolute power are those who know a better kind of life . . . . This is one of the grounds of his famous dictum that a community can never be properly governed unless its rulers are philosophers. . . .' It is clear that Plato believes that the supreme rulers must be not only of a philosophical temperament but trained metaphysicians, with a grasp of the ultimate nature of reality (the form of the good),[69] soldiers must be strong, active and spirited. If wisdom is the virtue of the rulers, courage must be that of the warriors. This account leaves the main masses of society behind, to constitute the third class of producers who are to cater to the material needs of people. They are farmers, craftsmen, traders and the like. Plato fails to recognize the existence of another class, i.e., of slaves or the servile class, although it is a historical fact that slavery existed in Greece in times of Plato. Perhaps Plato did not want to give them the status of a class, like Yājñavalkya, who confined his society to the first three classes (twice born). As a matter of fact, there seems to be great parallelism between the Platonic scheme of social organization and the Hindu concept of the class system (varṇadharma).[70] Accordingly the scholars (brāhmin), soldiers (kṣatriya), businessmen (vaiśya) and servants (śūdra) correspond to Plato's guardians, warriors and merchants with the fourth class of slaves not mentioned.

In Plato's ideal state people of all classes live in perfect harmony, in a spirit of willing cooperation and mutual dependence. Social justice is characteristic of that organized society in which each class or member works according to his vocation[71] and natural abilities and contributes to the common good and unity of the whole.[72] This brings Plato closer to Kautilya's contention that 'social good is based on the maintenance of a class-system (varṇadharma) in which one should do duties according to one's station'.[73] Both of them prescribe a strict rule and administration for the preservation and maintenance of this social order,[74] but they differ essentially as to the type or class of people who should rule or hold supreme power and authority in an ideal society. Kautilya prefers the institution of a strong centralized authority in the form of a king, while, according to Plato, supreme rulers should be wisemen or philosophers. Kautilya provides a philosopher (purohita) for the wise counsel of the king, but it is far from the Platonic idea of separating wisdom from courage (soldierly) in society, power is vested in a class which is subordinated to the philosophers. Kautilya takes pain to epitomize the qualities of wisdom and courage in the same person of the ruler. Both of them ensure the common good so that the rulers work for the good and happiness of all, and get the willing cooperation from the ruled.[75]

This inevitably leads to the problem of the best form of government. Plato describes various forms of government arranged in a descending order of merit to give an idea of their relation to the ideal state (republic).[76] The type of government in each society depends on the dominant standard of value or the mental attitude of the public. Field observes, 'Thus, any city in which the acquisition of wealth is regarded as the natural aim of human endeavour will inevitably tend towards an oligarchy, the concentration of political power in the hands of the wealthy. . . . It is condemned because it puts political power in the hands of the wealthy.[77] Plato here refers to the inevitability of a class conflict in which he anticipates Marxism[78] and which may result in a revolution. 'Plato has no faith in revolution of the masses as the solution of the evils of the plutocratic state. It leads to a further lower order of state, i.e., democracy because it contradicts the basic feature of the good state, the principle of division of labour, and fails to secure unity and harmony between different classes.'[79] Plato's concept of the ideal state is an organized society in which the wise rule, and all other forms of government can only approximate to this perfect type, a "pattern in Heaven" as he calls it.

If the Platonic analysis of the ordering of the forms of government is followed, Kautilya's concept of an organized society ruled by a powerful king belongs to a timocratic form of government. It is rightly based on a standard of value to be called acquisition of wealth (artha) as the natural aim of human endeavour. 'Wealth gives power and power is used to acquire more wealth, with the result, that both tend to be concentrated in fewer and fewer hands.'[80] This should be the aim of a king who should always try to maximize wealth and power by whatever means, according to Kautilya. Field writes, 'For the warrior class who in the good state looked on the rest of the citizens as in Plato's word, "free men and friends and providers of necessities" in return for the protection they gave them, now come to treat the producers as serfs and dependents, existing merely for the sake of the rulers'.[81] Kautilya may defend that a king is guided by the sacred law (dharma) and the public welfare (lokahita);[82] but he himself has raised the king above all sanctions. Now suppose a king becomes a tyrant as he is liable to become according to Plato's analysis, he throws the moral control over board and does not bother about public welfare, what is the principle which can hold him in check from his evil plans? Kautilya's fine touch of ideality about the personality of a king holds out no guarantee for the public good. Hence, power will have to be subordinated under wise leadership as provided in Platonic ideal state. Plato's description of a historical process of decadence in which he places his three forms of government closely resembles in theory with a similar description of the evolution of the institution of kingship in the *Mahābhārata*,[83] in which the first state of society ruled according to one's own dharma (dharmarāja) is the best and resembles Plato's republic, the period of decadence with Platonic democracy, and monarchy with timocracy. Monarchy is clearly accepted as a matter of necessity and not that it is an ideal state.

Kautilya thinks that the institution of kingship is the only ideal form of government which can guarantee social order and stability and public welfare. It is because of his fundamental stand, viz., that the social organization and social good (dharma) and happiness (kāma) depend on power and wealth (artha). Without it, the former cannot exist. Plato on the other hand, subordinates power under wisdom which is knowledge of the good or viture itself.[84] Justice is the social harmony of classes and virtues of wisdom, courage and temperance which corresponds to the concept of harmonized trivalues (anubandhatrivarga). There is a difference of approach between Plato and Kautilya; Plato's account is based on axiological gradation of all values under the form of the good[85] and Kautilya's concern is ontological in as much as he thinks that maintenance of life is the *sine quo non* of all valuational achievement.

Critical Remarks

Artha intimately belongs to the existence and maintenance of human life. It arises out of man's will-to-live and is a practical value. It bases itself on the necessities of human existence and social needs and points out to the intrinsic importance of their satisfaction. Maintenance of life means continuation of the psycho-physical existence in good health and efficiency. That which promotes life as such or is conducive to its maintenance is the artha-value. If survival is a value (life is a value that conditions the content of all values), it cannot be regarded as a disvalue from any point of view which has validity in value-consciousness.

But exactly here Indian views are divided into two contradictory positions; arthaśāstras regard artha as the supreme goal while the spiritual and religious traditions, including the Jainas and Buddhists consider it as positively evil in as much as it strengthens the bond of psyco-physical existence and blocks spiritual emancipation (mokṣa) or the descent of the Holy. This ambivalent attitude owes itself to their different metaphysical stands. But no moral and spiritual culture can negate the paramount importance of life, for it is not only the most powerful instrument (sādhana), but also a metaphysical presupposition of all culture. 'What would be if life were not' strikes the keynote of artha-value. Hence, the value of human life cannot be negated by any philosophy of values. The obvious contradiction about the valuational character of artha seems to originate from the axiological and ontological status of values. An exclusive concern with moral and spiritual uplift generates a distorted perspective which is deadly for the values of mundane existence, which, when seen from that point of elevation seem to sink into abysmal depths of insignificance; but an arthaśāstrin (a scholar of life-value) confines his concern to this-worldly existence and thinks of ways and means of its maintenance. The truth, perhaps, is that both material and spiritual welfare are values, one may be lower and the other higher; but they are values, for the higher does not or cannot negate the lower. The higher and the lower values may both be reconciled and harmonized into a system of values.

As soon as will-to-live is recognized as the basis and source of life-value, the struggle for existence becomes the law of human life. Might is right or the law of the fishes (matsya-nyāya) is not the true expression of it, for it is not purely biological; it is social, ethnic, anthropological and also moral, along with it, economic, physical and political factors are also involved. All this depends upon the conditions and levels of existence. The struggle for existence for fishes is not the same as for human beings. The law of survival of the fittest operates in the economic field in the form of competition, demand and supply and in the political and social spheres, in the form of power-politics. The struggle for life or survival throws man into the vortex of an intense activity. If he comes up to the task, he survives, otherwise he goes down into oblivion and non-existence. Anything that motivates and activates man for this keen struggle must be valuational and anything that depresses the human spirit for work or clamps or tones down life-activity is disvaluational. Human effort cannot be altogether written off although natural factors in the shape of fortune or misfortune come down on it with their dead weight. But faith in the absolute dependence upon fate or Providence is a retarding or negative value. This leads again to a cleavage in Indian views: the division is between the activistic and non-activistic philosophies of human life.[86] The attitude of the spiritual tradition cannot be called non-activistic, for it demands struggle and activity only at higher plane. But what it actually generates in the life-attitude of Indians, in the form of other-worldly and supramoral outlook, is deplorably non-activistic. But the ethics of the arthaśāstras is definitely activistic.[87]

The keen sense of life or will-to-live becomes a nucleus which expands and becomes a generating centre of many other values so that life itself becomes a system comprehending within its fold, values such as wealth, social stability, power, etc. These values may be extrinsic in so far as they are instrumental or form part of the self-same life-value. Any attempt to tear these values off from the systematic harmony or integration with life-value will result in an imbalance of values and a confused perspective according to which we may wrongly consider wealth or power as goal in themselves, and deprive them of their essential valuational character by virtue of which they are values. Wealth must be pressed into the service of man without which perhaps it is evil. Thus, concentration of wealth may be wrong. 'When wealth accumulates and men decay' is deplorable. Distribution of wealth assumes great importance in modern economy. Money is a powerful factor in the satisfaction of the economic necessities of life. Proper development and exploitation of natural resources, an organized system of management and distribution of commodities or wealth, so as to maximize the economic satisfaction of human beings is, therefore, an ideal. An economic system needs certain social or moral controls with a view to achieving maximum human good, otherwise it lapses into exploitation and corruption. Hence, economic values point to values of social organization and moral regulation.

Artha, as a value of social organization, law and order, belongs to the political aspect of human life. Men must be ordered in society if social existence is to be made useful and happy. Indian culture attaches an unerring rigidity to the varṇāśrama scheme, through its divine origin. Ordinarily, Puruṣa (the Divine Person) is nothing but man written in capitals which in turn signifies society. Society is divine, and it extends before and after men, brings them into being, influences them and controls them. The merits of an ideal scheme of four classes, namely scholars, warriors, businessmen and servants may derive from a functional and psychological division of labour but caste-system in its rigid and exclusive form has little claim to world recognition. Occupational division refuses to be based purely on birth or blood which may be sole indicator of some hereditary differentiation but not of other individual differences like aptitude, intelligence, personality, emotional stability, etc., on which occupational success depends. The four-fold class-system is too simple and neat for modern society.

Social organization may not be able to sustain itself altogether on conventional and religious grounds, for at times, historical and military factors tilt the balance of social forces which calls forth for a new adjustment under different schemes and orders. Social order depends upon governmental control which is the vehicle of all sorts of politico-social sanctions. Government is the caretaker or custodian of the values of social organization. Monarchy has been considered to be the only form of government which can deliver the goods according to

Kautilya. The institution of kingship divides society into two parts—the king who is the supreme authority, called god among mortals, and the subjects or the public. The Indian view of statecraft and government depends on power-politics and demands that the king should be all powerful in his kingdom and for the achievement of this ideal, he should always exert himself. Political power in the absolute sense is an ideal. The ideal king is a world-monarch (chakravartin) leading to the idea of world-government. The Indian ideal of a king is, no doubt, that of a well-bred, politically aware and responsible ruler who identifies himself with the people so as to not only know them but also look after their welfare and happiness. He is subjected to a number of social and moral controls. Law (dharma) is an impersonal moral principle which is considered to be the source of a king's authority. But in so far as it is an ideal of social aspiration, it is alright but as soon as an irresponsible king gets absolute power and control, maintaining it through rigid social patterns, governmental machinery, a vast army and secret police, there is no actual guarantee of social welfare and freedom. The charters of human rights do not also guarantee political freedom and social welfare unless there is a well-established machinery to implement it, for they are usually flouted by power-lords and experts of the game. Education, both of kings or politicians and members of the society, is essential for the realization of better social order and world-government—which are still distant ideals for mankind.

Artha is intimately related to satisfaction of desires including economic, physical, social and emotional ones, and hence it leads to pleasure-value (kāma). Artha (wealth and power) and kāma (pleasure and love) are the values for which householders aspire and which constitute the pravṛtti. Artha means life-value; but kāma which means emotional and artistic pleasure, adds a new qualitative dimension to life, and is, therefore, axiologically superior to artha.[88] Emotional and qualitative culture, however, depends on the ontological basis of life. This relationship is sometimes confused and one value is asserted over the other. Artha as life-value is a value on its own; but can lead to qualitative richness in kāma so that kāma becomes its intrinsic goal.

Values pertaining to life and its maintenance are bound to be related to moral principles, without which they may have to lose much of their valuational colour and tone. Acquisition of wealth is good, but looting it from those who legitimately own it, is certainly not so; it is good to live in so far as it does not interfere with the similar right of another, and likewise absolute power which borders upon tyranny, is a negative value.

But the question is: How are artha-values and moral values (dharma) to be related? Plato subsumed all values under the "Idea of the Good". The idea of harmony (anubandha) of values is suggested by Indian writers. But harmony, like the subsumption of values under the highest, which works against the interest of any one value, is not valid. When Kautilya asserts that moral value (dharma) is the root of happiness (sukhasya mūlam dharmaḥ) and material gain (artha) is the root of moral value (dharmasya mūlamarthaḥ), the ground of dependence is purely ontological and not axiological and if axiological ground is applied, the process of valuational preference may have to be reversed. Hence, in accordance with the twin criteria of strength and height, artha is ontologically superior to dharma and conditions its content, while dharma is axiologically higher than artha.

Artha is a name for all values belonging to life, wealth, power, socio-economic set-up, etc., which can be known as the material, biological and political values of life. So far as it is a value, it is a value in its own right, as absolute, self-existent and intrinsic as any other, although in the axiological status, it stands at the lowest level. Ontologically, however, it is the essential condition of all higher values of kāma and dharma, and though in any system of values, it may be graded as lower, it will not be ruled out as insignificant.

CHAPTER FIVE

Kama as Hedonistic Value

VATSYAYANA'S KAMASUTRA

There is a conscious tendency in Indian culture to appreciate values concerning the cultivation of sex and love in life and the pursuit of hedonistic culture. The doctrine of kāma as the technique of love-making and pursuit of pleasure has been the exclusive theme of the literature called kāmaśāstra. It was the culmination of all that was implicitly present in the ancient traditions of Indian culture. The art of love-making and magic was the dominant concern of pre-upanisadic literature.[1] Vātsyāyana's Kāmasūtra (aphorisms on the art of love) is a systematic exposition of sex and love in life and makes the art of love and the pursuit of pleasure the subject-matter of a science. The work is often considered to be of much later times,[2] but a clear reference in it is made as to its origin and development, from Kāmasūtra written by Nāndī (the vehicle of Śiva)[3] and developed by later sages (ācāryas).[4] Vātsyāyana condensed it into the present form of the treatise, known as Kāmasūtra.[5]

Vātsyāyana pays homage to the three values of life at the very beginning, viz., virtue (dharma), wealth (artha) and pleasure (kāma).[6] Perhaps he thinks that together they constitute the complete good of man, and likes to devote his work to their pursuit. His motive becomes clear when he accepts the pursuit of these three values so far they are harmonious, as the chief goal of human life.[7] What constitutes their harmony is not clear from his words. He divides life into three stages: (i) childhood, (ii) youth and (iii) old age; (he is making a departure from the traditional conception of the four stages of life, the fourth being āśramadharma), and wants the first to be devoted to education and thereby to the acquisition of wealth (which later on is made the prerequisite of a life of enjoyment);[8] the second part (youth) to enjoyment (kāma) and old age to virtue and salvation.[9]

He thinks that education and vocation is a preparation for a life of pleasure, which, according to him, is of topical importance. He recommends that, after the study of the sciences concerning virtue and wealth, a youngman should study *Kāmasūtra* and its sixty-four auxiliary sciences.[10] A girl should study it before her marriage, for after it, it is difficult to study.[11]

He describes the sixty-four arts concerning the science of love and enjoyment (kāma).[12] They can be classified into four groups, viz., first, fine arts like music, dance, painting, etc., numbering twenty-four in all; second, the gambling arts numbering twenty in all; third, arts of mating, numbering fifteen in all and fourth, later arts like promising, cursing, etc., five in all. A man who is well versed in these sixty-four disciplines is a man of culture, successful and lucky with women.[13] He says that some people doubt the utility of the study of the science of love, because they feel that sex-behaviour is natural and universal, and if birds and beasts can do it without any training, there is no point in studying this science.[14] Vātsyāyana, however, feels that manners, morals, and culture distinguish men from beasts, and he decides that by the study of this science alone, can married life be fruitful.[15]

A study of the science of pleasure (kāma) cannot be useful, unless the pursuit of pleasure is a laudable goal. Vātsyāyana has accepted the concept of the three values (trivarga) as a desirable goal of human life. He enjoins everybody to cultivate virtue (dharma) by studying dharmaśāstras[16] and work hard for the acquisition of wealth and other necessary things of life.[17] He takes up the traditional gradation of the three values, viz., virtue is to be preferred to wealth and wealth to pleasure.[18] He disputes such a gradation on the ground of vocation first, e.g., acquisition of power and wealth (artha) is usually recommended for kings[19] and hence it is preferable to virtue and pleasure because it is their cause.[20] In the same way, for ascetics a life of virtue and spiritual culture is preferable. But vocation as the ground of preference of values is not tenable, for vocation itself is based on principle of selection which is nothing but valuational.

Vātsyāyana resorts to a metaphysical principle which differentiates between naturalistic and supernaturalistic attitudes towards values. He writes that people tend to avoid duty and virtue because they do not get their rewards for them in this life.[21] It may be noted here that this naturalistic transvaluation of values refers directly to the tradition of the Cārvākas who were popular (before the time of Vātsyāyana) for their naturalism (lokāyatavāda). They validated it on the epistemological ground of perception as the only source of knowledge.[22] Whatever can be perceived, exists or is real. Inference is no validity. They repudiated supernaturalism and the idea of hell and heaven. They advocated a hedonistic and secular goal of human life. Pleasure (kāma) is the supreme goal of life.[23] They recommended pleasures on the basis of their quantity and not on quality. Pleasures of the senses and sexual gratification, which are certain, concrete this-worldly and not illusory, are to be preferred.[24] They also prefer pleasure to virtue on these grounds.[25] We have only one duty and that is towards the hedonistic goal of life.

Vātsyāyana definitely has this argument in mind when he refers to naturalistic tendencies among people; only he is not so bold as the Cārvākas. Perhaps he wants to subscribe to the vedic line rather than be branded as an indefile (nāstika) like the Cārvākas,[26] in as much as he accepts virtue as one of the aims of life.[27] He combines the naturalistic principle with another premise, i.e., perceptibility of results of acts (dṛṣṭārthatvam), but does not work out his thesis any further and, therefore, it is not certain whether or not he believed in the Cārvākas' epistemological stand. On the basis of the knowability principle, it seems to be difficult to prefer pleasure in the face of wealth (artha), which belongs to the life of this-world. But he twists this principle to apply it to the acquisition of wealth which needs hard labour and favourable fortune (bhāgya).[28] He declares that every thing depends upon fate which disposes for man's richness, poverty, success, failure, happiness and grief.[29] But he does not rule out the usefulness of human effort; rather he recommends a life of hard labour for happiness. An inactive person cannot be happy.[30] Fate is another form of the principle of unknowability (adṛṣṭa). As a matter of fact, he is not so keen in applying the metaphysical principle of adṛṣṭa as he seems to be inclined in favour of a valuational criterion of certainty or surety of value-achievement (artha-prāpti). On this basis, virtue can be condemned, because its results or rewards are not sure.[31] Nobody is a fool to give up that which is already achieved for that which is not yet achieved.[32] But on the authority of the śāstras, he recommends a life of virtue.[33] He does not seem to subscribe to any of these criteria according to which values should be preferred in actual life.

Even with regard to hedonism, Vātsyāyana takes up some of the grave doubts as to the desirability of pleasure.[34] He seems to be aware of the traditional arguments against the value of pleasure. A man may fall prey to detestable vices on account of an indulgent life, take to bad company, be attracted towards other people's wives, a life of profligacy and debauchery which may lead to loss of wealth and virtue.[35] Out of perverted sex are born confusion, ill-fame, accursedness and faithlessness which make a person condemned.[36] He clearly maintains a distinction between the healthy and unhealthy or normal and abnormal aspects of sex in man, and demonstrates that much of the condemnation of sex[37] is due to its perverted manifestations and abnormal expressions rather than due to a healthy concern for it. He emphatically lays down that, like food, sex-gratification is essential for physical health.[38] Hence, he finally establishes that because of fear of its perversions and vicious expressions, one should not eschew its rightful gratification.

He thus comes to his final argument, viz., pleasure is an intrinsic and absolute goal. Whereas Kautilya and other writers on dharma make instrumentality the sole ground of value-preference, Vātsyāyana changes the ground of preference from instrumentality to intrinsicality of values, and thus he provides for a radical transvaluation of values, which was originally initiated by the Cārvākas.[39] Vātsyāyana argues that pleasure (kāma) is the goal of both virtue and wealth.[40] It is undoubtedly true about money that it is never an end in itself, it is ultimately for the comfort, health and satisfaction of man that it is required. Money as an end in itself will be self-defeating.

Similarly, it is argued that virtue must lead to happiness.[41] The deontological point of view, according to which the possession of a virtuous character is a goal in itself, even in conditions of misery, is ruled out in favour of the utilitarian thesis which makes good character a sure means of happiness. If virtue entitles a person to plentiful and superior enjoyments in an other-world (heaven), then pleasure of similar enjoyments in this-world cannot be condemned as immoral.[42]

Vātsyāyana further maintains that happiness which is based on virtue and wealth must be most desirable. A balanced achievement of the three values leads to happiness, both of this-world as well as that of the other-world.[43] He maintains a hedonistic criterion for moral life when he writes that a gentleman's ethic is to do that which is sure to bring him happiness and delight in this world and about the consequences of which he is not doubtful in the next.[44]

Vātsyāyana places pleasure-value (kāma) in the proper perspective with the other values such as virtue and wealth, and argues that one should do that which helps realize all the three values (trivarga) or which promotes two of them (dvivarga) but is not opposed to the third or that which achieves one of them (ekavarga) but is not opposed to the other two. Too much charity may lead to loss of money and happiness or severe penance may destroy health and happiness.[45] It may sometimes be felt that the pursuit of sensual pleasure may clash with virtue or achievement of wealth. Manu believes in hunting, gambling, daydreaming, conversation, sex-indulgence, drinking, music, dance and aimlessly wandering as the ten occupations of a man of pleasure.[46] But if hunting is for protection, sexual intercourse for progeny, drinking for war, music, dance, etc., for devotion, then they can never be opposed to virtue and wealth. Hence indiscriminate pleasures are not desirable. The value of pleasure depends on its qualities or on its sanctification. Here Vātsyāyana makes a major departure from the Cārvākas who did not distinguish between pleasures qualitatively.

The Nature of Kama

Vātsyāyana's argument in favour of a hedonistic goal further depends upon the nature and character of what he designates as "kāma".[47] In Sanskrit, the word "kāma" is used for a whole range of psychic states, ranging from passion, sex, lust, desire and love to pleasure, sensuous gratification and sensual delight. The use of this word in the *Bhagavad-Gītā* in the sense of interest (sakāma) brings out yet another range of connotations comprising motive, interest, intention, wish and desire. Affecto-conative tendency towards the attainment of a definite object is desire. Vātsyāyana defines kāma[48] as a tendency or deposition which when excited into action, operates at four distinct levels, viz., (i) mind, (ii) self, (iii) senses and (iv) the objects of senses. It is a disturbed state of the organism which is technically called emotion; but having its origin in the mind it involves the self (ātman)[49] in so far as the responsibility and resultant delight is ascribed to the self; the mental disposition for gratification compels sense organs to come into contact with objects and the quality of agreeability and fitness results in a state of mind which can be known as pleasant, gratifying or pleasurable.

Kāma follows the definition of instinct. According to McDougall, 'instinct is an innate disposition which determines the organism to pay attention to an object of a class, to feel an emotional excitement in its presence and an impulse to a specific mode of behaviour'.[50] Vātsyāyana does not define it as inborn. It is not the behaviour which is innate; but the tendency to do it. McDougall takes pains to disprove Lloyd Morgan's contention regarding unlearnt behaviour. Vātsyāyana's definition of kāma identifies it with any affective-conative tendency towards pleasure which may be better termed as desire,[51] wants, appetites. Blind urges are psychic tendencies, but they are not conscious and thus do not involve the self (consciousness) and are not, therefore, kāma or desires which involve conscious pursuit of agreeable feelings. A person may be intensely hungry, but may not desire food on account of its undesirability at that time. Hence desires or kāma works at the conscious level, at which we do discriminate between right and wrong.

Vātsyāyana further delimits his definition of kāma, by distinguishing between general and specific desires. At the general level, desire is confined to sensuous gratification; but it reaches its final culmination only in sexual gratification which is specific and constitutes the true nature of kāma.[52] Thus, he defines it as desire culminating in sexual gratification.[53] For it, according to him, the meeting of man (hero or nāyaka) and woman (heroine or nāyakā) is necessary.[54] Sex is one of the permanent sentiments (rasa) and its corresponding emotion is love (ratibhāva). Sex (sṛṅgāra rasa) is believed to be of two kinds, according as it results in union (saṁbhoga) or separation (vipralambha).

Vātsyāyana develops his doctrine of sexual gratification (kāma) on the basis of both physiological and psychological conditions which are essential for it. Among the physiological requirements, he mentions the proneness of the organs of pleasure. These organs are of two kinds, (i) sense organs and (ii) sex organs. The most natural and elementary feelings of pleasure are the result of the contact of sense organs with agreeable objects, but since the pursuit of pleasure is an art, therefore, a man of cultivated taste (nāgraka)[55] should train his senses, through the fine arts and disciplines like music, painting, etc. But the sexual urge for its awakening needs the maturation of sex-hormones at puberty. Three physiological criteria are laid down for proper sexual gratification, viz., (i) the physical compatibility of man and woman, (ii) proper time and (iii) state of preparedness.[56]

Psychologically, when the sexual urge is born in the mind, it is manifested in two kinds of expressions: (i) gestures (hāva) which are classified as sixteen and (ii) emotions (bhāva) which have also been subjected to intense study and are of two kinds, overt and subtle. Sexual emotion not only depends upon the physiological conditions, but also on psychological ones. On this account, Vātsyāyana has stated four bases of such emotion (prīti), viz., (i) habit and physical gesticulation (abhyāsa), (ii) thinking (vicāra), (iii) memory (smaraṇa) and (iv) sense-objects (visya).[57] Dance, music, etc., arouse desire through gesticulation; by willing we can get it, by remembering it is stimulated and through sense organs the stimulation can lead to an emotion. Vātsyāyana devotes many chapters to the proper technique and other considerations[58] of the sexual union which, according to him, is the central principle of his theory of kāma. In the last book he even discusses the desirability of using aids and arts of beautification for a fuller life of pleasure (kāma).[59]

Socio-Moral Sanctions for Hedonism

Regarding the social sanction for a hedonistic ideal of human life, Vātsyāyana is thoroughly convinced that the pursuit of love and pleasure pertains to the life of the householder which is considered to be the greatest of the four stages of life. The advent of this stage is marked by two events: (i) settling in a career and (ii) marriage.[60] He thinks that acquisition of wealth through a vocation is essential for the maintenance of a household. Education, landed property, house, money and friends are some of the desirables for a man of pleasure.[61] He discusses in some detail the situation and design of the house to be constructed for a happy household.[62] The second essential, i.e., married life provides the framework within which the pursuit of pleasure is to be confined.

A person who has amassed enough wealth and married a girl on the basis of her family, temperament and merit, is entitled to the life of a cultured man (nāgaraka). He upholds the sanctity of marriage on social and moral grounds. Only marriage with a girl of the same caste who is virgin, and in accordance with the rules of the śāstras, yields good progeny and not otherwise.[63] He rules out all marriages which are not strictly in accordance with the social norms of caste, even if they promise great pleasure.[64] The text could also imply that such unlawful marriages are bad, because they are not productive of happiness in the end. Social sanctity is, therefore, needed for an undisturbed pursuit of pleasure. Vātsyāyana's man of refined taste or voluptuary (nāgaraka) should plan well his daily life for a systematic pursuit of pleasure.[65]

Vātsyāyana recommends a healthy and rightful satisfaction of one of the primary instincts of man. Expression and refinement of sex leads to health and happiness[66] but at the same time he is well aware that if sex is denied proper expression or is suppressed, it is bound to cause perversions (kāmavikāra). He classifies these abnormalities, numbering ten in all,[67] viz., (i) vacancy in eyes, (ii) attachment, (iii) resoluteness as to the achievement of goal, (iv) disturbed sleep, (v) reduced state of physical health, (vi) loss of appetite for pleasures, (vii) shamelessness, (viii) infatuation, unconsciousness and (ix) desire for death.[68] It is on account of perverted desires for sex-gratification that such disorderly tendencies take their birth.[69] Vātsyāyana condemns these desires as not sanctified on moral and social grounds. A married person owes certain obligations not only to his or her partner but also to others. He should be faithful in marriage, but if he looks towards another person, outside the marital relation for sexual gratification, it is a case of perversion.

Out of the four kinds of heroines, only two, namely, wife and a woman married for the second time (punarbhū) fulfil the conditions for a rightful sex-partner; and the other two, namely, prostitute and another man's wife (paradārā) are declared wrongful sex-partners. Vātsyāyana's chief motive in discussing in such detail the life and conditions of prostitutes[70] is not to encourage its practice, but to expose the institution. But Vātsyāyana does not consider prostitution to be as bad as extra-marital relations.[71] He narrates the conditions under which they are established, and demonstrates that it is purely due to perversion.[72] He allows full freedom for sexual life though within certain intrinsic limits.[73] Vātsyāyana's earnest endeavour is to reconcile the freedom of sexual life with social control in the life of a voluptuary (nāgaraka) who has learned to be faithful to his goal (kāma) and refine its expression and also abide by the rules of social life. Disturbed sexual pursuit on account of social transgression is not only the cause of pathological perversions, but brings in its wake unhappiness. The notion of happiness (sukham) is different from that of pleasure (kāma).[74] In that case his position can be interpreted to imply that sexual pleasures (kāma) pave the high road to happiness (sukham).

It may be noted here that the meaning of pleasure (kāma) as understood by Vātsyāyana cannot be stretched to include spiritual delight (rasa) or bliss (ānanda).[75] Kāma has a rightful claim on aesthetic pleasure in so far as it culminates in true sensual pleasure (pradhānakāma). The pursuit of fine arts is ultimately conducive to sensual delight (ratibhāva). He will not subscribe to the traditional Indian view that art is a dedication to the Deity and is meant to attain a state of self-absorption and blissfulness[76] which has nothing to do with sensual delight (ratibhāva). Eros (sṛṅgāra rasa) is one of the sentiments[77] which leads to erotic pleasure (kāma). Indian Aesthetics demands a refinement of sensuous pleasures and emotional states so as to lead to bliss (rasa) which is not sensual in character at all.[78]

The Contention of other Hedonists

Vātsyāyana's point of view can be construed as a contention in favour of a hedonistic[79] view of life, and he, therefore, has the full support of a tradition of thinkers who believe that pleasure is the supreme goal of human life. Pleasure is an elementary characterization of a mental state which is pleasant or satisfying and psychologically attends upon the successful execution of an activity or satisfaction of a desire. Desires or activities are motivated by organic needs, instincts or other general tendencies which do not always have pleasure as their object. Perhaps pleasure is never the matter-of-fact goal of desires. That we desire pleasures (objects) is no evidence that we aim at pleasure (a pleasant state of mind). Thus, we have desires not because of pleasure, but we have pleasure because of desires. Pleasure without a reference to a definite desire and its object (which forms its content) is hollow and empty, signifying only a quality without the object. But this psychological analysis of pleasure cannot rule out the possibilities of desire under the conditions of learning; a smoker who is initiated into his habit by the sheer force of initiation learns to smoke for a special pleasure which acts as a reinforcing factor.

The questions as to what constitutes attraction, immediate or remote pleasures is very hard to decide, for reasons of individual differences in structure, temperament and moods Vātsyāyana definitely favours immediate pleasures to remote ones.[80] Most of our decisions are based upon a promise of future pleasures. Sitting in a dentist's chair may be agonizing, but promises the future pleasure of good health. "The Cārvākas believe in forestalling immediate pleasures in order to gain greater ones in the future. These activities like agriculture, trade particularly, require putting off some immediate gains for greater pleasures in future."[81] But the issue seems to point to another ground of preference, viz., certainty,[82] which Vātsyāyana forcefully advocates.

The conscious act of preference involves a moral choice rather than a purely psychological response and a person feels it obligatory to aim at the maximum quantity of pleasure. He does subscribe to this position implicitly, for he enjoins on man to endeavour systematically for the greatest sexual pleasure (rati-bhāva). This point of view is similar to that of Bentham who finds both psychological as well as ethical hedonism quite compatible. 'What they do is to seek pleasure (psychologically); and what they ought to do is to act as to realize the greatest possible amount (of pleasure).'[83] Bentham recommends seven factors in calculating the quantity of pleasures, viz., intensity, duration, certainty, propinquity or remoteness, fecundity, purity and extent. The dimension of pleasure, i.e., extension makes the hedonistic goal a universal one, 'the greatest happiness of the greatest number'. Bentham provides four sanctions for a hedonistic goal, viz., (i) physical, (ii) political (iii) moral and (iv) religious. Vātsyāyana implicitly works out similar sanctions for a hedonistic culture when he admits that the requirements of health and social norms permit the pursuit of pleasure; and his considerations of virtue and Providence correspond to moral and religious sanctions of Bentham.[84] All these sanctions are externally imposed, barring the moral sanction, which cannot be viewed as internal as it is a sort of psychological compulsion.

J.S. Mill adds another sanction—that of a sense of nobility; but introduces a formidable difficulty in the act of preferring pleasures on the ground of quantitative difference in pleasures. He disparaged Bentham's view on the basis of sensualism, saying that it insists on no qualitative difference in pleasures.[85] Vātsyāyana definitely abides by the principle of qualitative differentiation of pleasures while the Cārvākas resemble Bentham in maintaining only quantitative differences among pleasures. Once sublimated and refined, pleasures, such as those obtained through artistic pursuits are preferred. The ground of preference can never be pleasure itself, but it must be some high moral consideration in favour of which the hedonistic thesis will have to be surrendered, for pleasure will have to pay the price for its own refinement. The only way to defend the hedonistic thesis is to reconcile the claim of pleasure with that of moral or intellectual culture.

Henry Sidgwick took up the task of reconciling the hedonistic goal of life with an independent sense of duty in right earnestness. A full-blooded hedonist is obliged to feel one and only one sort of duty, viz., his duty to attain the maximum of pleasure, and any principle which seeks to diminish it is no part of his duty. Hence, all moral and aesthetic considerations which tend to enhance pleasure, are welcome in hedonism, but if they work against its true interest, they become intolerable.[86] Therefore, any principle of rational duty and social obligation shall create dualism in hedonistic thinking. For Sidgwick, the dualism is between egoism and altruism, but for Vātsyāyana, this problem does not exist as he has not thought on the lines of universal hedonism; he worked out a hedonistic goal for the individual. But the dualism for him exists between the pleasure-principle (kāma) and social control (dharma).[87] Sidgwick's arguments for reconciliation of the dualism on psychological and metaphysical grounds are vain attempts. Persons who derive pleasure from sadism are very real and they cannot be ignored as mere pathological cases. Perversions of sex, on the same lines, cannot be disparaged as mere antisocial aberrations unless they are self-defeating. Sidgwick's conception of duty as imposed by the divine authority to sacrifice pleasure cannot be held feasible either, because a true hedonist cannot have faith in a God who asks him to forego pleasure.

It is clear, therefore, that theory of the hedonism will have to vindicate two propositions, viz., (i) pleasure is the only value and (ii) pleasures differ in quality. We have found that both of these propositions are untenable, independently as well as together. According to the first, pleasure is value so that if pleasure increases in a psychosis, the value should increase. In the case of rape or sadistic actions, where sexual expression or the human libido is allowed the fullest freedom, pleasure increases but value does not. Hence, pleasure cannot be equated with value. It cannot even be regarded as an index of value-achievement. But pleasure can hold out a claim to be one of the values. In that case its relation with other intellectual, moral and spiritual values will pose a problem which brings us to the second position of the hedonists, for qualitative differences on the basis of refinement of pleasures means increasing accommodation of higher values in the hedonistic scale. We have seen that the true hedonistic thesis clashes with higher values. But once other values are admitted along with hedonistic values, there cannot be a state of war between them for both of them are values having claims on the value-consciousness of man.

Rashdall has resolved this tangle for hedonists by conceiving of a system of values in which pleasure, duty, virtue, character and happiness hold their proper places. He is inclined to give a prominent position to duty in the whole scheme.[88] Vātsyāyana has always worked on the concept of the three values (pleasure, wealth and duty). If the hedonistic goal (kāma) is to be combined with duty (dharma), the latter cannot be reduced to the status of mere instrumentality, for in that case, there is no real harmony (anubandha). He admits a view of harmony in which the pursuit of one value is not opposed to that of another,[89] and he leaves it to the individual to decide about the situations in which they clash.[90] It is on account of deficiency of intelligence, intense attachment, hauteur, confusion, simplicity, blind faith, wrath, madness, lethargy, thoughtlessness and misfortune that a person decides wrongly.[91]

It is clear that Vātsyāyana does not want to subordinate one value to another, except that in his original contention he makes pleasure (kāma), on account of its intrinsicality, the goal of other two values of virtue and wealth. We have already seen that values are always intrinsic and absolute; what we call as instrumental value affirms the truth of its being derived from another value. Hence, if artha and dharma are values, they are so in their own right and, therefore, cannot be regarded as instrumental or derived from pleasure (kāma) which they happen to lead to. The question of relationship between ends and means may be vitally important for consistent hedonist.[92] The controversy, whether means justify the ends or ends justify the means, is tacitly based on the presumption that means are separable from the ends; but as a matter of fact it is impossible to draw a line demarcating exactly where means finish and ends start. The two are, therefore, fused into a valuational situation which is always a complex whole in which one determines the other. It is difficult to tell apart a virtuous life from the happiness which it must cause and the acquisition of wealth from the comfort and pleasures it affords. The simple logic of the valuational situation will demand the determination of (kāma) by artha and dharma, and if values are held to be always independent and absolute, this determinism of one value by another can only be understood in terms of a system of values in which values influence other values and in turn are influenced by them. Hence, the consideration of means and ends cannot become the basis of the gradation of values.

Comments

Kāma refers to pleasure. Pleasure is a state of mind with a pleasant or hedonistic tone, which accompanies the successful accomplishment of an activity. It is, in this respect, an abstract quality of mental life, and characterizes all those states of human life which can somehow be called pleasant, happy, joyful, delightful and gay. Thus, pleasure has a wide range of application from sensuous to sensual pleasures.

If kāma means pleasure, i.e., an abstract quality or mental states experienced as pleasant, it may be an index of value-achievement and not value itself, for it does equally attend on the execution of an activity considered as evil; there may be a situation in which pleasure may increase and value may decrease. All hedonistic arguments in favour of pleasure thus must fail. To be acceptable it will have to provide concrete content to the pleasurable experience. The Cārvākas and Vātsyāyana provide some specific contents of pleasure.

Kāma means pleasure resulting from the satisfaction of desire. Kāma signifies desire in its entirety, from the rise to the finish. Desire is the affective-conative state in which one consciously seeks to satisfy some need, want, instinct and motive or to achieve an end. The mind has a number of instinctive dispositions or sentiments. When they come into contact with objects, desires are born. Desires dispose the person to achieve goals both natural and conditioned. Pleasure marks the achievement of the objective on the fulfilment of a desire, but it does not invariably characterize the process of fulfilment, unless it is imagined to be completed even though it is not actually so. This distinguishes between real and imaginary pleasures.

Desires, capable of giving rise to kāma-value, are further designated and specified as sensual, sexual, amorous, artistic and aesthetic. When sense-organs come into contact with agreeable objects, like rhythmical notes reach the ears which satisfy some natural or cultivated likes and tastes, they give rise to pleasure. Sex is an instinct geared to a biological function; but activities associated with sex are highly hedonistic in tone. Sex leads to the higher manifestation of love. Friendship, fellowship, comradeship, tenderness, sympathy, affection and humaneness which have always to share something with love, point to realms both higher and nobler with which sex may have little to do.[93] Freud surrenders the sex-principle when he admits of its sublimation. Much of the pleasure, is a result of the aesthetic and artistic cultivation of the senses and tastes. Kāma-value specifically belongs to the pleasures of aesthetic culture and enjoyment of artistic expressions of the human sense of beauty in literature, poetry, drama, music, painting, sculpture and other fine arts.

The qualitative gradation of pleasures may prove disastrous for any hedonistic thesis and the Cārvākas are the most consistent in recommending all pleasures, preferably sensual, because of their certainty and intensity; but since kāma does not mean an abstract pleasure, without a definite content, hence the whole of the hedonistic psychosis can be evaluated qualitatively on the basis of its contents. Vātsyāyana steals a march over the Cārvākas and wins over kāma for both sensual and artistic pleasures. The argument based on the principle of higher and lower pleasures itself points to some other principle of evaluation of pleasurable states. Hence, kāma will have to work in harmony with other values and not in complete isolation from moral and social principles (dharma).

But kāma is regarded as the only and the supreme goal (parama puruṣārtha) of human life by the Cārvākas, while the Vedāntic school regards kāma as an obstacle in the way of the attainment of highest goal of spiritual liberation (mokṣa). Both are extreme views born out of different preoccupations. Neither kāma alone nor mokṣa alone is the only goal. The seeming contradiction in Indian philosophy is due to the fact that an exclusive concern for one realm leads a scholar to neglect the other and the contradiction appears because of wrong emphasis.

Kāma, in its full scope, ranging from lust to love and from sensual pleasure to artistic delight, may not be antagonistic to spiritual life; it may share it or lead to it, even enrich it. Similarly spiritual freedom (mokṣa) and religious holiness only show the way to kāma for an axiological assent. Both can be, therefore, harmonized through a middle principle, i.e., moral discipline (dharma).

An uncontrolled and unregulated life of love and pleasure (kāma) is evil and is, therefore, not desirable. Kāma is confined to the life of a householder, who is also to satisfy it in consonance with the demands of righteousness (dharma), for control is the very condition of proper enjoyment. The principles of moral regulation may be rational, natural, moral and spiritual. Increasing regulation by the moral principle (dharma) is itself in the interest of kāma for the increase of its axiological significance, characteristic of the higher and final manifestations of kāma. Dharma rules kāma, chastens and ennobles it.

Kāma as the qualitative emotional experience of the amorous and aesthetic activities of human life must be related to the general value of the existence of life as such. Artha, in the form of power and wealth is the only means of subsistence for a man. If artha is a life-value, kāma is meant to enrich it with qualitative experience and culture. But without life, culture cannot subsist, and without cultural achievement, life is meaningless. Hence, artha is ontologically superior and kāma is axiologically superior. Kāma brings to life much of the worth, charm and tone after which it hungers and thirsts. Life itself is willing to admit of kāma's axiological richness and hence it can be harmonized with kāma.

Kāma, which means pleasure, is a necessary ingredient of what is called happiness, a general condition of durable satisfaction of purposes in human life. Happiness is a complex psychosis in which pleasure colours the various contents of human life including moral control and spiritual achievement, and kāma is only an episode in the life-history of happiness. Happiness is concrete and pleasure is abstract. It is, therefore, more true that happiness (sukham) is the supreme goal of life rather than pleasure alone (kāma).

Kāma, taken to mean pleasure resulting out of sensual, amorous, aesthetic and artistic enjoyment is an intrinsic value, and cannot be ruled out by any higher moral or spiritual principle. It is a value in itself, cherished and sought after by men of taste and culture. Kāma points to the human capacities of love and artistic expression which are to be developed, cultivated and fulfilled with a view to achieving the maximum of a peculiar value known as kāma. Kāma is an absolute and intrinsic goal of life which has its distinct but proper place in the total scheme of values. It is, therefore, wrong to assert that kāma is the only value, for it is one of the values of life.

CHAPTER SIX

Dharma as Moral Value

The Notion of Dharma

The concept of dharma seems to be quite central to the Indian concept of values. It has a comprehensive character in as much as it implies a variety of meanings and refers to many states which are valuational,[1] but its moral nature is consistently acknowledged. Its intimate concern with human conduct and moral life makes it focal in its position with regard to other values of life. This exactly is the theme of the treatises on law (dharmaśāstras). Though the use of the word 'dharma' was fully in vogue in the Vedic times,[2] it became the central concept of Hinduism only much later. A more important concept of ṛta was prevalent in the Vedic times which carried two meanings, one of cosmic law and the other of social and moral conduct.[3] Originally it referred to the law of orderliness which governed the course of things and provided the principle of human conduct, for 'orderly and consistent conduct is the essential feature of good life. Disorder often represented in the form of falsehood (*anṛta*), is the greatest evil and virtue is in conformity with the cosmic law.'[4] The metaphysical bond between the ontological and axiological characterizations of ṛta lies in truth (satyam) which is not only a synonym of ṛta but also significant in the cosmic as well as moral spheres. The concept of dharma preserves the two implications of ṛta in yet another unique manner, characteristic of Indian thought,[5] in which it is used not only as an ontological reality, such as in Buddhism, but also in legal, social, political and moral senses as in Hinduism.

Dharma as the Central Concept of Buddhism

The Buddhist treatment of the concept of dharma is original and unique in view of its positivistic approach to philosophical problems. Stcherbatsky is of the considered opinion that dharma is the central concept in all Buddhist philosophy.[6] According to him, dharma (Pali: 'dhamma') is an element of existence which is ultimate, subtle and real and an imposing superstructure of a systematic philosophy has been built on this central concept of dharma.[7] Accordingly, the four noble truths which constitute the spirit of Buddhism are, (i) discovering the elements of existence (dharma); (ii) their causal connection, (iii) the possibility of their suppression for ever (nirodha) and (iv) the way to do so (mārga).[8]

Buddhism which may strike one as a purely moral philosophy discloses itself to be a metaphysical doctrine, according to which existence is an interplay of a plurality of primal elements (pṛthakdharmas). These elements do not inhere in one another and hence there is no reality or substance (like matter or soul) apart from a mere combination of these (saṁskṛt) under the influence of forces (saṁskāra). These elements, of course, cooperate with one another to make things (saṁskṛta) in accordance with the law of causation (pratitya-samutpāda). Elements are non-substantial, soulless (anātman) impermanent (anitya, i.e , points in time stream) and restless (duḥkha). Hence, the world process is based on dharmas which cooperate, proceeding from causes (hetu-prabhava) and steering towards extinction (nirodha).

The concept of dharma in the Buddhist system has acquired a completely different connotation which is unique in itself and is not traceable to any other system. Dharma, as the basic element of existence is a purely metaphysical notion. The Buddhist doctrine of dharma, as the basis of samsāra cannot be interpreted to mean that dharma like ṛta is the Eternal Law of the course of things, for dharmas (dharmadhatus) cooperate under the influence of laws of causation which are different from dharmas themselves. It is far-fetched to say that dharma, in Buddhism, means the 'law of Nature, the chain of causation'[9] or the immanent order of the world process or the force binding things together and regulating human conduct.[10] More so, when we closely seek to understand the nature of dharma in Buddhism, we find that it is regarded as subtle, ultimate, unanalysable, evanescent and therefore an inconceivable and transcendental element.[11]

The purely metaphysical implications of dharma in Buddhist philosophy do not incline us towards considering its claims in the moral sphere. But nobody can help this unless dharma itself, as conceived in Buddhism has a moral implication. Remotely so, of course, dharma, in strict Buddhist terminology, does touch on the doctrine of karma which, in other Hindu systems, is inevitably linked with dharma. The Buddhist doctrine of karma instead of that of dharma, seems to have a closer bearing on moral philosophy. Karma in Buddhism is a phenomenon of moral causation. If Buddhism disposes us towards complete causality without any exception, operating in the world process, it has no other claim except fatalism in the moral field; but it distinguishes between material causation under the law of homogeneity (sabhagahetu), causation in the organic world under the law of growth (upacaya) and causation in the animate world under moral causes (vipāka-hetu).

Moral causation is different from other types of causation in the sense that our life (a group of elements) is determined firstly, by the previous elemental antecedents and secondly, by the mysterious efficiency of past deeds, if the person has a well organised, strong character of any sort, good or bad. The effect of a prominent past deed on the life of a person is another event and is, therefore, believed to be produced involuntarily. Such antecedents which are capable of moral causation (vipāka-hetu), constitute what is known as karma.[12] They may be intellectual or purely moral. The exact nature of these moral antecedents is not well-defined but it is certain that they cannot be material; they correspond to dispositions (psycho-physical). But the question is whether or not the law of moral causation in Buddhism (karma) amounts to a recognition of the freedom of will. If the event produced by karma is to be involuntary, it is ethically indifferent, for it is, according to Buddhism, the natural flow of past events (karmas) and even the past moral antecedents must be produced likewise under a similar moral causation and so on till there is complete continuity in causation without any break wherein the possibility of a new development may be visualised. Hence, the law of karma in Buddhism does not admit any free will. Moral causation is strictly causation only of a different type, where elements cooperate in a freer play of a greater number of permutations and combinations than in the physical world. (Buddhism confines the law of karma to the moral world only, wherein it is regarded as the chief factor or force disposing us towards nirvāṇa. Hence, the law of karma in Buddhism is not the same as ṛta in the Ṛg Veda or the law governing the entire world process.)

A persistent question as to the possibility of moral development and regeneration still awaits an answer in Buddhist view of causality. Buddhism maintains that the stream of life (santana) is influenced by two forces (i) avidya (ignorance) which predisposes the wheel of life to turn on and (ii) prajñā amala (transcending wisdom) which stops the wheel and prepares the elements for rest (nirvāṇa). All elements in an actual stream of life are in a state of unrest or commotion (state of duḥkha). But Buddhism has shown the possibility of the suppression of this commotion thus leading to eternal rest. Dharma (element) is thus something to be suppressed or vice versa;[13] in other words, an element capable of final rest is dharma. Hence, dharma is both an ontological entity as well as an axiological principle. Reality (dharma) has a value-structure which can determine existence. In the conversion of elements in commotion into elements at rest, a special force (prajñā, meaning a capacity of appreciation) is introduced. Prajñā is the only hope of mankind. The element of appreciative choice and will, which makes the stream of life or dharmas beyond influence (anasrava) and prepares for final extinction (nirvāṇa), is the biggest moral force believed to be operative in the character of man. The dharma theory of Buddhism implies a moral theory on the world plane of elements working themselves towards complete extinction or annihilation (universal nirvāṇa).[14]

The path, consisting of eight-fold virtues (aṣṭāṁgikamārga) shown by the Buddha, pertains to the element called prajñā which helps dharmas to be extinct. The whole of moral life, therefore, comes under the theory of dharma, for moral life is a force by which utpatti-dharmas are transformed into anutpatti-dharmas. Other moral disciplines mentioned in the Buddhist texts like cessation through wisdom (pratisankhya-nirodha), path of vision (dṛṣti-mārga) and mystical concentration (bāvanā-heya) point to the same process of disquietening of the dharmas. It is clear that existence (with all its potentialities), according to Buddhism, is distinct from the possible state of existence (its metaphysical potentialities realized) or that ultimate value and value-realization is not exactly automatic; but is contingently dependent upon moral force. Buddhist dharma reveals itself as an axiological concept, the ought-to-be in things (dharmakāya).[15]

Manu's Ideas

Dharma as one name for moral life and moral values acquires its full significance in the Hindu dharmaśāstras which are a systematic exposition of this concept. Of them, *Manusmṛti* is the most consistent and quite representative.[16] Manu defines his subject matter thus: 'Dharma is conduct sanctioned by the Vedas and Smṛti'.[17] He further elaborates that 'he shall give the dharma in its entirety including the moral distinctions of actions and conduct of four castes as obtained from traditions'.[18] At another place, he regards dharma as 'the practice of the saints and that which can be intuited by the conscience'.[19] Manu seems to waver between two different grounds of approved conduct, viz., tradition and conscience. According to him the four sources of dharma are: (i) the Vedas, (ii) tradition, (iii) conduct of virtuous men and (iv) individual conscience.[20] It is quite possible that there may be a clash between the various authorities of dharma. Manu thinks that the clash will arise only in the mind of the person who is confused about them, but in the ultimate analysis, all bases are one.[21] He favours Vedic authority (śruti) which is ultimate and cannot be challenged by the other three.[22] For him, the Veda does not simply mean knowledge as it is heard (śruti) but also revealed knowledge. Hence, moral conduct (dharma) is conduct duly sanctioned by authority.[23] If a distinction between customary and reflective morality is ever to be maintained, Manu would prefer the former and he is bound to do so by the nature of his job as the law giver.

Manu arrives at the true essence of all dharma which is

universal moral obligation. He accepts the spirit of disinterestedness (niṣkāmabhāva) as constitutive of moral obligation. Volition, according to him, is the psychological basis of all action and volition must imply desire. Hence such desire is the universal basis of all action and as such cannot be got rid of.[24] It is impossible to give up desire. He distinguishes between two types of interestedness (kāmyatā), (i) action with desire for fruits and (ii) action with no desire for fruits like the study of the Vedas. He prefers the latter to the former.[25] A man who performs all actions with a spirit of disinterestedness, comes to enjoy immortality and thereby all fruits of actions.[26] Perhaps it is not the enjoyment of fruits which matters but the spirit in which actions are performed.[27]

Manu makes a distinction between two types of dharma: (i) moral duty and (ii) virtue as the inner auspicious disposition. He enumerates ten virtues of man which are of cardinal importance, namely, perseverence, forgiveness, self-control, abstension from theft, cleanliness, sense-control, wisdom, knowledge, truthfulness and control over anger.[28] The duties of man are further divided into two kinds, social and individual. The social duties of man, according to Manu depend upon the four-fold division of society (varṇadharma) and personal duties are derived from the four-fold stages of life (āśramadharma).

It is clear, therefore, that Manu breaks no new ground in codifying specific duties and depends upon the same basis as the class system obtained from the Vedic traditions. Manu believes in the divine origin of classes. 'The lord, for the prosperity of the world, caused the four classes to proceed from his mouth, arms, his thigh and feet respectively,'[29] and he further maintains that the four castes derive their functions accordingly.[30] Originally, the four-fold division of society may have had functional base but with the passage of centuries, it was frozen into the hard form of the caste system (jātiprathā) which was based on birth and actions.[31] As a result the demarcation between the castes became rigid and social transgression (varṇasaṁkara) was considered to be the cause of social confusion and anarchy.[32] At another place Manu accepts ethnic and linguistic distinctions as the basis of social castes.[33] Radhakrishnan supports this view when he says that the transition from the class system to the caste system was due to historical cause.[34]

The four-fold division of the span of human life is the source of personal duties of man. A hundred years are equally subdivided into four consecutive periods of twenty-five years each. The stages are named as the student (brahmacārin), the householder (gṛahastha), the hermit (vānaprastha) and the ascetic (saṅyāsin),[35] and at every stage a person is to perform different functions and duties.[36] Complete renunciation (saṅyāsa) is the final aim which can be achieved gradually, graded through the stages of life. Manu regards this scheme of life to be the only one leading to a life of freedom (mokṣa). A number of sacraments (saṁskāra) are prescribed for man to make his āśrama-life more effective. Forty of them constitute the dharma of a Hindu. Starting from the time of conception of the child till death, these sacraments aim at building up and refining of the physical, moral and spiritual sides of the human personality.[37] Life of indulgence (pravṛtti) in the earlier stages and a life of renunciation (nivṛtti) in the later is prescribed.[38] Thus Manu's treatment of dharma brings out clearly the comprehensive character of moral values as moral obligation, virtue, social duties and personal duties which relate to the time and place to which an individual belongs.[39]

Manu never fails to place dharma in the proper perspective of values. There is no doubt regarding the relation of moral values to the ultimate goal of human life. Manu believes that spiritual emancipation (mokṣa) is the highest goal of human life and a life of moral duty (dharma) is only the way and preparation for the final achievement (parama-gati).[40] Manu describes the state of liberation (mokṣa) as self-realization (ātmadarśana).[41] A person who sees the same self in all beings knows the reality, and becomes Brahman.[42] As compared to the *summum bonum*, moral values are instrumental but such is not the case when other values are compared to dharma. Manu believes in the three value-concept (trivarga) which means that the harmony of hedonistic (kāma), materialistic (artha) and moral (dharma) values is most desirable.[43] Consequently, any pleasure or money-achievement which is opposed to the sanctions of dharma is morally evil and not desirable.[44] How dharma holds its sway over lower values, is not clear except that kāma and artha are lower and dharma is higher.

DUTY-ETHICS OF THE BHAGAVAD-GITA

A detailed and systematic account of dharma, with special reference to the notion of duty, is found in the *Bhagavad-Gītā* which is the most important book of the Hindus. Despite the wide philosophical synthesis of divergent doctrines of Indian thought undertaken in the book, we do not fail to discover a consistent answer to the problem of duty. Let us begin with Arjuna who was confused as to whether or not it was his duty to fight. He sought from the exalted Lord Krishna proper guidance.[45] The lord replied in categorical terms that it was his duty to fight because he was a soldier (Kṣatriya).[46] Obviously, caste system (varṇadharma) is the reference which determines the duties of a soldier. The four-fold classification of society is based on the aptitude (guṇa) and action (karma) of persons.[47] Being a soldier to the core, it was Arjuna's aptitude which enabled him to fight, for it is impossible to stay inactive (niṣkarmakṛta) for dispositions (guṇa) engage men accordingly.[48] Hence, the general answer to the problem of human duty is that one should do one's duty pertaining to one's station in life (varṇa).

Now the question arises as to what is the exact nature of the action which should be performed. 'What is right action and what is not, is really a difficult question on which even the wise are confused.'[49] Any action done according to one's occupation is not always right. The *Gītā* works out a solution between the conflicting paths of action and renunciation of action. If actions involve man in the shifting wheel of life (saṁsāra), and the complete cessation of all actions is impossible, then the essence of right action lies in the spirit of disinterestedness, which consists in neither giving up action altogether nor indulging in it but in giving up attachment for fruits of actions and the consciousness of doership (kartvatvabhāva) and desire for consequences (phalāsā).[50] Hence, duty is right action in accordance with one's station in life performed disinterestedly. Acting disinterestedly (niṣkāmakarmayoga) is not a mere external renunciation but means an internal transformation of human nature,[51] for which the *Gītā* wants to prepare man through a system of gradual training and psychological disciplines, which includes cultivation of the spirit of indifference (samatvayoga),[52] devotion (bhakti), controlled intellect (sthita prajñā) and sense-control (indriyanigraha).[53] The *Gītā* discusses the three famous paths of life, viz., the path of knowledge (jñānayoga), the path of action (karmayoga) and the path of devotion (bhaktiyoga) and brings about their synthesis by interpreting their real meaning to be that knowledge means realization as distinct from mere scriptural erudition; action means yoga as distinct from mere performance of rites and rituals; and devotion means surrender to the highest (Brahman) as against the worship of deities. Such disciplines alone can bring about the true internal transformation of human nature by destroying the desire for fruits and generating the true spirit of selfless and disinterested action.[54] A true spirit of disinterestedness entitles a man to liberation (mokṣa) or the highest status (parama-gati).[55] It recommends devotion to the Supreme God in the person of Vāsudeva as the sure means of attaining the highest goal (mokṣa) and an everlasting state of bliss.

Thus, the *Gītā* regards three elements as essential preparations for a life of duty, viz., (i) social classes (varṇadharma) as the broadest framework of duties, (ii) the spirit of disinterestedness (niṣkāmakarmayoga) as the essence of right action and (iii) God-realization through knowledge, devotion and meditation. The four-fold social classification (varṇadharma) is sometimes considered to lack in a truely universal and humanistic character, but the disinterested spirit coupled with a true internal change in human nature provides a secular and universal basis to human duty. Whereas the dharmaśāstras are concerned with social, legal and external implications of dharma, the *Gītā* provides an insight into the inner and deeper aspects of moral duty and remains the most authoritative account of dharma for the Hindu mind.

Comparisons

It has been seen that Plato's division of society envisaged in his "Republic" bears a deep resemblance to the Indian four-fold social order though the fourth class of servants is missing in the Platonic scheme. But Plato uses his scheme of social classes for an entirely different purpose which has little resemblance to the Indian dharma. Plato's concept of virtue dominates his entire consideration of social order. If virtue means exactly what dharma stands for, the virtues of the various classes, such as prudence, courage and temperance would mean the dharmas of the first three classes. Service, work and obedience as the characteristic virtues of the serving class (śūdra) do not have any place in the Platonic scheme. The Platonic idea of justice, which means the harmonious functioning of the social classes or proper subordination of virtues, will also mean dharma which regulates the achievement of artha. There is, therefore, no exact parallelism between varṇadharma and Plato's ideal social order as has been discussed in Chapter V. We often forget one important point in this connection that the Indian scheme of the four classes (varṇa) is essentially connected with the ideal of the four stages of life (āśrama) for which there is no parallel in Western thought. The four-fold stage of life is unique in quite another respect, viz., it is made subservient to the highest goal of human life (mokṣa) for the attainment of which man is trained and prepared gradually through the four stages. A life of indulgence consisting of the first two stages (pravṛtti), and a life of renunciation consisting of the later two stages (nivṛtti) are not distinct and opposite but form the continuous stages of a single effort to achieve the *summum bonum* (mokṣa). Dharma is a means to mokṣa.

Kant and Disinterestedness

Both Manu and the *Bhagavad-Gītā* agree on the universal character of duty, which is believed to be constituted by the spirit of disinterestedness (niṣkāmakarmayoga and akāmatā). Duties which are determined by the social order are to be discharged without any desire for consequences. There are two levels at which moral actions are performed, viz., teleological morality and deontological morality. If the moral quality of an action is believed to depend upon its consequences, it is called teleological ethics but when the consequences of an action are believed not to determine the moral judgment, i.e., an action can be judged as good or bad on its own account without any regard to its fruits, it is called deontological ethics. The duty ethics of the *Bhagavad-Gītā* is in line with the latter rather than the former.

Immanuel Kant holds a similar view in his *Critique of Practiced Reason.* He also thinks that motive and not consequences determine the moral quality of an action.[56] Kant regards three propositions as central to his theory of Ethics, (i) that to have moral worth, an action must be done from a sense of duty,[57] (ii) that an action done from a sense of duty derives its moral worth, not from the purpose which is to be attained by it, but from the maxim by which it is determined and therefore does not depend on the realization of the object of the action, but merely on the principle of volition by which the action has taken place without regard to the object of desire,[58] and (iii) that duty is the necessity of action forms respect for the law.[59] There may be two motives of action: impulse and principle. Kant thinks that only action done with principle as motive is moral and it should be done not on principle but for the sake of the principle.[60] The principle or law is of the nature of an imperative or command. Now all imperatives command either hypothetically or categorically. Writes Kant, 'the former represent the practical necessity of a possible action as means to something else that is willed. . . . The categorical imperative would be that which represents an action as necessary of itself without reference to another end.'[61] Finally, Kant gives us the form of the moral law. He writes, "the imperative of duty may be expressed thus: Act as if the maxim of thy action were to become by thy will a universal law of nature.'[62] The universality principle is purely formal and is derivable from the rationality of human nature. Passions and impulses may contradict, but a rational man must abhor self-contradiction.

It is, therefore, clear that Kant upholds the maxim—duty for the sake of duty—and in this respect, there is a close resemblance between Kant and the *Bhagavad-Gītā* in as much as both deny that the moral worth of an action depends upon its consequences, and both condemn the volition as determined by the practical necessity of realizing definite ends. But there seems to be an essential difference between the two so far the source of duty is concerned. Kant derives the moral law from the universal reason in human nature whereas the *Gītā* determines duties on the basis of social station and the stage of life. Kant seems to be too formal in his account of the principle of duty and it is criticised on account of its formalism which fails to provide a positive guidance to man. What are the specific duties which a man should perform? The *Gītā* provides a clear answer to it in the form of duties of the varṇāśramadharma but Kant fails to do so, though he recognizes the duties of imperfect obligation besides those of perfect obligation. The former are not universally binding on all human beings.[63]

The duties of imperfect obligation correspond to the duties of the varṇāśramadharma, while the duties of perfect obligation correspond to the spirit of disinterested actions (sāmānya dharma). There is another striking similarity between these points of views. The *Gītā* works out in minute detail the exact discipline and training by which the lower or sentient part of human nature is to be transformed to subserve the purpose of a smooth life of duty. The control of the senses, mental concentration and equipoise of intellect, etc., are recommended in the same direction. Kant also seems to favour transforming of the sentient side of human nature.[64] Emotions, passions and desires are as good constituents of human nature as reason. The *Gītā* and Kant, therefore, enjoin on us to refine human nature so as to make it fit for a life of duty.

Kant seems uncompromising as far as the independence of the moral ideal of duty for duty's sake is concerned. Goodwill is intrinsically good; it needs no other condition in order to be good. But on the other hand he believes that 'this will then, though not indeed the sole and complete good, must be the supreme good and the condition of every other things, even the desire of happiness'.[65] This implies that a life of goodwill ought to include something else in order to be completely good. Kant admits of happiness and perfection as ideal-ought-to-be as distinguished from ideal-ought-to-do.

In a similar way, the *Bhagavad-Gītā* and Manu show a supreme concern for a life of duty but accept the highest goal of liberation (mokṣa) to be of supreme status (parama-gati) to which even the life of duty (dharma) must be subordinated in the ultimate sense. Comparing the view of the *Gītā* with that of Kant on this point, B.S. Gouchhwal writes, 'Thus, what is actually revealed in the teachings of Kant and the *Gītā* is not that the agent should empty his will of all motive, but that the multiple purposes of the deeds that fall to his lot in life, should be replaced by a single purpose, namely, allowing its grip on its own law . . . with a view to determining the way in which this single purpose is to be realized, Kant and the *Gītā* turn to something immediate and concrete, namely, the doing of duties . . . thus there emerge two ends, one immediate and concrete and the other remote and transcendent, but they are conceived in such a way that the one becomes transmuted to be the birth of another.'[66] Kant mentions the twin goals of perfection of the individual and happiness for others as transcendental ends. The *Gītā* also is clear that 'of necessity certain duties devolve upon us the performance of which is inextricably linked up with the attainment of perfection'.[67] Both Kant and the *Gītā* regard the grace of God as necessary for the realization of moral good.[68]

Bradley and the Bhagavad-Gita

The essence of moral life as the disinterested spirit of doing actions and the ideal of duty for duty's sake on which both the *Bhagavad-Gītā* as well as Kant agree, have been found to be unsatisfactory on account of its formalism. It can only give us a form of the morals without a positive content, which is not possible without a concrete set of duties. Bradley on similar grounds finds this inadequate when he writes, 'So we see "duty for duty's sake" says only, "do the right for the sake of the right", it does not tell us what right is or "realize a good will, do what a good will would do, for the sake of being yourself a good will".'[69] He finds the universality and absoluteness of the moral laws debatable and impracticable.[70] He observes, 'Let us say then that to realize is at least to particularize. . . .' Realize asserts the concrete identity of matter and form which 'formal will denies . . . .'[71] The principle of universalization as duty for duty becomes meaningful only when a concrete content of moral life is supplied to it. 'What duty for duty's sake really does,' says Bradley, 'is first to posit a determination, such as property, love, courage etc. and then to say that whatever contradicts these is wrong. . . .' The particular duties must be taken for granted.[72]

It is exactly at this juncture that ethics of the *Gītā* differ from that of Kant. It is impossible for Kant to go from the universal form of duty to particular duties whereas the *Gītā* accepts the particular duties of a man on the traditional basis of social order and the four stages of life and from them goes on to the essence of moral obligation which is disinterestedness. It is presupposed that a person in a definite walk of life and at a definite stage of life has a definite set of duties, for which he alone is responsible and which he alone is to discharge. And again, Kant's acceptance of an ideal of virtue and happiness as the complete good is unwarranted in a system of duty for duty's sake. Realization of an end must be implied in all moral life. The *Gītā's* duty is after all subordinated to the supreme achievement of salvation (mokṣa). The twin considerations of concrete and particular duties and the aim of moral life bring us close to the Bradley's conception of "My station and its duties".

Bradley thinks that 'we have self-realization left as the end . . . morality implies a superior, a higher self or at all events a universal something which is above this or that self and so above mine'.[73] The self which is to be realized, according to him, is part of an organic whole,[74] for "the mere individual is a delusion of theory, and the attempt to realize it in practice is starvation and mutilation of human nature, with total sterility or the production of monstrosities".[75] A man is a member of a moral organism; "it is in its affirmation that I affirm myself, for I am but as a heart beat in its system. And I am real in it, for when I give myself to it, it gives me the fruition of my own personal activity, the accomplished ideal of life which is happiness. . . . We have found self-realization, duty and happiness in one".[76] But every individual shall assert his essence only when he functions effectively in the social whole.[77] In other words, every person occupies a definite place in society as a teacher, doctor, lawyer, father, adolescent, etc., and certain duties on that very account devolve upon him which he alone will have to discharge if he is to be himself what he is.

'What is it then that I am to realize?' asks Bradley and replies, 'we have said it in "my station and its duties", to know what a man is, you must not take him in isolation. He is one of a people, he was born in a family, he lives in a society in a certain state. What he has to do, depends on what his place is, what his function is and that all comes from his station in the organism'.[78] The good of the individual connot be sundered apart from the good of the social whole which is promoted when a member functions in it, because he finds himself as "an organ in the social organism".[79] Compare this theory: "My station and its duties", with the *Gītā's* candid injunction to Arjuna, "Since you are a soldier, therefore, it is your duty to fight, for soldiers fight".[80] It seems to commit the fallacy of *petitio principii*, for the argument moves in a circle, but Bradley says that there is no way out of this situation, for every person will have to do his own duty which pertains to his station in life.[81] Any ideal scheme of moral life which accrues to itself the merit of being absolute and universal, will prove to be not only impracticable but also a mere abstraction. In the ultimate analysis, morality is relative to the social order to which a man belongs, it is relative to the times and stage of human development and it is relative to the station and state of the man. The four-fold division of society and the four stages of life (varṇāśramadharma) are facts in Indian society which determine the specific duties of an individual.

Elaborating on the ideal of self-realization, Bradley says that a man is to realize his true essence of being in order to realize himself, and the true self is the social self, it is the social organism which is higher than the subjective self. The community is the real moral organism which in its members knows and wills itself and sees the individual to be real just so far as the universal self is in his self as he is in it.[82] 'Realize yourself as an organic whole.' There are, therefore, two selves in a person, the universal self and the individual self which constitute the basis of moral judgment.[83] To the question: 'how am I to know what is right?' Bradley replies, 'the universal self judges the individual self, the higher self is the man who has identified his will with the moral spirit of the community. If an immoral course be suggested to him, he feels or sees at once that the act is not in harmony with a good will.'[84] Similarly, the *Gītā* develops a thesis of the distinction between the empirical self (jīva) and the transcendental self (ātman)[85] and enjoins that the moral life lies in the gradual realization of the true essence as the real self (ātman).[86] It is in this context that the *Gītā* accepts the ideal of self-realization as the supreme goal of life[87] and further develops it by identifying the true self of man (ātman) with the universal self (paramātman) which is the same as the Absolute (Brahman). Hence, self-realization is at the same time Brahmā-realisation or God-realization.[88] Manu also agrees on this point, in so far as he accepts self-realization as the highest goal of life and that the true self is the universal consciousness or the Absolute. Bradley also reaches out in the direction of the realization of the absolute as the ultimate goal of human life, when he writes, 'Against this ideal self, the particular person remains and must remain imperfect. The ideal self is not fully realized in us'.[89] In the chapter on "Ideal Morality", he develops his point of views regarding the Absolute as the object of moral realization, but thinks that morality must always fall short of the Absolute and thus negate itself. 'Morality', he says, 'does involve a contradiction . . . . No one ever was or could be perfectly moral and if he were, he would be moral no longer. Where there is no imperfection there is no ought, where there is no ought, there is no morality . . . the ought is self contradiction.'[90] Thus, he raises the Absolute above moral effort whereas for the Indian mind, the Absolute (Brahman) is the highest object of realization.[91] Bradley's Absolute is a community of selves or a society of individuals, but the *Gītā's* Absolute is the absolute which is a totality of consciousness, existence and bliss (saccidānanda). Bradley's conception of the absolute reality has some resemblance with the Buddhist dharma as the ontological existence (dharmadhātu) while the *Gītā's* conception of the Absolute reality resembles Buddhist *dharma* as the axiological entity (*dharma-kāyā*).

CHAPTER SEVEN

Moksa as Spiritual Value

THE CONCEPT OF MOKSA

Mokṣa which ordinarily means liberation,[1] is regarded in Indian philosophical tradition as the final destiny of man and as such, it has been accorded the highest importance in the scheme of values.[2] There seems to be no doubt as to the valuational character of the state of liberation (mokṣa), and since it is the highest goal of human life, a keen study of the concept must bring to light the nature of ultimate values. It is on account of its ultimate quality that sometimes it is considered in isolation from other values of life like the economic, hedonistic and moral values. The distinction between them is maintained on the difference between empirical and transcendental values. The state of liberation (mokṣa) seems to transcend empirical categories; its transcendental nature is thoroughgoing. It is, therefore, imperative to know exactly the mode and ground on which empirical and transcendental values are related, and whether or not there can be a positive transition from the empirical to the transcendental. It is sometimes said that on the attainment of the highest, there remains nothing to be attained.[3] This implies that in the face of the spiritual, other so-called empirical values must lose their value. But this position jeopardizes the very basis of the four-fold aim of human life. Hence, a further study is needed to characterize spiritual values in relation to other values. The problem of mokṣa has been the primary theme of many philosophical systems called the science of liberation (mokṣaśāstras). They concern themselves with the concept of liberation and the means of its attainment (mokṣasādhana).

The problem of the destiny of man (mokṣa) is linked with the problem of self, for according to classical view it is not the attainment of something foreign to self but constitutes the realization of its own essential nature.[4] The nature of self is the metaphysical ground of the state of liberation (mokṣa). There are various views as to the nature of self. They can be classified into two main groups, viz., those who do not believe in the existence of a soul substance (anātmavāda) like the Buddhists, and those who believe in the existence of self (atmavāda). The latter view is further divided into those who maintain many selves (anekātmavāda) and those which believe in one supreme self (ekātmavāda). The Buddhist concept of nirvāṇa and Sāṁkhya's view of release (mokṣa) represent the first two groups and are taken up for discussion in the present chapter, while the study of the theory of oneself (ekātmavāda) is postponed to the next chapter which is concerned with the Brahman as value. Śaṅkara and Rāmānuja, the two stalwarts of the Vedānta school, have made valuable contributions towards the problem of liberation (mokṣa) and without a discussion of their systems, no account of the concept of liberation is considered complete. It is on account of their significance that a full chapter is found necessary to discuss their point of view. Brahmanvāda is unique and yields us an exact rationale of value-philosophy and it is not proper to mix it up with any other point of view on liberation (mokṣa).

THE BUDDHIST NIRVANA

The Buddhist concept of the highest destiny of man as nirvāṇa affords an opportunity to study mokṣa from a more positive and more intellectual point of view (unless nirvāṇa itself is altogether different from mokṣa) as against the spiritualist and absolutist approach of the Upaniṣads. The pessimistic strain of the Upaniṣadic view of human life influenced Buddhist teachings and was rather more prominently stressed. Nirvāṇa is advanced as the solution of the problem of human suffering. The whole Buddhist philosophy is based on the problem of suffering and the solution to this problem. Buddhism centres round nirvāṇa. The old Buddhist credo "Ye dharma hetu-prabhāvaḥ" which is the briefest formula of Buddhist philosophy, sharply expresses the idea that 'the Great Recluse has indicated the (separate) elements of existence (dharma), their interconnexion as causes and effects and the method of their final suppression'.[5]

The whole philosophy of elements (dharma), which according to Stcherbatsky forms the central concept of Buddhism,[6] is subordinated to the practical end (which is so pronounced in the Buddha's teachings) of preparing for an understanding (prajñā) of the separate elements, which results finally in the state of rest (nirvāṇa). The Buddha laid greater stress on rousing humanity to attend to moral life[7] rather than merely philosophizing about the abstract goal. This provided scope for varied interpretations at the hands of later Buddhist thinkers, regarding the exact nature of nirvāṇa. The historic silence of the Buddha over the final goal of human life on account of metaphysical difficulties in its positivist description[8] cannot be ultimately maintained and its nature must be discussed.

The word "nirvāṇa" is derived from the verbal root "nirvah" which means to blow out or to cool down. Nirvāṇa amounts to blowing out the flame of life. In this sense, it means extinction[9] or death. But this cannot be the correct interpretation of nirvāṇa, for death is considered to be a link in the chain of suffering. Nirvāṇa must be a solution to death. Extinction may mean nothingness or blankness equivalent to Non-being. But that also seems to be an incorrect interpretation, for the law of universal causation of the Buddhists is ultimate and Being cannot result in Non-being. Therefore, nirvāṇa must be only another type of Being or life—a life which has ceased to draw from the fuel of desire. The second sense of the verbal root 'nirvah' as 'to cool down' perhaps comes nearer to the point arrived at here.

What is to be cooled down in nirvāṇa? The passions (klesha) which lead life towards duhkha (sorrow) through their influence (sasrava), are to be cooled down or appeased.[10] Cooling of passions, as understood in the ordinary sense, must mean a psychological discipline of self-control or control over passions and attachment or desires. If this is the case, nirvāṇa must mean a life of harmony and mental poise and thus it must be an empirical concept and such a life must be of an intrinsic as well as moral value. But the word passion (klesha) used in the Buddhist terminology can only be understood in the proper perspective of Buddhist metaphysics. According to it, only the separate elements of existence (dharma) are ultimately real. They are found in two conditions, (i) life-influenced elements (sasrava dharmas) and (ii) elements not influenced by life (anasasrava dharmas). The former are in a state of ceaseless commotion (duhkha) and the latter, in a state of calm (śānta). The former is the notion of existence and the latter, that of value.

If it is in the nature of elements (dharma) to be always in commotion (duhkha), it is impossible for them to be in rest (śānta). The Buddhists characterize element (dharma) as suppressible.[11] Hence, value is the condition of reality; nirvāṇa is, therefore, the ultimate goal of the world process in which the elements in commotion come to final rest. The ordinary course of life (santana) is constituted by sasrava-dharma influenced by passions (klesha). Pure life (arya) is constituted by anasasrava dharma free from passion (klesha). Klesha here means a tendency towards life or a will to live or 'elan vital' of Bergson. It is by suppression or elimination of passion (klesha) that the final rest of elements is achieved. Nirvāṇa is a process of converting all uttpati dharmas (elements producing life) into anuttpati dharmas (elements not producing life).

The way to achieve this nirvāṇa or the final rest of all elements in life is knowledge—a discrimination of elements (prajñā) which ordinarily means appreciative understanding. It is capable of development and cultivation and becomes immaculate wisdom (prajñā amalā) which is at the same time anasasrava prajñā (understanding not influenced by passion for life). This anasasrava prajñā joins the life process as a force thereby disquieting or suppressing every element one by one, and increasing the area of blankness. This is cessation through wisdom (pratisankhya nirodha) and is called dṛṣti-mārga, which can result in suppression of some of the movements of elements.[12] This stage is lower than the final nirvāṇa which means extinction of all elements. After dṛṣti-mārga has done its works, the remaining elements are suppressed by mystical concentration (bhāvanā-heya). This concentration comes nearer to Hindu Yoga (nirbījasamadhi). By the dṛṣti-mārga [realization of the two-fold truth of elements (dharmatā) and not-self (anātma), some mental elements like feelings, ideas, volitions are stopped and by bhāvanā-heya, all the remaining impure and material elements as well as sensuous consciousness is finally suppressed.

This suppression is not illogical in view of the basic notion of elements, which are subtle entities not exactly material or mental. This is still not the final nirvāṇa. Mystical concentration (bhāvanā-heya) can lead to a spiritual or transcendent existence or being in which consciousness and mental phenomena are brought to a complete standstill (corresponding to nirvikalpa-samādhi). This spiritual being has the purest elements (dharma) which come to an absolute and eternal extinction in the state of nirvāṇa when an eternal blank is substituted for them all. Nirvāṇa means the eternal blankness or absolute annihilation. This does not mean that nirvāṇa amounts to achievement of nothingness or extinction. Nirvāṇa only implies that elements (saṅskṛta-dharmas) are extinct but the presence of asaṅskṛta-dharma (which has been sometimes understood as pure essence) cannot be ruled out on account of the Buddhist stand on universal causation. What is the nature of this essence if it ever exists in nirvāṇa? Prof. Stcherbatsky in his discussion arrives at negative results. It is extinction of consciousness; it is inanimation. 'It is neither birth nor death and also it is not fit to say that it is neither birth or death.'[13]

Nirvāṇa cannot be regarded as a state of bliss since all feelings or conscious states are absent. It is just cessation of manifestation. It is a negative concept. Prof. Stcherbatsky believes that nirvāṇa is not a state of consciousness, hence it is not spiritual. Others collaborate this view.[14] But Max Muller and Childers repudiate this stand. They observe that 'there is not one passage which would require that its meaning should be annihilation'. This pertains to the essential difference between the Hīnayāna and Mahāyāna formulations of the nature of nirvāṇa. A.K. Lad writes that Hīnayāna maintains a negative attitude in so far it makes nirvāṇa an egoistic ideal (arhathood), annihilistic with a negative means to its attainment; and Mahāyāna is positive in approach and views. Nirvāṇa as altruistic, Bodhisattva, and spiritual with a positive means of its realization. Thus he observes that Mahāyāna nirvāṇa is far superior to Hīnayāna nirvāṇa. The Hīnayāna nirvāṇa is only a step towards the goal, a halting place on the way to the goal and not the goal itself.[15] Radhakrishnan is constrained to observe that 'Evidently, two different views were developed very early on the basis of Buddha's utterances. Buddha's real attitude is probably that nirvāṇa is a state of perfection inconceivable by us',[16] and we are obliged to give negative descriptions of it. T.R.V. Murti holds that 'The vaibhāsikas or any school of Buddhism never took nirvāṇa as nothing but as some sort of noumenal unconditioned reality behind the play of phenomena. . . . Only it is inexpressible. . . . It is not being nor Non-being'.[17]

Nirvana and Moksa

In view of the discussion on the nature of nirvāṇa, it is abundantly clear that the concept of nirvāṇa does not strike a discordant note in Indian philosophy which centres round mokṣa or mukti as the highest goal of life. Both the concepts are based on the premises that (i) there is suffering in life and (ii) nirvāṇa or mokṣa is the state of liberation from suffering. The fact of human suffering has been more emphasized in Buddhism. But this fact and the rejection of vedic authority have hardly made any difference in this regard. The state of nirvāṇa is believed to be achieved through three stages, (i) stoppage of the movement of elements (nirodha) through vision (dṛṣṭi-mārga), (ii) complete appeasement of passion and desire (nirodha-samāptti) when a spiritual being emerges (this is the ideal of Bodhisattva) and (iii) nirvāṇa at this stage is an absolute and unconditioned reality which is considered to be an essence beyond any characterization and on account of its indescribability some say that it is pure extinction, non-being which cannot be described as spiritual or blissful, but others regard it as a state of perfection. Mahāyāna and Hīnayāna differ essentially in their characterization of the third stage.

Nirodha is definitely an empirical state which can correspond to liberation in this life (sadhehaṁukti); the second state is transcendental in so far as the spiritual being is asserted at this stage. This, therefore, corresponds to the meta-empirical concept of liberation (mokṣa). The third stage of unconditioned reality comes closer to the view of the Absolute (Brahman) in so far as both are beyond description, absolute and transcendental (neither being nor Non-being). Thus, concept of nirvāṇa and mokṣa have deep affinity. If mokṣa, as the release from psycho-physical existence and the realization of some spiritual essence, is capable of varied characterizations, nirvāṇa can be one of such formulations. It presupposes the same metaphysical grounds which are the Law of Karma, the cycle of birth, suffering and moral disciplines as means of mokṣa. It is, therefore, not an alien doctrine.[18] In its negative interpretation, akin to vaibhāsika's nirvāṇa, it is comparable to Nayāya Vaiśeṣikas conception of Mokṣa as cessation of suffering in an inanimate existence without any spiritual essence. And if nirvāṇa means unconditioned absolute reality behind the phenomena as according to Mahāyāna, it comes closer to brahmvāda of Śaṅkara. T.R.V. Murti, however, brings out an essential point of difference between the Mādhyamika and Advaita's notions of release. Nirvāṇa is not identified with consciousness and bliss, but for the vedānta, release is identified with absolute existence, consciousness and bliss (sadcidānandam). 'The Mādhyamika seems to stop short at that or the bare assertion of the Absolute as the implicate of the phenomena, the Vedānta proceeds further to define what is the nature of the Brahman.'[19]

The Doctrine of the Samkhya

The Sāṁkhya[20] is one of the six philosophical systems which are mainly concerned with liberation and the means towards it. The system seeks to find out the certain and permanent way of ending three-fold affliction, which is intrinsic, extrinsic and supernatural. The known ways to end suffering are not sure and effective.[21] The Sāṁkhya recommends the way of intimate knowledge of the manifest (vyakta) and the unmanifest (avyakta).[22] The manifest is defined as caused, perishable, not all-pervading, manifold, dependent, mergent, having a form or that which is supported, while the unmanifest is the opposite of these.[23] The duality of the spirit (puruṣa) and Primal Nature (mūlaprakṛti) constitute the unmanifest, both being causeless (ahetumat).[24] There are infinite number of spirits (puruṣa)[25] which are of the nature of pure consciousness, witness (sākṣin), isolated and neutral (udāsīna), perceptive and inactive.[26] It is the manifest nature (pradhāna) which evolves for the enjoyment and ultimately for the separation of the spirit (puruṣa).[27] The entire activity of Nature (prakṛti) has its teleology in the spirit.[28] The spirit is neither bound nor liberated.[29] It is due to ignorance as to its original nature, distinct from nature, that it finds itself subjected to the rule of three qualities (guṇa) and experiences the effects of this self-imposed bondage in the form of the three-fold miseries.

The Sāṁkhya attaches very little importance to moral life which is again confined to the operations of the sense-world and it thus fails to generate true knowledge, essential for final release (mokṣa).[30] The seven forms of virtue and dispositions are properties of the will and as such are categories of Nature (prakṛti). There is only one form of such activity, i.e., wisdom or knowledge to discriminate spirit from Nature which is the true cause of release (mokṣa).[31] This discriminative knowledge (vivekākhyati) is the result of the repeated study of the truth, 'I do not exist, naught is mine, I am not'.[32] At the dawn of this pure knowledge, the puruṣa affirms its isolation from the body and by reason of the fulfilment of Nature's purpose, it, having been seen by the spirit, ceases to act and the spirit (puruṣa) attains eternal and absolute isolation (kaivalya) which is final (mokṣa).[33] At this stage, having intimate knowledge of its own separateness and being restored to himself, the self (puruṣa) sees like a spectator from a distance and Nature (prakṛti) becomes unproductive and devoid of its forms.[34] On being disassociated from the body, and Nature having retired after doing all that was necessary, the spirit (puruṣa) attains the release which is both certain and final.[35] The achievement of release (mokṣa) is nothing but affirmation by the self (puruṣa) of its own essence as pure consciousness, absolute detachment, neutrality and complete inactivity.[36] In other words it is not identity with something, but a realization of the essential difference of the spirit from Nature. Self-realization is realization of a spiritual essence and detached existence (kaivalya).

Thus, according to the Sāṁkhya, the highest goal of man is liberation (mokṣa) from the clutches of nature. Both bondage and the fact of release are phenomenal; pure spirit never suffers from any such change. In this respect, the Sāṁkhya view differs from that of the Nyāya-vaiśeṣikas, according to which both bondage and release are real and true to the self. They accept a negative concept of mokṣa as the cessation of suffering without any positive attainment of any spiritual essence; the Sāṁkhya fares better by starting from the postulate of a positive essence of the spirit (puruṣa) and by virtue of the same, it is expected to affirm its own essence as pure consciousness, freedom and singleness. But if bondage is phenomenal, release (mokṣa) must be so and, therefore, it does not constitute any real gain for the self (puruṣa) who is ever free, detached and conscious. The puruṣa, due to ignorance, feels bound and released without causing any real modification in the essence of the self. If the experience of bondage and release does not effect in any way the transcendental shine of the spirit, it is as good as absent. The question is straight: 'Does self emerge better after every experience of bondage and release?' According to the Sāṁkhya there is no question of better or worse, because change is phenomenal and not true of the spirit. Hence, all valuational accomplishments are phenomenal and absolutely speaking, they are not accomplishments and therefore they are not valuational.

Can we say that liberation is the highest value and yet it is not a value? This contradicts the whole teleological account of Sāṁkhya's view of the world. If Nature (prakṛti) works towards a purpose, value must determine reality. The Sāṁkhya does not admit change to be real. The spirit is the absolute reality and is beyond all change and causation. But on the other hand, the spirit (puruṣa) as experiencer and self-conscious entity must be appreciater of values which are nothing else but its own fulfilment and self-affirmation. Thus, either the teleological account is wrong or mokṣa is not a value. This situation arises out of the basic postulate of pure consciousness being the essence of the spirit (puruṣa). The consciousness modified by the objects of experience is not true of the self. 'If experience, then both pain and pleasure', is the only logical outcome of the argument arrived by the Nyāya-vaiśeṣikas; if ever misery is to be got rid of, consciousness must go altogether and along with it the pleasure too. The self (puruṣa) in that case cannot be spiritual, it will be reduced to inanimate bare existence as contended by the Nyāya-vaiśeṣikas.

Now if the Sāṁkhya in spite of such consequences, persists in postulating a spiritual essence of the self, the position becomes vulnerable on account of an assumption, without any ground, of a multiplicity of selves. If pure consciousness is the essence of the self, then multiplicity will have to be ruled out, on account of its phenomenality, so that one absolute whole of pure consciousness remains as the undisputed truth, as maintained by Śaṅkara. Mokṣa in this case will not be an affirmation of distinction, detachment, singleness, but a realization of identity, unity and wholeness of pure consciousness. In order to be logically consistent, the Sāṁkhya should either stop short at the Nyāya-vaiśeṣika's position, according to which mokṣa is not a spiritual value or absolutistic view of the vedānta. The arguments advanced by Sāṁkhya to prove the multiplicity of selves[37] are valid in the phenomenal world. They hold good for the empirical self (jīva) and not for the transcendental self (ātman). A.K. Lad levels the same charge on the Sāṁkhya, namely, that it cannot explain the plurality of selves and evolution of Nature and the state of bondage.[38] He concludes that 'the Sāṁkhya represents the second stage in the logical development of orthodox Indian thought. The first stage is represented by the Nyāya-vaiśeṣikas and the third by vedānta.[39] At the first stage, the soul exists devoid of consciousness; at the second, it is conscious in essence and at the third it is consciousness, existence and bliss.

Śankara's View of Moksa

The concept of a pool of pure consciousness as the ultimate essence of the self seems to be the logical consequence of the Indian way of thinking about the highest goal of human life. This has found its fullest expression in the advaitavāda of Śaṅkara. The highest expression of his philosophical idealism is the Absolute (Brahman) which is eternal all knowing, absolutely self-sufficient, ever pure, intelligent, free, pure knowledge and absolute bliss.[40] Its essence is pure consciousness. The Absolute (Brahman) is one without a second and is the only reality. The purest and highest self (ātman) is also universal, pure and blissful and therefore, the same as the Absolute (Brahman); Śaṅkara maintains an absolute identity (without qualifications) between the highest self (ātman) and the Absolute (Brahman).[41] The world, which consists of things differentiated by names and forms, and the individual self (jīvātman) which is embodied under the limiting conditions of body, senses and mind, are the products of ignorance (avidyā) which is of the nature of non-discriminative knowledge.[42] The individual self (jīvātman) enjoys pleasure and pain and lives in the transmigratory existence (śaṅsāra) because it does not understand its true essence as the blissful, highest self.[43] 'So long as the individual self does not free itself from ignorance in the form of duality (which ignorance may be compared to the mistake of him who in the twilight mistakes a post for a man) and does not rise to the knowledge of the self, whose nature is unchangeable, eternal cognition which expresses itself in the form "I am Brahman" so long it remains the individual self. But when, discarding the aggregate of body, sense-organs and mind, it arrives by means of scripture at the knowledge that it is not that aggregate, that it does not form part of the transmigratory existence, but is the True, the Real, the Self whose nature is pure intelligence; then knowing itself to be of the nature of unchangeable, eternal cognition, it lifts itself above the vain conceit of being one with the body and itself becomes the self. . . ."He who knows the highest Brahman, becomes verily the Brahman".'[44]

Mokṣa is release of the individual self from the limiting bodily adjuncts and a dispelling of the thick powerful veil of ignorance and realization of the truth that everything is the self and the self is Brahman. Mokṣa means the realization of the unity of the self with the highest self or Brahman which is already there, but was blocked by ignorance and its products—the limiting conditions.[45] This realization is affected only through knowledge;[46] the merits of one's deeds only prepare the ground for it.[47] But all the same, he who is desirous of knowledge must be possessed of calmness, subjection of the senses, etc., since these are auxiliaries to the attainment of knowledge, hence they are necessary.[48] Effects of good and bad deeds will have to be destroyed ultimately by fruition and with the knowledge of the Brahman,[49] the self becomes one with the Brahman.[50]

Mokṣa according to Advaita-vedānta is the final aim of the whole logical procedure of working out an idealistic account of the highest destiny of man. Mokṣa, according to Advaita philosophy of Śaṅkara, is the realization of the absolute identity or oneness of self with the highest reality (Brahman) whose essence is not the only existence (sat) and self-revealing consciousness (cit), but also bliss (ānand). But since consciousness and bliss are already accomplished facts of the highest reality, how can they be accomplished by human effort? Śaṅkara has already answered this by holding that the fulfilment of the individual self (jīvātman) does not mean that of the highest self (ātman),[51] just as its limitations (ignorance) do not affect the latter.[52] Bondage and release do not apply to the highest self or the Absolute. The accomplishment of the self through mokṣa is comparable to the sense of gain of the person who discovers the lost necklace round his own neck or the state of the man who realizes his mistake having taken a rope to be a snake. It lies in the realization (prāptaprāpti) of that which is already realized or rejection of that which is already rejected.[53] The Absolute (Brahman) is accomplished in its essence from eternity to eternity.[54] Man's desire to realize this essence is born of illusion, which is dispelled on attaining mokṣa. Mokṣa, being absolute reality, is eternal, ever accomplished, without change.[55] The upshot of the whole argument is that Śaṅkara identifies existence with value and value with reality, which is both self and the Absolute. Does the release of a person (mokṣa) result in any improvement in the totality of reality? Śaṅkara would rule it out, since absolute reality transcends all change, be it progressive or retrogressive. For him, the starting point is the same as the destination from the absolute point of view. On this ground, Dr. R.P. Singh argues that mokṣa is the definition of absolute values which are not something to be derived 'nor is it within the power and scope of human agency to create them; values are not "Karmasādhya", says Śaṅkara, they are intrinsic and Absolute. Ātman being the same as mokṣa or Brahman, is spoken of by him as akarmaśesa'.[56]

Śaṅkara's followers may assert that the ideal of man cannot be other than the self which is ever realized by him in whatever he does.[57] Self-realization is the meaning of mokṣa, and on Śaṅkara's own ground, self-realization is a realization of the self's identity with the existent, the real and the eternal, which is not only the highest self but also the Absolute (Brahman). Self-realization is, therefore, mere affirmation of the eternal identity or non-duality of the self and the Absolute. It is sometimes believed that the self ceases to be before it becomes the Absolute so that self-realization means self-destruction which is undesirable.[58] Mokṣa means self-annihilation, according to Śaṅkara, if self means the narrow self or the false self. The destruction of the false self and the realization of the true self must be a value. The self is the highest self as well as the universal self. Hence Śaṅkara's argument that mokṣa is the identity between self and Absolute leads us to the identity between value in the absolute sense and existence. Dr. R.P. Singh also reaches a similar conclusion when he writes, 'the way in which Śaṅkara characterizes ātman, Brahman and mokṣa leave no room for doubt about their identity and their nature as values and not mere existents'.[59] Mokṣa is an absolute value, it is transcendental self-existence and an ideal ought-to-be implied in human life and the world. Thus, Śaṅkara's account of mokṣa is the highest stage of the Indian concept of the final goal of man, and marks an improvement upon those of the Buddhists and the Sāṁkhya.

Ramanuja's View of Moksa

Rāmānuja regards Śaṅkara's Brahman as the void in which discernible values do not get asserted. Mokṣa will mean being lost in the void. He, therefore, tried to proceed from value-premises, from which he discovered reality. The *Bhagavad-Gītā* precedes him when it declares that the highest dharma is performing actions befitting one's caste, stage in life and qualities with a spirit of disinterestedness (niṣkāmakarmayoga). It is at the same time the highest state, goal and happiness of man (parama-gati);[60] it heralded a more empirical, activistic and concrete goal for man. The idea of personal God was conceived. "Vasudeva sarvam" refers to God in every thing.[61] The Purumīmāṅsā, the doctrine of mokṣa as the realization of eternal happiness with active participation (pravṛtti) in the discharge of unconditional duties on the realization of the moral imperative as duty (niyogasidhi), disposes for consideration a purely positive and activistic view of mokṣa. The *Bhagavad-Gītā* is inclined to accept the unity of the self with the highest reality, only to steer clear of the absolutism of the Vedānta, a consequence more favourable for a tangible and activistic view of the goal of man; but the Purumīmāṅsā has consciously argued against the phenomenality of the world and the individual selves, which are ultimately sublated like products of illusion, and maintains that worldly pleasures and pain are transformations of the non-spiritual part of the self and mokṣa lies in freedom from the world and thereby from such transformations.[62] The self enjoys the eternal happiness of the effect of meritorious actions in this state. The view that moral activity and self, as the centre of such activity, is ultimate and indestructible matured itself in the thought of Rāmānuja, though within the folds of absolutistic idealism.

Rāmānuja criticises absolute non-dualism on the ground of the epistemological difficulty of the proof of such identity; knowledge presupposes the thinking subject and the distinct object.[63] The self is of the essence of a subject and things in the world as objects. God is the highest subject and the world and selves are distinct from them. All of them, of course, constitute the Absolute (Brahman) which is undifferentiated essence, and consciousness or intelligence and blessedness are its attributes and not essence. Similarly, the self which is of the essence of a thinking subject is ultimate and eternal and consciousness is only an attribute of it; the latter cannot exist if the former were not to be. Hence, the conscious self persists in the state of release. Rāmānuja's great achievement lies in formulating the indestructibility of selves. The selves can have intuition of the supreme self (God). Rāmānuja's Brahman is subtle, conscious, unconscious and qualified (sūkṣmacidacid-viśiṣṭa). The individual selves are mere modes or aspects of the Brahman (śārīrin) as they constitute its body (śarīra). The true nature of these selves is, however, obscured by ignorance, which means not illusion (māyā), but the influence of a chain of works without beginning and mokṣa or release which follows on the destruction of such ignorance, means understanding the highest self by intuition which is the natural state of the individual selves. Hence the goal of a man is to restore himself to his natural position as one of the factors of the highest reality which is again a society of many distinct selves. Mokṣa is merely the affirmation of our harmony with the Absolute (Brahman) and thus gaining an eternal life of felicity or blessedness (ānanda) arising out of the consciousness of favourable objects presented in their true essence as having their being and harmony in God.

Rāmānuja's concept of liberation implies neither the accentuation of the singleness of self nor annihilation into the Brahman, but preservation of the self's distinctive essence as the unique centre or conscious subject in the society of selves in the state of natural intuition of the Brahman. But what is the relation of the self after release to the Brahman? The view of an organic unity between the parts of the Brahman (śarīrin-śarīra) is the answer. If there is a society of selves, the relation of one individual and the whole may further affect the status of the selves in the Brahman. In the total picture, the Lord (Iśvara) or God, in Rāmānuja's philosophy assumes to Itself the role of the Governor, and the whole society of selves might be subordinated to the Supreme Will of the Lord. Rāmānujites admit that mokṣa means the restoration of harmony by subordinating the individual will to the Divine Will or self surrender so that His Will may prevail. This consequence spells disastrous results regarding the highest goal of man. Man will always be subordinate to God and will not be able to reach the highest status of Godhood. Rāmānuja's concept of the highest goal for man is not the highest, for there is still a scope for him to travel and reach his final destiny. Rāmānuja, like other thinkers of the Saguṇa-Brahmavāda, believes in four types of liberation, (i) sālaukya in which a liberated self resides in the same abode with God, (ii) sāmīpya, humble living in the nearness of God, (iii) sārūpya which implies assuming the same form as that of God and (iv) sāyugya union with God. They mark the four stages of the soul according to the increasing depth of relationship and unity with God. The whole matter is considered valuationally. Rāmānuja does not conceive of the absolute merger of self with God as Śaṅkara does. The distinction between the self and God remains and man is not allowed to achieve the status of God. This condition of maintaining some distance between God and the free soul is itself, according to the religious point of view, valuational, because it intensifies the longing for God eternally. This may be true from the religious point of view, but in the presence of a something higher, greater and nobler, man cannot be made to stop short at something lower. The tendency to achieve the highest condition conceivable by man must constitute the content of an ultimate value like mokṣa. True autonomy must be the goal. Rāmānuja succeeds in demonstrating the distinct reality of selves in the body of the Absolute, but has failed to restore to them the highest glory of being ultimately autonomous. The condition of subordination of man to God is itself not the highest value and is morally degrading.

It is clear, therefore, that Rāmānuja's theory of the Absolute is a religious account of the highest goal of man, while Śaṅkara's concept of the mokṣa is metaphysical. Mokṣa, according to Rāmānuja, is the highest religious value; it constitutes the realization of the absolute values of Truth. Beauty and Goodness. His concept of the highest condition does not go beyond the moral domain, for he thinks that there is no supra-moral plane of being, wherein there is a complete cessation of a life of duty (karmasaṁnyāsa). Even in the state of mokṣa, a person is supposed to discharge unconditional duties with a spirit of disinterestedness, for they are believed to be conducive to the power of enlightenment (sattvavivṛddhijanaka). In this way, he has made the highest state (mokṣa) to be morally activistic. The state of mokṣa, therefore, cannot be conceived as a condition of complete disembodiment, for moral activity presupposes empirical life, unless mokṣa means an internal transformation and realization which is possible in this very life. Śaṅkara's concept of Jīvanamukti implies this. But the view that a life of selfless duty conduces to enlightenment, disposes us to look towards a state of complete enlightenment farther from the moral life which is higher than it. Metaphysically, this condition of highest enlightenment must be the goal. Hence, Rāmānuja's concept of the highest state of man is the highest from the religious point of view; it is, undoubtedly, not the highest from the metaphysical angle. This is exactly the point of difference between the approaches of Śaṅkara and Rāmānuja.

COMPARISONS

The concept of liberation (mokṣa) as found in Indian thought is unique, an exact parallel to which in Western philosophy is hard to find out except a similar view in Spinoza. A.K. Lad writes, 'If any single conception can be taken to distinguish Indian philosophy from the Western, it is the conception of mokṣa which is usually translated into English as liberation, salvation or release, though none of these words reveal the full meaning of the original. The conception of salvation or release in Western theology implies that the soul has fallen in the dearth of the world at some particular time due to certain sin and we have to release it from it. But (the) Indian conception of mokṣa implies that the soul is eternally free, but it has wrongly identified itself with certain extraneous elements and we have to realize its true nature.'[64] Apart from the religious significance of the concept of mokṣa, it has been subjected to much of philosophization at the hands of Indian thinkers, who may seem to differ wildly from full non-spiritualist to spiritualist views about the final destiny. The problem of liberation (mokṣa) finds its crux in the notion of the self even though the Buddhists may not believe in a permanent self.

In Western philosophy if any view of the highest destiny of man as freedom or salvation comes close to the Indian concept of mokṣa, it is that of Spinoza, who has conceived of the two distinct states of man, namely of human bondage and of human liberty, on the same pattern as most Indian thinkers do. He devotes Books IV and V of his *Ethics*[65] to the considerations of the two states respectively.

Spinoza works out his views on the final destiny of man as a strict deduction from his general metaphysical standpoint. He believes in only one substance which can be truly independent and that is God. Everything else is dependent on God. Thus, all individual things are partial, limited and determined; and this is true of man who is a part of God. Man's imperfection is mainly due to an imperfect knowledge he has of God, Nature and himself. His salvation lies in the attainment of true knowledge which Spinoza terms as intellectual love of God (*Amor dei*), but on true realization, man does not become God, as Śaṅkara holds, for the knowledge only reveals man's essential dependence on God as a part of God. This again is not the state which Rāmānuja thinks is the final destiny of the liberated soul, for Spinoza's liberated man keeps on loving God without being loved by God in return.

Spinoza thinks that human bondage due to the importance of man in governing or restraining the affections (passions) which cloud his power of discrimination and consequently, he is forced to choose the worse in face of the better. It is clear, therefore, that the path towards liberty is paved by the power of the intellect which can control the affections. Reason alone, according to Spinoza, leads to blessedness. It is reason again which enlightens man as to his true nature as a part of God. The highest knowledge proceeds from understanding the nature of individual things and their dependence on God. The more we understand it, the more we understand God.

From the highest knowledge arises the highest possible peace of mind and finally the intellectual love of God which is an eternal state. Spinoza believes that so long as the body remains, the mind, which is otherwise eternal, is subject to the effect of passions; but when the body ceases to be, the mind (soul) stays eternally as a part of God. This state, according to him, is blessedness and this is what is known as intellectual love of God, for it is eternal. Thus, Spinoza's view of salvation can be compared to the Buddhist concept of the attainment of enlightenment (bodhi), because both imply a cancellation of the effects of passions (affects or kleśa), but there will always be some metaphysical differences which distinguish their standpoints.

Self-realization[66] as the supreme goal of life can be used as a starting point in the comparison of Eastern and Western thought, as it is acknowledged by most of the idealists both in the East and the West. Self-realization, if it means anything, must mean realization of the self which is considered to be higher or more true than the actual personality.[67] It may mean self-development, and in this sense, it implies the realization of certain potentialities of human nature which are at present undeveloped. Aristotle's conception of Eudaemonism will be closer to this. He maintains that to energize the soul (which should be taken to mean the rational part of human nature) according to the point of virtue which provides the form to moral life, gives joy (Eudaemonia) which is the aim of life. Self-realization, therefore, will not mean the development of all the capacities of human nature, for that is not only well nigh impossible. A choice of capacities is, therefore, necessary for a theory of self-realization which would mean the realization of those capacities which are better or higher than others, for the self to be realized must be full of value.

F.H. Bradley suggests that both the spheres of knowledge and conduct be developed,[68] but that comprises almost the whole of moral life. A choice will have to be made between higher and lower, true and false, in order to make self-realization a practical ideal. Hegel maintains that reason evolves in the form of an idea both as the self as well as the world through the dialectical process culminating in the all comprehensive intelligence which is God or the Absolute. T.H. Green is more explicit and in the restatement of the Hegelian thesis. He accepts the idea of self-realization as the final goal of human life, and goes on to define the nature of the true self which is to be realized. The true essence of self is its rationality or self-consciousness, which is the differentia of man. Apart from it, man resembles animal, for both of them have sensations, appetites, etc., but it is on account of the presence of the spiritual essence in human nature which disposes it to have perceptions instead of sensations and in him appetites become desires. He elaborates this idea of the spiritual element by the process of human volition in which man dreams of an imaginary goal and then sets about realizing it. He, on account of this spiritual capacity, transforms his ideas into reality. He is a little creator and resembles Providence in this respect. After having confirmed the spirituality of self, he proceeds to demonstrate that reason or spirit is all-pervading; it is unmanifest in certain things and manifest in others. As we go from stones to trees and from them to animals, we see that the reason in stones is so latent and implicit that it is as good as absent, it becomes slightly explicit in vegetable organisms while in the case of animals, it is revealed in consciousness. But in human nature it is quite explicit in the form of self-consciousness and reason. Even man is not completely spiritual or rational. It is God or the Absolute which is all reason, pure intelligence. There is much gap between man and God. The ideal of man is to realize his true essence which is self-consciousness or reason. Self-realization, therefore, means realization of the spiritual self. Self-realization is at the same time God-realization, for God is the truest essence of man and is complete Reason. T.H. Green answers the most important question with respect to the problem of self-realization, that it is the spiritual capacities which are higher and more worthy of realization than others.

In order to face the charge of selfishness on self-realization, the nature of self will have to be further explored, for a self in order to be itself will have to exclude other selves from itself and is bound to be selfish. T.H. Green will argue that true self is not selfish or parochial, it is true simply because it is social; the social self alone is higher and it is this sociality which is an essential characteristic of spirituality. Bradley contends that we are to aim at a society of selves of which our self is a part.[69] How one person can involve others in his own essence, does not present any formidable difficulty to idealists who believe in the theory of internal relations. The social relations of a person are internal and constitute his essence which is spiritual and which is to be realized.

Let us see how we can answer some of the fundamental questions raised by Western thinkers in their discussion on the subject of self-realization from the Indian point of view of liberation (mokṣa). The Indian concept of liberation implies two states of man, viz., bondage and freedom. We do not find the exact equivalent of this in the philosophy of self-realization, except that a distinction is made between the false self and the true self. The former is the actual or empirical (jīva) and the latter is the real or transcendental, (ātman, puruṣa). The false self is false because it is changeable, limited and miserable according to the Indian point of view, and the cause of this bondage is inevitably ignorance of the true nature of self. Self-realization lies in the removal of such ignorance and thus breaking through the limitations on the free life of the spirit, the liberated soul realizes its truest essence as consciousness and bliss. Self-realization cannot be selfish ideal, because according to Indian philosophy, selfishness is a characteristic of the false self, and self-realization means rising above narrowness and selfishness. The true self must be the same in every body, because distinctions of body, mind, etc., are external to the spirit. The highest state of self-realization is the realization of absolute identity with the Absolute (Brahman) according to Śaṅkara. Rāmānuja comes closer to Bradley in his concept of a system or organism of selves. But the Absolute is an undifferentiated whole of spiritual essence, according to Śaṅkara.

Distinct metaphysical standpoints mark the difference between the Western concept of self-realization and the Indian view of liberation (mokṣa). The distinction between true and false selves has been metaphysically validated by Indian thinkers, so that false self is designated as empirical and the true as transcendental. The former is the state of bondage and the latter the state of liberation. We do not find any attempt made by Western thinkers to investigate the cause of such bondage. For Indian thinkers, ignorance of the true nature of the self is the cause of bondage. Self-realization for the Indian mind is spiritual awakening or wisdom, which dispels this ignorance and helps break through the bonds of the false self, and usher in the free life of the spirit. Indians have been so fascinated by the ideal of liberation that ever since they have been thinking of it as the most practical ideal. The basic difference between the Indian and Western approaches lies in the difference in original motivation. Indian philosophy takes its origin from the problem of suffering and the natural tendency to remove it. It shows a more humanistic approach than Western thought for which philosophy is more or less an intellectual activity.

Critical Remarks

The twin propositions, namely, (i) that worldly life means suffering and (ii) that mokṣa or liberation from it is the highest goal of human life are acceptable to the whole of Indian thought (with the sole exception of the Cārvāka school, which believes in a pure and simple naturalism or lokāyatavāda); and it moves within them which form its extremities. The Jainistic and Buddhistic (hetrodox) views about the highest goal of man also revolve round the same conception of mokṣa and can be viewed, not as antagonistic or dissensionistic but only variationistic in as much as the concept of mokṣa itself is capable of various interpretations at the hands of orthodox philosophers.

The concept of mokṣa implies a number of theories as its metaphysical grounds: (i) the theory of suffering, (ii) the theory of universal causation (karma), (iii) the theory of the transmigratory existence of man or the cycle of birth and death (saṁsāra), (iv) the theory of transcendental freedom (mokṣa) and (v) the theory of the path to it (mokṣa-sādhana). These five theories constitute the basic minimum of the concept of mokṣa, acceptable to all Indian thinkers despite their diagonally opposite views about the details of these theories. It is on account of this common area of pure agreement in Indian thought that the theory of self is left out here, because it is opposed point-blank by the Buddhists although it is found to be quite central to the concept of mokṣa in the rest of Indian thought. Similarly, the theory of the highest reality is not invariably essential for the theory of mokṣa, for whereas it is considered absolutely essential in the Advaita-Vedānta, the Nyāya-vaiśeṣikas stop short at the reality of the self in their view of mokṣa although the highest reality is different and the Buddhists, only by implication of their original stand, have been led to believe in it.

The theory of suffering has been the problem with which Indian thought has been preoccupied through the ages. It was first mooted by the Upaniṣadic mystic sages and later the Indian philosophers took it up. Those thinkers who do not accept the authority of the śruti (veda, including the Upaniṣad), accepted it. The Buddhist theory, i.e., duḥkhavāda which originally means belief in the unrest or commotion (duḥkha) of the elements of existence (dharma), ultimately points to the fact of sorrowful existence. The theory of suffering may be stigmatized as a pessimistic view of life. In so far as it is an account of life based upon the hard facts of poverty, disease, fear and the slavish subjugation in which the majority of mankind is writhing, even at present, it is true and realistic and can hardly be denied. So the Indian view is not pessimistic because suffering is a judgment of fact. But the presence of happiness is also a hard fact, in as much as we do enjoy our life. The question as to what is pessimism and what is optimism, can be referred to the tendency of accentuating one aspect of life over the other, unwarranted by facts themselves. Pessimism, accordingly, means a prejudice in favour of the dark side of human existence. Again, the question escapes a solution unless a factual balance between the two aspects of life is struck one way or the other. But much seems to depend upon classifying and ultimately recognising what is pain or pleasure. The Indian mind has found, on analysis, the transitory and uncertain nature of empirical pleasure. But again, this might be due to its pessimistic bias. The question whether a view is pessimistic or not is, however, important.

The theory of the cycle of birth and death is the logical result of thinking about this basic problem, for if suffering is the essence of life (empirical), to be (in the empirical sense) is to be miserable, then the solution seems to lie in death, which ends all life in the form of psycho-physical existence and suffering along with it. Most people misunderstand mokṣa as to be the release from the psycho-physical organism. (The concept of nirvāṇa is subject to this misunderstanding to a geater extent.) But Indian philosophers think that death does not put a stop to suffering because it is no end of life which persists through the rigours of death and emerges phoenix-like from the ashes of the previous life on the force of past cumulative psychic dispositions (saṁskāra) as germ-carriers of life-elan. With every new life, the tendency to suffer is repeated until the cycle of human existence (saṁsāra) becomes a formidable and vicious circle (bhavacakra) hard to break through. Hence freedom from suffering means freedom from the transmigratory cycle (saṁsāra). The belief in transmigration can hardly be advocated on factual evidence, which is totally lacking. Man does live, as a matter of fact, after his death not in the form of another similar life, but in the life of his progeny and future generations to whom he has hereditarily transmitted much of his dispositions (saṁskāra) and in the form of his creations, which continue to act on the future generations. If this is the case, then the only way of overcoming human suffering is to plan human life so as to eliminate chances of suffering and to pass on only noble characteristics to the progeny and noble deeds for the future. But Indian thought, in the absence of positive evidence in favour of the theory of transmigratory existence, resorts to metaphysical reasons in the form of the theory of universal causation, which is a valid argument for a metaphysical belief may be justified on metaphysical grounds.

The theory of universal causation (karma) is the metaphysical basis for the theory of cyclic human existence. The theory of universal causation implies the intrinsic necessity with which the effect follows cause. It is also a law recognized by the scientific world and is true in the case of psychic occurrences; psychic disposition determines future mental states. But the Indian theory of karma is peculiar in one respect—the belief that the consequences of the acts of one person must revert to him alone, and he must live on until the whole potential of Karmic energy in the form of consequences is exhausted. This prolonged life means fresh actions (karma) and fresh reserves of such energy, which results in a vicious circle, which leads to the cycle of transmigratory existence. But transmigratory existence may not be the inevitable logical consequences of the theory of karma, which holds good also in the case of living through the life of one's progeny, and the future generation which one has determined. According to this view, we enjoy the consequences of good acts, and suffer those of evil ones in this very life though the consequences of some of our acts, which mature after our death, revert to future mankind. But the Indian mind seems to prefer universal justice and proper dispensation to be worked out in detail on the basis of individual, who perpetrates certain consequences through his actions, must be bound morally to bear their brunt also. Hence, the belief in the theory of bondage (bandha) is based on the metaphysical postulate of an inherent moral world-order and universal justice. Another postulation, viz., the immortality of soul or self is also necessary in view of the fact that it must be responsible for the everlasting consequences of its actions. However, the necessity for it is ruled out by the Buddhists, who believe in the persistence of impressions (Saṁskāra) in the absence of a permanent soul substance or self. Once the belief in the theory of karma and the theory of transmigratory existence, which together constitute the belief in bondage (bandha) is confirmed, the theory of mokṣa follows from it as a logical consequence.

Human bondage is the basis of the theories of karma and saṁsāra; but it is viewed differently by different Indian thinkers on account of their different metaphysical standpoints. Despite variations in the nature and cause of bondage, ignorance (avidyā) or wrong knowledge (mitha jñāna) or wrong belief about the true nature of things is always regarded as the basic cause of bondage. (This postulate is refused by some thinkers, like Rāmānuja, who only takes it in a definite sense.) Ignorance as the absence of correct knowledge of the fundamental reality differs from one school of thought to another. It is wrong knowledge of the materialistic conception of reality (mithya jñāna) according to the Jainas and the Nyāya-vaiśeṣikas. It is wrong belief in the permanent self etc. according to the Buddhists. It is of the nature of illusion (bhrama) which facilitates and strengthens false superimpositions on the highest self (ātman) according to Śaṁkara. It is wrong understanding about the true nature of the self, as thinking subject due to the effect of past impressions, according to Rāmānuja. Ignorance in the form of non-discriminative knowledge of puruṣa and prakriti is the cause of bondage according to the Sāṁkhya. All agree, however, that ignorance results in bondage, i.e., empirical existence. In other words, a person in bondage is limited by his psycho-physical organism, i.e., material body, sense organs, mind and intellect (buddhi) which act as the operating agencies of basic ignorance. Embodiment results in life and life in activity and activity takes man round the cycle of existence (saṁsāra) by the force of causation (karma) and there is no end to it on its own. Both good and bad acts are acts and all action binds man. Hence, both kinds of action operate under the influence of karma, within the domain of bondage (bandha).

Ignorance by itself cannot constitute human bondage in the cycle of existence, for ignorance is purely an intellectual category and as such can hardly be believed to determine activity, life and birth and death. The postulation of a force is necessary, a force which may owe itself teleologically to ignorance, and att he same time operate in the domain of life as a category of the law of causation (karma). This force is believed to be the same as 'life-force' or 'will-to-live' or 'elan vital' of Bergson and 'horme' of McDougall. It, by itself under the influence of ignorance, determines life, birth and death in the cycle of existence. The passion (klesha) of the Buddhists which issues forth in the life-prone-elements (sasrava dharma), the Karmic energy of the

Jainas which pollutes the soul, the cosmic will (ahaṁkāra) of the Sāṁkhya which works itself out in all details of life, and the cosmic delusion of Śaṁkara are all pointers to the same principle of life-force or passion or passion for life. Due to this cosmic power the bondage is hard to break or overcome.

If some sort of ignorance, non-knowledge, nescience or wrong knowledge is the cause of human bondage and suffering, then wisdom, knowledge or true cognition of discriminative understanding must be the way of release (mokṣa-sādhana). In fact, three well-defined paths to mokṣa are current in Indian thought: knowledge (jñāna), devotion (bhakti) and action (karma) corresponding to the cognitive, affective and conative aspects respectively. Various thinkers have emphasised different paths, for example, the original concern of the Buddhists and the Jainas was to recommend right conduct for mankind, while Rāmānujists wanted to make devotional meditation of the Lord the only way to mokṣa. But in the last resort they all revert to the same path of knowledge. This was because of the direct influence of the Upaniṣads, which the Indian mind could not shake off. In the Upaniṣads, besides knowledge (jñāna), austerity (tapas) and mental concentration (yoga) are also recommended. Right renunciation (saṁyāsa) and disinterestedness of action (niṣkāmakarmayoga) are given prominence in the *Bhagavad-Gītā.* The difference in these approaches is superficial, for all mean the same and ultimately result in the destruction of the life-force and ignorance. Everything which is action oriented (pravṛtti) must result in activity and thus strengthen the life-force by the law of karma; hence, moral life by itself is ruled out as the way to freedom. for good acts bind in the same manner as the evil ones. Knowledge of the highest truth, helped by moral, mental, physical and spiritual disciplines is the only way to cut off the roots of the life-force and release the soul from bondage.

If the law of causation is universal, every effort to escape from it itself will be subject to the law and, thus, release from the world (saṁsāra) seems to be impossible. Knowledge (pure cognition) is as good an activity, with mental antecedents and consequents, as action itself. If action is believed to bind, knowledge must do so too. Actions are more effective in shaping man's destiny than knowledge, for knowledge does not always lead to action. Moral discipline seems to play a more important role in a good life than mere knowledge. But Indian thinkers implicitly believe that to know means to be, that knowledge results in being, wrong knowledge in bondage and correct knowledge in freedom. The unpaniṣadic injunction "One who knows Brahman, becomes Brahman" seems to run like an undercurrent in the whole gamut of Indian philosophy. A parallel belief is that of Socrates who said "Knowledge means Virtue". The power of knowledge in determining being or even becoming being can be doubted, for it is itself the product of being in as much as knowledge cannot subsist apart from the knowing apparatus, objects, sense organs, mind and the knower.

Knowledge is a factor which affects, influences and purifies the being. But knowledge too, is condemned by Indian thought as mundane or worldly, therefore, ineffective in achieving mokṣa, for it is the product of sense organs, mind, etc., which themselves are products of ignorance or absence of knowledge. Knowledge (pure cognition) recommended by Indian thought is higher than worldly knowledge and can be understood as cosmic and transcendental realization or a vision which closely resembles Plato's synoptic vision. The question remains as to how such knowledge can usher in a type of being? The answer to this is very simple: by knowledge, we become Brahman, because Brahman is itself knowledge, intelligence, consciousness. The answer points to another level of being whose essence is knowledge or pure cognition. So actions (karma) being operated upon by the law of causation, cease having consequences on reaching full fruition in the life of a person with true realization, and the seed of life is destroyed in the fire of pure cognition. The soul, due to seedlessness (nirbījatvam), becomes free from the worldly cycle (saṁsāra). But the idea of destroying the seed by knowledge does not become clear until it is referred to the view of ultimate reality.

The concept of mokṣa must imply a belief in two kinds or levels of being: (i) the empirical and (ii) transcendental. The transition from empirical existence to transcendental means mokṣa. A positivistic philosophy, confined within the observables by sensory experience cannot demonstrate the reality of mokṣa. The Buddha's historic silence meant helplessness in explaining transcendental reality, although his concept of nirvāṇa did imply it. Every Indian thinker, in expounding mokṣa gives an account of the higher level of existence. Unity, union or mergence or becoming one or living in harmony with this transcendental being is the nature of the state of mokṣa. Usually, these levels are thought to pertain to the self of man or soul or spirit and the nature of mokṣa becomes a state of the soul. Though, this is not the case in Buddhism which does not believe in the soul-substance or self. Based on this difference, the theories of mokṣa are divided into two groups: (i) those based on self and (ii) those on not-self. Theories of self refer to the pure spirit as the essence of self in transcendental existence and are further differentiated on the basis of different characterizations of that spiritual essence. The Jainas endow pure spirit with perfections of all kinds as their essence whereas Rāmānuja refers to them as attributes of the transcendental self. The souls of the Nyāya-vaiśeṣika are bare existences with any consciousness while the Sāṁkhya considers pure consciousness and inactivity and neutrality as the essence of puruṣa. Śaṅkara's Brahman is existence (sat), self-revealing consciousness (cit) and bliss (ānanda). But theories of the soul are also divided on the basis of (i) those who believe in the many souls or selves (ultimately) and (ii) those who believe in one absolute self or Brahman. Śaṅkara's view belongs to the second category while all others to the first. (Rāmānuja's selves, as modes of the Brahman, are not many but expressions of the self-same Brahman). The theories of the plurality of selves are metaphysically unsound since it is not possible to adduce a principle of multiplicity of selves which are pure spirits, and pure spiritual essence must be undifferentiated. Hence, Śaṁkara's Brahman is the soul logical conclusion of all spiritualistic account of selves and the idealistic view of human life.

Mokṣa, according to the soul-theories means mergence of the self in the Absolute, which is self-annihilation. Mokṣa or nirvāṇa proceeding from the premises of not-self Buddhist theories means pure extinction or annihilation in the absence of any definite positive essence. Hence Mokṣa based on either premise is an annihilistic state, and as such cannot be a value, for value means accomplishment or something capable of accomplishment. In so far as annihilation is accomplished through mokṣa, it is a value, though a negative value. The negative character of mokṣa does not simply lie in negating life, for it posits a definite existence, but in the negative valuational qualities of mokṣa. The argument in favour of a positive value on the basis of a positive realization of the Brahman-essence is false, on the obvious ground that Brahman is itself not a valuational category because it transcends all valuation and is supramoral or amoral. But the process of achievement can remain valuational. The argument is also not acceptable on account of the fact that mokṣa implies a change and, therefore, is not real, and again if, every time a soul achieves mokṣa neither Absolute reality (Brahman) nor the liberated self, which ceases before it achieves the top, stands to gain, then mokṣa is not an achievement of value. Idealists, like the realists of Indian thought, hold that the real and the valuable are ultimately one so that the ultimate reality is at the same time ultimate value. But the Absolute (Brahman) is existence and any attempt to unite value with existence spells disaster for an idealistic account of life. Existence cannot be a value and an unchangeable total existence, like the Brahman, has hardly anything to do with the ideal of man, for it is already existent. The question cannot be settled unless the nature of the Absolute is studied deeply, for Śaṅkara maintains an absolute identity of value and existence and reality and value.

There is another and very important implication of the concept of mokṣa. Freedom comes closest to the literal meaning of the word mokṣa. Freedom is the minimum and maximum connotation as the common denominator of all theories of mokṣa. Freedom, as the content of mokṣa seems to have the most cogent claim on value. But freedom by itself does not constitute such a claim unless it is clearly made out as to what it is from which freedom is sought and what it attains. It is both the negative as well as the positive aspects which constitute its case for a value. If freedom is sought from evil, it is a positive value, again if by freedom, good is attained it is good. Indian thought is quite consistent in holding that mokṣa is freedom from suffering and it must be a positive value. But suffering has been confused with life and mokṣa is taken to mean freedom from life itself and in this sense, its claim as a value is doubtful, because life is itself a value which conditions the content of all values.

The original motive-force of Indian philosophy, viz., to find a way of emancipating the human spirit from suffering can be justifiably put to a pragmatic judgment. Once pragmatic grounds are admitted, the ideal of a planned human life and society as the sure way of eliminating human suffering, can be considered which is a more positive approach. Release from life must mean death, but that is not the meaning of mokṣa, for death is supposed to bring fresh life. Thus, mokṣa must mean eternal death so that there is no fresh life, no return from death. But the word 'eternal death' is distasteful to Indian thinkers, for, according to them, mokṣa is eternal life, higher and nobler, transcendental and spiritual. The matter cannot be left at identifying mokṣa with freedom, call it eternal life or eternal death.

This brings us to the positive aspect of mokṣa. What is the positive attainment of a liberated soul? It is believed to become pure consciousness, bliss, etc., but the possibility of happiness in the mokṣa state is doubtful. What constitutes happiness? Can it exist without consciousness? If ever consciousness is posited, both pleasure and pain must appear, even in the highest state attainable by man. This is the most forceful point made by the Nyāya-vaiśeṣika. If consciousness is negated of all attributes in the mokṣa state, there is nothing left except bare existence which is nothing but emptiness, void, extinction, desolate materiality and soul-destroying solitude. In the absence of a genuine case for a positive content of the state of mokṣa, mokṣa cannot be regarded as eternal life. It must mean eternal death to all intents and purposes.

But Śaṁkara distinguishes between consciousness and pure consciousness. The former is subject to modifications, and the experience of pain and pleasure, but the latter is self-revealing and blissful. The experience in samādhi bears testimony to the fact of consciousness without states (nirvikalpa). Mokṣa is Brahma-realization and it is attainable through factual experience. Mokṣa is a fact as much as Brahman is. Existence, consciousness and bliss are the positive achievements in mokṣa. It is Śaṁkara's view that mokṣa is an absolute value, an ideal of human life. Śaṁkara's ideal of liberation in this very life (jīvanamukti) rules out the avowed belief that mokṣa is eternal death and self-annihilation. Mokṣa, which is Brahma-realization, is nothing but spiritual awakening and internal transformation which can be achieved while living. The state of mokṣa, therefore, does not necessarily imply release from the psycho-physical organism. Mokṣa is an absolute and ultimate value, which can be integrated with other values of life, including the economic and mental, for without their ontological basis, life and its higher realizations cannot be maintained. Mokṣa is a value in the system of values, only it is the highest and supreme, though it does not and cannot swallow up the rest, for artha and kāma refuse to be derived from mokṣa. All values are held to be absolute and self-existent; some of them are regarded as higher and some lower. The apparent monism supposed to be implied in the Indian concept of values is, in fact, pluralism, because the consideration of a supreme value implied in the concept of mokṣa is found to be quite consistent with the idea of various values forming a system.

CHAPTER EIGHT

Brahman as Value

Self as Value

Self is involved in every act of value-realization which can be viewed as a process of transition from an unfulfilled self to a fulfilled one. Self is the end of all activities, the object of all volitions. It initiates the search for a goal and directs it to itself. This point has been abundantly demonstrated by Śaṅkara in his *Updeśasahasri* and F.H. Bradley in his *Ethical Studies.* If true self is the perfect self, it must be the highest goal of man and in this sense, self means the universal self which pervades in every being, for a narrow self is bound to be imperfect. The perfect self must include everything released to it through internal relations; so long as anything remains external to the self, there is a tension which is the basis of value-realization. The act of desiring points to an object external to the self and achievement results in satisfaction of the desire. This process of self-fulfilment goes on in an ascending scale till the most satisfied or fulfilled self is achieved, which is the highest value; this is regarded as the ideal of ātmaprāpti or ātmalābha when nothing remains foreign to or unachieved by the self.

On the other hand, it is established that it is because of the self that man desires other things; Self is the dearest, in other words, the most valuable object in the world, and all other objects are dear because of the self to which they are related. *Bṛhdāraṅyaka Upaniṣad* declares that 'it is the love of self, (*ātmakāma*) that reflects itself in all other forms of desires. Thus, the husband is dear to the wife not because of the wife's love for the husband but for the love with which she loves her own self. Gods are dear to us because of Self.'

Śaṅkara develops his theory of value on the basis of satisfaction of the self. He defines value as that which satisfies self. There are two different notions of self, (i) empirical and (ii) transcendental. The former arises when some external object is achieved and when the true self is attained, there results true bliss (ānanda). Empirical pleasures are desired only as a means to the attainment of the true self, and every such effort, based on self-deception (avidyā) as it were, amounts to groping in the dark; this hankering ceases with the attainment of bliss when the true self is realized. According to Śaṅkara, bliss is infinite, absolute and unexcelled (niratiśaya). There is no higher and better attainment than self-realization. Self is the *Summum bonum*.

The Concept of Universal Self

The enquiry into the nature of the Absolute (Brahman) has been the thematic essence of Sanskrit literature called "Science of the Absolute" (Brahmaśāstra).[1] This branch of knowledge is designated as metaphysics of the Absolute (Brahmavidyā or Brahmatatvajñāna). Such metaphysicians also concern themselves with mokṣa, which is the realization of the essence of the Absolute (Brahmasvarūpa). Hence, for them even mokṣa depends upon the value-character of the Absolute (Brahman). They call themselves mere commentators on the vedic text (śruti), but they have developed original propositions on the basis of their interpretation. All of them take their cue from the Upaniṣads and the *Vedānta-Sūtra,* which accept the Absolute as the ultimate reality and unity of self and the world. What is the relation between self and the Absolute? How can we reconcile one and many (ekāneka)? This constitutes the problem of unity in diversity or identity in difference (bhedābheda). Most renouned scholars, such as Śaṅkara, Rāmānuja, etc., start by answering these questions and develop comprehensive philosophies. These idealistic systems are important from the point of view of value in so far as they promise to throw light on the nature of absolute values, the relation of value and reality and value and existence.

Śankara's Concept of Brahman

The problem of self and the principle of unity are quite central to all Brahmavāda. The problem of unity is the key to any epistemological approach to metaphysical reality, for unity is knowledge and truth. Śaṅkara examines the problem of identity-in-difference (bhedābheda) and finds it true in the empirical sense, for unity (permanence) cannot be equated with difference (change), anything identified with a changing process must also change. The only way out of the impasse is to seek unity in some esoteric principle which is neither identity nor difference, neither one nor many, neither unity nor diversity, but that which transcends all these empirical distinctions.[2] Unity-in-difference belongs to the realm of appearance and is a purely relational category. The reality transcends both unity and difference, it is non-relational (asparśa),[3] non-phenomenal, immutable and one. Śaṅkara calls it Indeterminate Absolute (Nirguṇa Brahman). Since it cannot be known by any subject-object (dṛka-dṛiśya) categories, it is beyond thought, concept and word (anirvacananīya). It can be negatively defined as "not this, not this" (neti, neti).[4] It is unanalysable, partless (niravyava) and indefinable. Silence describes it.[5]

But against this negative approach to the Absolute, Śaṅkara also gives a positive account of it, because he holds that it is not possible to deny without affirming. Negation implies affirmation. This argument is sufficient to refute all negative accounts of the highest reality, like those of the Buddhists who acquiesced in pure negation and the Nyāya-vaiśeṣikas who could not affirm anything. Śaṅkara declares that "neti neti" yields place to "that thou art" (tat tvam asi). He pulls his Brahman out of Buddhistic nihilism. He is not a disguised Buddhist (pracchanna Budha). His Absolute has a positive content; it is pure spirit, pure consciousness (akhanda caitanya), existence (sat).[6] The greatest affirmation of the Advaita is that Nirguṇa Brahman is identified with the ātman which is the truest self of man. Ātmādvaita is the same as sattadvaita.[7] This is the approach from the inner self, but starting from the world of objects, we can arrive at the Absolute all the same. The three affirmations about all objects, i.e., existence (sat), consciousness (cit) and bliss (ānanda) are ultimate and therefore they affirm the Absolute.

But how can the negative and positive approaches to the Absolute be reconciled? On the negative side, we should not form the impression that Brahman is a mere blank (śūnya), a mere nothing.[8] Śaṅkara writes in chapter eight of the *Chandogya Upaniṣad*, "The Absolutely true Brahman, being one without a second, is regarded by dull persons as non-existent (asat)."[9] The negation of appearances will not in the least affect the underlying reality.[10] It is clear that Śaṅkara, to use Bradley's terminology, does not deny "thatness" by denying logical predicates which affect only "whatness" of the Brahman. "Thatness" or existence of the Brahman is unchallenged. Brahman is an entity which is real in the absolute sense, highest of all, eternal, all penetrating like ether (ghatauākāśa-vat).

This acosmic nature of Brahman may be found totally unrelated to life (in the empirical sense) and the world, which according to Śaṅkara are appearances and therefore unreal. They are both existent and non-existent (sadāsadabhāva). The denial of the world is not, therefore, ultimate. They are not absolutely unreal; nor are they real. Here Śaṅkara introduces the concept of three orders of reality (sattātraya), viz., (i) illusory reality (pratibhāsika-sattā) which is epistemologically based on dream-consciousness, (ii) empirical reality (vyavahārika-sattā) based on sensory experience and (iii) transcendental reality (paramārthika-sattā), based on intuitive experience (anubhava) or stateless and objectless consciousness (samādhī).

It seems to be clear that a negative characterization of Absolute reality, according to Śaṅkara, touches only its "whatness" and its "thatness" remains unaffected. "Thatness", according to him is pure existence and nothing else.[11] Other positive contents such as consciousness (cit) and bliss (ānanda) are purely inferential (anukūlatarka) based on empirical reality as the premises, hence they merely touch its essence, which is beyond characterization. On the same epistemological grounds, Absolute reality cannot be declared as pure intelligence, permanent and pure spirit, for they are only pragmatic assertions made for the sake of discourse. But existence cannot be treated at par with other predicates for reasons of a contradistinction between "thatness" and "whatness" and besides, "that" is affirmed in the mystic experience. How can a mystic convey what he has experienced? He talks in parables and symbols (e.g., om). It is, therefore, impossible to communicate existence which lies in the giveness of experience and cannot be inferred or conveyed. Communion is Union. One who knows Brahman, becomes Brahman.[12] Bradley also subscribes to this when he writes, 'Fully to realise the existence of the Absolute is for finite beings impossible. In order thus to know, we should have to be and then we should not exist.'[13]

The existential aspect of the Brahman should be treated at par with other positive essences which are found to be concerned with its "whatness". It would have been fair for Śaṅkara to stop philosophizing at this point and start experiencing, for it is only in the immediate experience that the essence of the Absolute is given. Now if the positive contents as existence, consciousness and bliss are acknowledged, they together constitute a definition of Brahman and this definition is true of any absolute and intrinsic value. There seems to be no doubt that Śaṅkara identifies the Absolute reality with absolute and ultimate value. Brahma-realization is at the same time the final and supreme goal of human life.[14]

Interpretations of Venkatarama Iyer and R.P. Singh

Value is a relational category and is, therefore, not applicable to Brahman which must, therefore, be best called as supravaluational. On the contrary, any non-value characterization of the Brahman can be refuted on the ground that it is the highest reality which underlies all experiences and appearances, the world and men. The absolute reality of Śaṅkara is above two other levels of realities, the illusory and the empirical, and transcends them. The levels may be valuational so that the degrees of reality are also the degrees of value, and the highest reality is at the same time the highest value. Do levels of reality imply any degrees of value? Is highest reality, highest value? Śaṅkara seems to relegate notions of value to only the empirical level which cannot hold good at the transcendental level.

It is hard to agree with Venkatarama Iyer that "Advaita is essentially a value-philosophy".[15] He develops his view on the epistemological nature of the undifferentiated experience which leads us to affirm the metaphysical reality of the Brahman on the one hand and beauty and goodness on the other, because according to him "Aesthetic and moral experiences also lead up by stages to the same consummation".[16] Apparently, he is correct, because the Upaniṣads declare Brahman to be surpassing beauty, bliss and goodness (sat). But it is untenable on Śaṅkara's own epistemology which makes completely undifferentiated experience as the basis of the absolutely real, but aesthetic and moral experiences are not so undifferentiated that the relational distinction between the subject and object is absolutely abolished. They may approximate to it but are not the same. They are the stages to it, in as much as the subject in an aesthetic experience loses himself but not entirely; he retains a slim distinctness. This mergence of the subject and object, in which aesthetic value is experienced, is only temporary. "The aesthetic feeling or the sense of the beautiful is due to a temporary suppression of individuality and objectivity to an unconscious realization of oneness."[17] There is harmony, but that cannot be interpreted in the sense of absolute unity as Śaṅkara defines it. Iyer feels the need of transcendence in a moral and aesthetic experience to arrive at unity.[18] Hence aesthetic, moral, and religious experiences are approximations to the ideal experience of Śaṅkara's concept (Ātmānubhava).

Śaṅkara has, therefore, successfully argued as to the metaphysical reality of Brahman being truth (satyam) but has failed to justify the Upaniṣadic assertions about it as beauty (sundaram) and goodness (śivam) and God (īśvara). This was the main target of attack by other vedantins, especially Rāmānuja. Śaṅkara's Brahman seems to transcend all such values.[19] Iyer admits that 'the deficiencies and contradictions that are inherent in Logic, Ethics and Religion arise from our attempt to view from a lower standpoint a reality which belongs to the higher plane . . . they can be overcome by passing beyond relations to what is non-relational'.[20] Bradley also thinks that moral life is ultimately full of contradictions and raises his Absolute above all values, of truth, beauty and goodness.

Iyer seems to accept our conclusions with regard to Śaṅkara's attitude towards values when he inadvertently writes at another place that it is Śaṅkara's uncompromising passion for the truth, the whole truth, and nothing but truth that marks him out as a philosopher of the highest order. 'He did not allow other considerations to interfere with the free march of his thought. He considered the interests of even morality and religion to be extraneous to the interests of philosophy proper . . . a true philosopher must not be wedded to partial truths but must be ever intent on knowing and realising the highest truth.'[21] Beauty, goodness and holiness are condemned as lower because they are partial truths and truth as such, the whole truth, which is metaphysical reality must be the highest. But there is one limitation: when one skips over truths which are found to be partial, in a rush for the highest truth, what one discovers is truth which must be the highest value. Even the identity of value with truth (reality) cannot be accepted without examination. There seems to be a tendency in the whole Indian tradition to fuse value with reality.

If reality and value on the one hand and value and existence on the other, are identified, as most of the absolute idealists may do the entire philosophy of Śaṅkara may turn out to be a philosophy of value. Dr. R.P. Singh has taken pains to demonstrate this truth, which, according to him, is responsible for the misinterpretation of Śaṅkara's advaita. He writes, 'The one great truth which has escaped the attention of the interpreters of Śaṅkara who have consequently found in his works a system of pure and undiluted rationalism is that it is primarily and pre-eminently a philosophy of value.'[22] Most of the critics of Śaṅkara, according to him, confuse axiological and existential categories in his system. Śaṅkara has used categories like substance, cause, universal and particular, existence, reality, levels of reality, etc., which are all value-categories.[23] Dr. R.P. Singh thinks that 'the relation of value to being—this is the key problem of Śaṅkara's philosophy.'[24] He writes further, 'His notion of reality is that of value, value and reality being identical in his system. . . . The Vedānta of Śaṅkara is ruled by the idea of a highest good, a *summum bonum*, a perfection which it is the great business of life to attain. . . . This good is not merely ethical or religious good but is identical with what the metaphysicians call the highest reality.'[25] Thus, degrees of reality are at the same time degrees of values. According to Dr. R.P. Singh, existence is rooted in reality and therefore in value. There is no duality between the actual and ideal, world and Brahman, existence and value. 'Śaṅkara shows that in its essence the world of existence is an expression of the world of value, the actual of the ideal, the not self of the self.'[26] He elaborates this point, 'valuational consciousness is led to recognise Brahman as the self of the Universe and its innermost essence, as the goal towards which the world process can be said to be moving . . . the absoluteness of the Bra man and inseparability in it of value and existence, cannot be expressed in a better, more intelligible and more exquisite way than by calling it the ātman or the absolute ground (of the world of fact).'[27] He writes further that for Śaṅkara ātman, Brahman, and mokṣa are values and not mere existents.[28] Brahman is described as Saccidānanda, it is the self of the universe which is itself grounded in existence, consciousness and bliss. According to Dr. R.P. Singh, 'the values of sat, cit and ānanda are absolute and intrinsic values and Brahman is the embodiment of these absolute values.'[29] Absolute values are the results of moral or religious efforts and they are not derivative. 'Values are not karm-asādhya says Śaṅkara. They are intrinsic and absolute. Ātman, being the same as mokṣa or Brahman, is spoken of by Śaṅkara as akarmaśeṣa.'[30] According to Dr. R.P. Singh, 'Value cannot be defined in terms of anything else; it can only be defined in terms of itself.'[31] He argues that definition will have to be *per genus et differentiam* and the absolute has no differentia. Existence, knowledge and bliss do not qualify the Absolute, they constitute its essence. Hence absolute value is indefinable; it can only be experienced as the very essence of our own self.[32] So he concludes that in Brahman value and being come together and fuse in one, Brahman is said to be Advaita by Śaṅkara. *Brahman* is above all duality, duality of value and existence, of self and not-self, of ideal and actual, of is and ought.'[33] Existence (*Sat*), consciousness (*cit*) and Bliss (*ānanda*) are dimensions of value to be expressed by the term "*tattva*" which means value (essence) as opposed to mere existence (*tat*).[34] *Brahman* is, therefore, the Absolute value, "*tattva*". Thus Dr. R.P. Singh has brought an aspect of Śaṅkara's advaita to light which is not found in other absolutist idealists of the West, and by his value point of view, he has rendered it more intelligible. Value in its true and ultimate character is absolute value, which explains all other approximations to it and becomes the basis of reality and existence, from the idealistic point of view.

Śankara and the Determinate Absolute of Ramanuja

Rāmānuja, although a full-blooded vedantin, was dissatisfied with the conclusions of Śaṅkara which drove him to admit only indeterminate Absolute (nirguṇa Brahman). Śaṅkara's Absolute is a mere void, a blank which fails to serve as an object of devotion and moral aspiration. Rāmānuja wanted to shift his approach from the logical to the moral and religious point of view. Rāmānuja contends that thought alone cannot bring us face to face with reality. It can be envisioned by intuition which is conditioned by devotional fervour.[35] There is an inherent necessity in the nature of knowledge which enables the indeterminate cognition to pass over into the determinate.[36] Our judgments are attempts to relate parts to larger wholes. The most perfect knowledge is a single organized experience, consisting of parts having specific functions in the whole. Rāmānuja as opposed to Śaṅkara, argues that bare identity is useless and insignificant. Identity is a relation and every relation requires two terms. The judgment asserts an identity in and through difference.

Once we admit the principle of identity-in-difference (bhedābhedavāda), it logically follows that the real cannot be a bare identity. It is a determinate whole, which maintains its identity in and through differences. Rāmānuja, therefore, believes in an Absolute (Brahman) which is a whole of parts such as an infinite number of selves, the World and Lord (God). 'Souls and matter are comprehended within the unity of the Lord's essence and are related to the Supreme as attributes to a substance, as parts to a whole or as body to the soul which animates it' (śarīraśārīrina).[37] Rāmānuja used another expression to term the relation between elements and the Absolute, i.e., modes (prakāraprakārī). They qualify the Absolute, they are its modifications, and determinations. The unity of elements (śeṣas) in the Absolute is organic in type, after the analogy of parts and the organism. Souls and matter do not entirely exhaust the content of the Brahman, for the whole is always more than the mere sum of the parts. They predicate the whole. There are internal differences in Absolute reality (svagatabheda) which are dissolved into a synthetic unity.

Existence (sat), consciousness (cit) and bliss (ānanda) characterize the Absolute (Brahman). Rāmānuja's Brahman is, therefore, full of qualities (saguṇa) of which knowledge, power and love are the most pronounced. A liberated soul enters into a real fellowship with God and other personalities. Rāmānuja thinks that by his concept of a determinate Brahman (saguṇa-brahman), he has done full justice to certain assertions of the śṛuti according to which the Absolute is full of noble qualities, values and excellences of the world. The same were not fully justified in Śaṅkara's concept of Absolute reality. Rāmānuja approaches Absolute reality from the various points of view of the (i) metaphysical, (ii) aesthetic and (iii) moral. From the metaphysical point of view, the Brahman is the real of reals (satyāya satyam), it is defined as real (satya) conscious (jñāna) and infinite (ananta). It is the supreme sat which sustains all beings and the world as their ultimate ground. It is the absolute self, super-subject. The term "higher than the highest" used in the Upaniṣads is used for Brahman which is the supreme self and also is the home of all eternal values. The Absolute as a notion of the all-comprehensive reality, the unity-in-difference and a whole of parts and a universal present in particulars is the ideal achievement of vedantic quest which arrives at the Absolute truths. But the same Absolute is not only the logical highest but also the embodiment of all moral values. He is the righteous ruler of the universe. The evil in the world is not a foil to the infinite goodness, and holiness of God but is traceable to the moral freedom of the finite self. The ultimate moral goal of man is the attainment of Godhead; he is therefore the supreme Good and the *summum bonum*. The same Brahman is infinite beauty from the aesthetic point of view. The Upaniṣads define the Absolute as inner beauty, the effulgent one. The cosmos is the expression of the spontaneous will of the Lord to be beautiful. He is delight (raso vai saḥ) and bliss (ānanda). Hence the Absolute is the embodiment of absolute values of truth (satyam), goodness (śivam) and beauty (sundaram).

Rāmānuja is successful in giving an exposition of Absolute reality from the value point of view. From the religious point of view God is regarded as the embodiment of values like holiness and inspires reverence, devotion, faith and humility. The reality is the ultimate basis of absolute values, goodness, truth and beauty. Here again is present, implicitly or otherwise as in the whole tradition of Indian thought, a tendency to equate reality and value. The word 'sat' which means both existence (reality) as well as goodness, conveys the fullest import of the fusion of reality and value. The uniqueness of Rāmānuja's philosophy lies in a value-approach to the real, which helps us in arriving at goodness which is the ideal of Ethics, truth, the ideal of Logic and Beauty, the ideal of Aesthetics. This implies that value conditions reality. The true is what represents the real, and what is practically useful (yathārtha vyavahāramguṇa). The essential difference between Rāmānuja and Śaṅkara is that of approach. Śaṅkara shows an exclusive concern for metaphysical truth and relegates religious and moral concerns to the lower level, whereas Rāmānuja approaches reality from the point of moral and religious values so that his concept of the Absolute is the embodiment of truth, beauty and goodness, all the absolute values.

Śaṅkara and Bradley

Of all the idealist thinkers in the West, Bradley comes closest to Śaṅkara. Their absolutism undoubtedly has a good deal of agreement. Both believe that reality in its complete and most perfect form is the single Absolute and everything short of it is "appearance" or "māya". 'There is but one reality', says Bradley, 'and its being consists in experience. And reality in the end belongs to nothing but the single Real. For take anything, no matter what it is, which is less than the Absolute, and the inner discrepancy at once proclaims that what you have taken is appearance.'[38] Both Śaṅkara and Bradley define their Absolute to be above all religious and moral characterizations of it as

God or goodness. Śaṅkara makes a clear distinction between the conditioned and unconditioned natures of Brahman.[39] The former characterization of Reality belongs to the vyavahārika level while the latter to the transcendental level. Similarly, Bradley holds that God, as the highest object of religious devotion is an appearance. He writes, 'Religion naturally implies a relation between man and God. Now a relation always is self-conrtadictory. It implies always two terms which are finite and which claim independence.'[40] He brings out the inherent contradiction in the concept of God when he says, 'Hence, short of the Absolute, God cannot rest and having reached that goal he is lost, and religion with him.'[41] Similarly, both of them believe in the transcendence of morality in the Absolute, since it implies a difference of good and evil and all differences are relative and thus cannot survive in the Absolute. Śaṅkara argues that the knower of Brahman transcends morality; for him there is no moral obligation. Bradley also regards his Absolute as supramoral. He argues that goodness is an appearance, because it involves the separation of idea and existence,[42] and possesses an adjectival character.[43] He defines "good" as 'that which satisfies desire', and covers up all forms of goodness—intellectual, moral and aesthetic. The self-discrepant nature of goodness is evident from the satisfaction of desire. Thus, according to him, 'goodness' as such is but appearance which is transcended in the Absolute.

So far, there is general agreement between Śaṅkara and Bradley, but how religion, morality and beauty are transcended in the Absolute is a fundamental issue which reveals the basic differences in their approach towards value. For Śāṅkara, they are transcended in the undifferentiated unity of the Absolute, while for Bradley, they are transcended in the sense of being transmuted. The objects of ignorance (avidyā) are totally destroyed in the transcendental experience; but Bradley's concept of transmutation of appearances in the Absolute is different from the Śaṅkarite notion of sublation in as much as in transmutation appearances lose their individual natures, but they are retained as entities. He writes, 'In the Absolute no appearance can be lost. Each one contributes and is essential to the unity of the whole.'[44] He believes in the concept of unity in difference and thus comes closer to Rāmānuja than Śaṅkara.

Shrivastava finds Bradley's "concept of transmutation very intriguing".[45] He thinks that 'Bradley's Absolutism is particularly vulnerable on the point of the relation of appearances to the Absolute.'[46] According to him, 'The discord of an appearance is removed in the Absolute, says Bradley; it is transmuted to harmony. If so, the appearance as an appearance is really annulled or lost. Where all is harmony, no appearance can conceivably exist. If an appearance is still to be there, then the discord has not really vanished, and the Absolute is infected with numerous discords. Thus Bradley's Absolute cannot be unity or totality of appearances.'[47] But we find that Bradley's endeavour is to arrive at a concrete unity and not a mere abstraction. Perhaps Shrivastava has failed to understand clearly the import of the distinction between "that" and "what".[48] It is on account of the individual character or "what" that an appearance is an appearance, for "that" is the same Absolute to which "what" is predicated, and when it sheds off its "what", "that", i.e., existence of an appearance must remain. But Shrivastava is not able to reconcile himself to the idea of appearances having "independent ontological status alongside of the Absolute".[49] This controversy is the same as that between Śaṅkara and Rāmānuja. Both Bradley and Rāmānuja think that harmony or unity means a unity of entities, otherwise it is a mere abstraction or void.

Rāmānuja's concept of unity in diversity (bhedābheda) protects the interests of ultimate values of truth, beauty, goodness and religion, but Bradley seems to lose this argument in conceiving of his Absolute as supra-moral, because for him, all human pursuits, moral, aesthetic and religious involve a self contradiction between the ideal and reality.[50] On his own premise, Absolute reality which is identity of fact and idea, must be the supreme good as in the case of Śaṁkara's Brahman. But Bradley denies this when he contends, 'Goodness is not absolute or ultimate; it is but one side, one partial aspect of the nature of things. . . . Goodness as such is but an appearance which is transcended in the Absolute.'[51] On the other hand, Bradley accords a differential treatment to goodness when he argues, '. . . the Absolute is good and it manifests itself throughout in various degrees of goodness and badness. The destiny of goodness in reaching which it must itself cease to be, is accomplished by the whole. And since in that consummation idea and existence are not lost but are brought into harmony, the whole, therefore, is still good.'[52] He therefore maintains that 'the good is a main and essential factor in the universe'.[53] Shrivastava points out the glaring self-contradiction in Bradley's position, because if good could survive in the result, it is not lost and, therefore, not an appearance.[54] This contradiction is due to the confusion between "that" and "what". Specified goods are good because of their "what" which is destructible in the Absolute, but their universal "that" or existence remains. It is this absolute existence which is good ultimately, for ontology becomes axiology. Hence, Bradley's Absolute is a notion of absolute value and it is exactly the same as Śaṅkara's Brahman.

But we will have to concede one essential point of difference between the approaches of Śaṅkara and Bradley which has been brought to light ably by Shrivastava, viz., that while Śaṅkara's Brahman is attainable by factual experience, and is a fact, Bradley's Absolute is only an abstract metaphysical notion. Shrivastava writes, 'For Bradley, the Absolute is a logical postulate only an Idea of Reason in the Kantian sense, and not a fact or verity of human experience. Śaṅkara belongs to the band of those vedic sages of India who have ever been affirming from the depths of their own experiences such as I have known this Infinite Being.'[55] Hence, for Bradley, the supreme good exists only in faith; he observes, 'And hence our common life and our supreme good escapes once more to take its place in an invisible world. It is in some city of God, in some eternal church, that we find the real goodness which owns and satisfies our most inward desire.'[56] On the other hand 'the supreme Good of Śaṅkara cannot only be experienced but is our very self'. The highest good lies in the realization of the Brahman. But Bradley tells us that 'we never have or are a state which is the perfect unity of all aspects'.[57] In other words the Absolute is unattainable.

Comments and Observations

In philosophy there are two opposite standpoints from which the nature of absolute reality is discussed. Subject and object in the epistemic situation constitute the polarity. The subjective approach has been preferred in Indian idealism. "Know thy self' is the golden rule. By an analysis of the thinking subject truth can be known. The inward gaze discovers reality in the innermost depths of the subject, which is the self and the centre of the cosmos also. This line of approach is sure in so far as the existence of the self (ātman) can never be doubted.[58]

The concept of self develops through three logical stages, viz., psychological, epistemological and transcendental.[59] At the first it is defined as speech (vāc), mind (manas), wind (āpas), ether (ākāś), etc. At the second stage, it is conceived as bhūmān which is a self-maintaining principle and the ground of finite objects. At the third level, it is the presupposition of all knowledge, which is beyond proof (svayaṁsiddha), self-revealing (svaprakāśa), infinite (ananta) and suprarelational (asaṅga). This transcendental notion of self rises above the subject and object categories.

The essence of the transcendental self (ātman) is consciousness, it is the all-pervasive spiritual principle.[60] It is both existence and consciousness, for knowledge and existence cannot be distinguished.[61] Western theories of self lead either to empty abstractions or to the agnostic position. Consciousness cannot be regarded as the separable or inseparable accident of the self as the Nyāya-vaiśeṣikas and the Jainas do. Self is of the essence of consciousness.

Self, which is pure consciousness, cannot be other than the universal self (paramātman), and therefore, it must be the same as the Absolute (Brahman), for it rises above diversity and distinctions, it is the universal in particulars. The principle of multiplicity of selves (ātman) cannot be ultimately maintained in face of the spiritual essence, which is pure and simple, and beyond division. The Sāṁkhya's argument goes the same way as Rāmānuja's does, because individuation is empirical and not ultimate. Śaṅkara's simple equation of self (ātman) and the Absolute (Brahman) is the only logical conclusion of all idealistic argument. Even Hegelian and Bradleyan conceptions of the Absolute fall short of this. The Absolute as the society of selves or the organic unity of selves and the world, is approximation to the truth. The Absolute (Brahman) is, therefore, not a distinct principle from the self (Ātman).

Absolute reality cannot be proved through discursive

knowledge; it cannot be known, for it is knowledge itself. It is existence and existence can only be felt in an experience. Differential approaches to the Absolute stem from the various experiences which are preferred. Rāmānuja's concept of the Absolute is built on the ground of aesthetic or religious experience in which the distinction between the subject and object is not completely dissolved. His analysis is bound to land him on a concept of unity in which diversity is preserved. Bradley begins from the analysis of feeling in which "that" and "what" cannot be distinguished. Śaṅkara makes samādhī or dreamless sleep the approximation to the experience in which subject and object are ultimately sublated. This differential approach is again due to the original motivational force. Rāmāṇuja's approach, for example, is religious, moral and aesthetic; he adopts a value point of view which becomes the conditioning principle of reality. Reality as value may not need value as the conditioning principle, for it can be known as the very essence of truth or it may not be conditioned by any extraneous consideration at all. Śaṅkara and Bradley raise their Absolute, above the moral, aesthetic and religious experiences which fail to grasp the totality of the content. It is, therefore, the metaphysical point of view which can help grasp the Absolute, and is superior to them.

The true natuie of the Absolute is pure existence (sat) self-revealing-consciousness (cit) and bliss (ānanda). In this, the very definition of absolute value is also self existence, and an ideal essence, non-relational and aprioristic. This positive characterization of the Absolute (Brahman) is sometimes believed to fall short of it which is, in fact, indescribable. This again constitutes the indefinable and unanalysable character of absolute value. The Absolute (Brahman) is, therefore, an absolute value. To consider the Absolute (Brahman) as the highest object of moral, aesthetic and religious pursuits is to specify the character of absolute value from extraneous points of view. Truth, beauty, goodness and holiness are specific absolute values. The Absolute (Brahman) as the embodiment of truth, beauty and goodness, as according to Rāṃānuja is a determinate entity with a specific essence. It cannot serve as the highest object of religious, moral and aesthetic life at the same time unless it transcends them all in essence. Hence the

Absolute (Brahman) is the absolute and supreme value and truth, beauty and goodness are absolute, concrete and discernible, and specific values. Their absolute nature cannot be doubted as far as their specific fields are concerned.

The logical conclusion of absolute idealism in India is the nature of the Absolute (Brahman) as the highest reality, which is an expression of absolute unity and identity of reality and existence; existence and consciousness; knowledge and existence, value and existence, self and the world, particular and universal. The complete identity between value and reality or being or existence makes the Absolute (Brahman) the supreme value, which implies that all other lower orders of reality must possess lower value as compared to the Absolute. This "higher" and "lower" pertain to the axiological status of values and to nothing else. It is contended by Hartmann[62] that no value can be regarded as supreme unless it is emptied of its contents; but the Absolute (Brahman), which is a supreme value like the "Good" of Plato, is full of contents such as existence, consciousness and bliss. It is so complete and perfect that nothing falls out of it. On that account, it is unknowable and indescribable. Hartmann would say that the Absolute is indiscernible absolute value.

If both the Absolute (Brahman) as well as liberation (mokṣa) are believed to be the highest values by the Bṛahmavādins, they must be identical. Mokṣa is Brahman, and Brahman is mokṣa.[63] This simple equation will have to be understood with certain reservations, because liberation (mokṣa) as the highest value has been held by thinkers who do not believe in the Absolute. The Nyāya-vaiśeṣikas and the Sāṁkhya, for example, maintain the highest value without the Absolute. Mokṣa is, therefore, a more popular concept than the Absolute (Brahman).

If the Absolute (Brahman) is a supreme value, it is supreme axiologically. But it is defined to be existence (sat) and as such, it must retain to itself the highest ontological or existential status. Existence of the Absolute, truly speaking, is not an existential category, it is a being (bhāva) of the highest order and is, therefore, superior to being (existence in the spatio-temporal sense). This ordering or ranking of being must be axiological and not ontological. Existence in the Absolute means self-existence of the essence of Absolute (Brahmasvarūpa) and is purely an axiological notion. It is, therefore, wrong to conclude that the Absolute is beyond the axiological and ontological categories. It is the highest value axiologically speaking, while the lower values can be acknowledged in face of the Absolute. The ideal of liberation in this life (jīvanamukti and Bodhisattva) implies the coexistence of the highest with other lower values. Hence, the Absolute (Brahman) or liberation (mokṣa) can be regarded as the supreme value in a system of values. The lower is transmuted in the higher, but is not destroyed in this process. Śaṅkara's lower order of being is sublated into the higher order. This means that the lower achieves more axiological significance; but the existence persists as the common factor which is never destroyed nor diminished ultimately. On the other hand it remains in the Absolute (Brahman) as the richest spiritual essence. The principle of sublation of the lower into the higher is an axiological principle of ordering values which may form hierarchical system (sopānakrama).

CHAPTER NINE

Conclusion

The problem of value and the gradation of values have been found to confuse many students of Indian philosophy as to their true character, import and significance. Various schools of Indian thought have been studied and examined, looking upon the problem from different angles. A proper study of the precise problem of gradation of values has inevitably led to the study of nature and importance of various values. During the course of this study, the following conclusions have been arrived at:

THE AXIOLOGICAL CONCERN OF INDIAN THOUGHT

A keen awareness of values is at the root of most philosophical investigations in India. Axiological concern constitutes one of the original motivations of ancient Indian philosophy. Knowledge-oriented curiosity leads the thinker to a vision of reality (darśana) or an attempt at a realization of truth. A true spirit of enquiry does not stop short at a mere intellectual abstraction but finds its fulfilment in emotional appreciation; thought and practice and philosophy and religion are found to influence one another. Many schools of Indian philosophy show a humanistic concern in making the problem of universal suffering its original preoccupation. This frame of mind makes value the guiding principle of knowledge.

The entire Indian philosophical literature can be classified on the basis of its axiological concern, which is announced by every author at the very beginning of his enquiry. Dharma, artha, kāma, mokṣa and Brahman indicate thematic notions, which are at the same time values of life.

Theory of Value

To make axiological concern the motivating principle of philosophical investigation is one thing and to develop a systematic theory of value is quite another. There has been a lack of a proper and intensive enquiry into the nature, definition and problem of value in Indian philosophy. The sole exception is the system of Pūrva-Mīmāṁsā which originally promises to enquire into the nature of dharma which connotes the good (artha). The good is defined as an object worthy of desire. Pleasure and pain constitute the basis of valuation, which consists of both positive and negative judgments. The quantity of pleasure is, therefore, the criterion. But once the division between the empirical good and the non-empirical good had been made and the former relegated to the sphere of the amoral (or the ethically neutral), the enquiry shifts away from an objective and secular study of the value-notion to a mere interpretation of the scriptural texts (śṛuti). Other writers like Śaṅkara and Rāmānuja have only touched upon the problem without dwelling upon it for a thoroughgoing study. Two reasons are found to be at the root of this utter neglect of a theory of value.

In the first instance, Indian thinkers have failed to isolate the notion of value from other concepts like kāma, dharma and Brahman, etc., with which it comes to be associated. The keenness for the concrete values of life makes them miss the abstract and philosophical aspect of the problem.

Secondly, the very fact of a straight division of the subject-matter of values illustrates the point that there was specialization in each field so that value as a theme was left to take care of itself. There has been a lop-sided development of the value-philosophy; the total picture of the entire spectrum of values is not clear until one is in a position to apiece all the aspects of the problem together and harmonize them into an integrated whole, which alone can give a true perspective of values. There is no doubt that such a compartmentalization has paved the way for a good deal of specialization and expert knowledge in various fields, and writers have shown due awareness of other value-fields, but it has unconsciously confused students not only as to the true perspective of values but has also made them lose sight of the original subject of value. Consequently, we find that Indian philosophy has lagged behind Western thought in respect of the development of a theory of value. A discussion of the problem of value amounts to a rediscovery of Indian philosophy in terms of value-notions.

THE REALMS OF VALUE

An understanding of the concept of the four aims of life (catuṣ-puruṣārtha) is fundamental to the Indian concept of values. It is the basis of the division of the entire subject-matter. The four values of artha, kāma, dharma and mokṣa together with Brahman are exhaustive of the entire value-spectrum. On an intensive study of each value, we have found that each is a realm or sphere in itself in which many values are involved, rotating around the self-same nucleus. Each realm signifies four distinct characteristics of value, (i) situation and context in which value-phenomenon takes place, (ii) content and condition of value-experience, (iii) criterion of value-judgment and (iv) "height" of value or its ideality.

Value-realms refer to the various aspects of human life and personality which are found to be the prius of all values, such as economic, psychological, moral, spiritual and religious. Naming the value-realms is fraught with difficulties which have been found to stem from two authentic sources:

In the first place, words like "artha", "kāma", "dharma", "mokṣa", etc., have found to be used in a variety of meanings. The terms may be taken to mean all those objects, states and conditions which they denote otherwise there may be confusion over the exact connotation of the concept. That is why Potter likes to designate them as "attitudes of life, instead of values of life".[1] But it is better to call them values since the concept of value implies both objects and affective-conative attitudes as well as ideals and norms as their transcendental essence.

Secondly, there has been a gradual development in the

spheres of the values. Kāma, for example, originally meant sex-satisfaction but has been extended to imply aesthetic and hedonistic pursuits of life. One word has been applied to such a diversity of situations, states, and objects that one is left in a state of complete bewilderment. Axiological and ontological aspects get confused. It would be a good past-time to disentangle the various shades of meanings centring around each word to arrive at its true character and import.

Four values of life have been current in the thought and life of Indian people from ancient times and during the course of their history they have come to acquire rich connotation and various shades of meanings. This has made the four-fold concept practical and comprehensive. It is, therefore, proper to name them as such or designate the value-realm by the aspect of human personality to which they pertain.

THE POLITICO-ECONOMIC VALUES

Artha is one name for biological and economic values. It denotes object, aim, money, power, success, etc. The object of desire is one meaning which can be said to exhaust the entire connotation of the word, "artha". Indian thinkers have authoritatively delimited the scope of this concept to what may be called the value of the maintenance of life in this world, which can be truly characterized as biological and economic values having their own situations, contents and criteria.

Artha refers to the survival and maintenance of human life. It arises out of man's will to live. Based upon the economic and social necessities of human existence, it points to the imperative importance of the satisfaction of those necessities. Maintenance of life means continuation of the psycho-physical existence in good health and efficiency. That which promotes life as such or is conducive to its maintenance is artha. If the will-to-live as the subjective condition is the source of value, the struggle for existence bocomes the law of human life. This law depends upon the level of existence, for a purely biological struggle is not a true expression of human beings for whom the struggle goes up into a wider situation in which biological, economic, social, political and moral factors are also involved.

This struggle for survival throws man into the vortex of an intense activity. If he wins, he survives, if he loses, he goes down into non-existence or is extinct. The will-to-live, activity, effort, volition, desire for mastery and success, self-assertiveness, self-confidence are some of the subjective conditions of this value while survival, life, self-maintenance, health, success, power, prosperity and mastery are the criteria of the valuational achievements on account of artha.

A keen desire to live becomes a nucleus which expands and becomes the generating centre of many other values so that life itself becomes a system of values such as wealth, social stability, political power, etc. Money is a powerful factor in the satisfaction of the economic necessities of life. Proper development and exploitation of natural resources, an organised system of management and a proper distribution of commodities or wealth so as to maximize economic prosperity and satisfaction is, therefore, an ideal. This points to another situation which calls forth a social organization and a moral regulation of human conditions. Men must be ordered in a society if social life is to be made useful and happy. The varṇāśrama scheme is ideal if based on inner merit, occupation, economic and functional factors, but it is too simple to be of much use to a modern urbanized society in which social grouping is based either on socio-economic factors or on industrial and commercial needs.

A social organisation cannot maintain itself without proper governmental control which is the authority for all sorts of socio-political sanctions. The state is the custodian of the social values of stability, law and order, social welfare, etc., to which all political agents or organs must be responsible. A monarch, parliament or a dictator holds power in so far as he or it guarantees social stability and political welfare.

Artha is instrumental in the satisfaction of a large number of desires including the economic, physical and social, and hence it is the source of pleasure (kāma). Both artha and kāma are grouped together for a path of pravṛtti. Artha refers to life-value and kāma as the value of emotional and artistic pleasure adds a new dimension to life. It is for an enriched life that man wants to survive. Similarly situations pertaining to artha demand a principle of self-regulation which is truly moral in nature.

Providing a moral basis to the struggle for existence which is so characteristic of the individual human being at the biological level are purely moral principles based on dharma without which life, wealth, power and existence may create chaotic conditions giving birth to disvalues. Artha, therefore, is related to kāma and dharma.

Psychological and Hedonistic Values

Kāma which originally meant sex-enjoyment, has been used to signify desire in its entirety. Desire is the affective-conative state in which one consciously seeks to satisfy some organic needs, wants, instincts, motives or to achieve some goal. Desires may take their birth from learnt or unlearnt dispositions, instincts or sentiments, and every fulfilment of a desire is marked by a pleasant feeling. Desire may be regarded as the motive-force leading to physical activity and resulting in psychological satisfaction; but the contents of kāma are further specified as sensuous, sexual, amorous, artistic and aesthetic. Sensuous pleasure results from the contact of senses with agreeable objects as determined by natural and cultivated tastes. Sex has a biological function but sexual activities have been found to be highly pleasure-giving. Sex-sublimation and refinement open up into its higher manifestation like friendship, fellowship, comradeship, tenderness, sympathy, affection, love and philanthropy which have very little in common with sex. Pleasure (kāma) also includes enjoyment of aesthetic and artistic expressions of beauty in literature, drama, poetry, music, painting, sculpture and other fine arts. Kāma in its highest refinement is ecstacy (rasa) which is akin to bliss (spiritual joy).

Kāma, therefore, inevitably refers to pleasure which is a state of mind, hedonistic in tone, resulting from the successful execution of desire. It is in this respect, an abstract quality of our experience characterizing all those mental states which can be called pleasant, happy, joyful, delightful and blissful. But any argument making this abstract quality of experience an intrinsic and absolute value, as hedonistic do, is bound to fall, because pleasure may be an index of value-achievement but not value itself. It is perhaps not even a sure index of value-achievement, because in a particular case, value may decrease and pleasure may increase. Hence, a concrete content of pleasure is essential for a hedonistic argument as the Cārvākas and other kāmaśāstrins do provide. Any attempt to grade pleasures on qualitative basis shall prove disastrous for a hedonistic thesis, because it is not pleasure, but its content that can be graded. Kāma will have to absorb more of culture and artistic refinement in order to show more of value-ascent. Hence, all psychological values admit a principle of regulation on an aesthetic basis. Kāma will have to work between two poles, viz., self-indulgence and self-regulation. It will have to ward off the deprivation of desires which can lead to fear, anxiety, boredom, frustration, a sense of shame, guilt psychosis and mental regression as evils or disvalues on the one hand and uncontrolled gratification and sensualism on the other. This points to the necessity of a principle of moral regulation of kāma which may be based on rational, natural, aesthetic and spiritual grounds. This increasing regulation of kāma by dharma is in the true interest of kāma itself in order to achieve an axiological ascent which comes to life and existence (artha) as its qualitative cultivation and culture. Kāma forms an essential ingredient of the wholesome life.

THE MORAL VALUES

The literal meaning of "dharma" (dhāryate iti dharmaḥ that which integrates, holds, or maintains is "dharma") is quite central to the concept of dharma, because it brings out clearly its intrinsic character as a principle or law which may have both ontological as well as axiological status. The Indian tradition is not in favour of maintaining an ultimate distinction between being and value. The concept of ṛta also indicates a fusion of existence and value; the cosmic principle of the universe is the same as the moral law which regulates man's life. Macrocosmos is governed by the same laws as the microcosmos. The Buddhist definition of dharma as the elements of existence and the universal law of karma (causation) are descriptions of the self-same dharma. The principle of value as "ideal-ought-to-be" is inherent in the very constitution of the universe, and exerts a normative influence which has a moral basis on the course of things.

However, the ontological significance of dharma does not eclipse its axiological character. Dharma means moral value par excellence. The word "law" connects the two concepts. The law operates in two more spheres—society and the life of man. It becomes the principle of social order and organization, without which society disintegrates and withers away. It is the expression of social and legalistic norms, and the eternal relation between rights and duties which is the basis of social contract and cohesion. It also refers to religious and spiritual culture. The moral nature of dharma is believed to comprehend the entire gamut of human life including its social, moral and spiritual aspects, for a distinction between value and moral value is as hard to maintain as between dharma and value, for it exhausts the full content of moral life and it is implied in the basic notion of "good", "right" and "duty". It is both a moral universal as well as a moral particular, the norm, the judgment and the action, duty, virtue and end. The dimensions of dharma range from the lower rungs of the value-ladder of artha and kāma to the middle level of social norms and moral values to the uppermost level of life in a spiritual and religious culture. Dharma, therefore, occupies a pivotal position in any scale of value.

A great divergence and variety of views exists in Indian culture about the nature of dharma. It is both existence and value, being and ideal, empirical and transcendental, instrumental and absolute, personal and impersonal, teleological and deontological, subjective and objective, naturalistic and supernaturalistic. But once we accept dharma to be identical with moral values, whatever the nature and character of moral values is also true of dharma. If a valuational approach to such problems is adopted, one is always constrained to prefer the objective over the subjective, the absolute over the instrumental, the transcendental over the empirical, the deontological over the teleological; but this pragmatic approach will itself depend upon the above grounds of justification. The differences in views about the actual content of moral values are usually justified on the ground of changing times, conditions and circumstances; for the notions of duty, virtue and norms will have to be dynamic in order to be really effective and normative, otherwise they fail to be moral. The sets of moral duties and virtues, obtainable from different cultural traditions have been different, but the law of moral regulation of both inner and outer life, society and social organization has always been the same. Hence, various characterizations of dharma serve only to illustrate its outer limits and enrich its contents.

Spiritual Values

The concept of mokṣa implies a metaphysical belief in two levels of being, viz., empirical and transcendental. A transition from the empirical existence to the transcendental one is called mokṣa. Existence in the form of a psychological organism is characterized as empirical. Suffering is the essence of empirical life; to be (in the empirical sense) means to be miserable. The only sure way out of suffering is to be released from empirical existence once for all. But death which is a temporary release from life, is no solution, for life persists through the rigours of death and the force of cumulative dispositions; it leads to a new life with a renewed tendency to suffer. Man is taken round in a cycle of empirical existence (bhavacakra) and is condemned to suffer eternally unless this vicious circle is broken. But breaking the circle is a formidable task so that the way to a transcendental existence is not easy. Indian thinkers have been keen on finding out ways and means of breaking through the bonds of empirical existence and they have thought radically about it.

The gist of the main currents of thought, regarding mokṣa or nirvāṇa in almost all schools of Indian philosophy particularly in the orthodox systems and in the heterodox Buddhism, could be stated as follows: Most of the schools do not question the need for liberation, the differences in opinion are only regarding the nature of the ultimate state.

A release from empirical life is possible only by suppressing its cause, which is ignorance (avidyā) or wrong knowledge (mithya jñāna), non-discriminative knowledge (aviveka) or wrong belief, or illusion (bhrama). This nescience determines empirical existence through the ontological forces of the ego (ahaṅkāra), intellect (buddhi), consciousness (cit) and mind (manas) and the transmigratory cycle revolves according to its own law of causation. The relation between ignorance and the principle of life (life-force in the form of kleśa), kārmic energy or cosmic will (ahaṁkāra) is teleological. If ignorance is the cause of bondage and suffering, true knowledge must lead to an emancipation from it (mokṣa). Many means, viz., knowledge (jñāna), devotion (bhakti), action (karma), renunciation (saṁnyāsa), mental concentration (yoga) and austerity (tapas) have been recommended for the achievement of true knowledge. True knowledge is not theoretical or intellectual understanding, but true realization (darśana). A life of both mental and moral discipline is a preparation for it. How can true knowledge help to attain mokṣa?

True knowledge or realization ushers in transcendental being by destroying the very seeds of ignorance and life élan and thus negating the cause of empirical existence. Knowledge determines being, it becomes being. To know means to be, for knowledge is being, it is the essence of the ultimate reality. One who knows Brahman, becomes Brahman, because knowledge is the essence of Brahman. Unity or oneness with the true being is already an accomplished fact.

Mokṣa is a negative concept in so far as it means negation of the conditions of psycho-physical existence or empirical life, unless a systematic account of the positive content of transcendental existence is given. The central meaning of mokṣa is freedom[1] which is itself negative. Redemption from empirical life must be considered a value, because life means suffering, and a relief from suffering must be a value. But this negative character of mokṣa can be changed by positing a definite content of transcendental existence. This is sometimes believed to be doubtful, for there is an epistemological difficulty in knowing that which transcends this process of knowledge (transcendental reality). One thing is logically certain, however, that mokṣa, which is a release from psycho-physical organism, must be a state of life of the spiritual in man in contradistinction to this material state. That must be acknowledged as the character of mokṣa.

Further, mokṣa is spiritual freedom which is the essence of transcendental existence. The term "spiritual freedom" remains hollow unless a positive content is provided or a definite view about the spirit is held. Two groups of philosophies are available regarding spiritual life, viz., theories of the negation of the self and theories of the self. According to the former, the self is false and empirical, and on achieving nirvāṇa, it is totally destroyed and a void substitutes it, leading to pure annihilation or extinction. This negative view has been found to imply a positive basis of nirvāṇa. According to the latter, self in its truest and absolute essence must be one, a multiplicity of selves must be a falsification of reality, one undifferentiated spiritual essence is the sole logical outcome of the spiritualistic account of reality. Hence, mokṣa according to the latter view means realization of an essential identity with transcendental reality. But this realization of the Absolute (Brahman) seems to be unreal, for it implies change and change is empirical and cannot touch the Absolute, in so far as total existence is unchangeable. The release through mokṣa, however, does not imply change, for it is never achieved. The soul is ever free, it is existence (sat), consciousness (cit) and bliss (ānanda), and bondage or release are merely denying or affirming the reality as such and are, therefore, not true absolutely. Mokṣa means the affirmation of absolute values which are identical with reality and existence. It has been found that all the negativistic and nihilistic accounts of mokṣa (Nyāya-vaiśeṣika and Vaibhāṣika) are based upon epistemological difficulties of describing the transcendental but do inherently imply a positive reality, without which the explanation is not tenable. Hence, the vedāntic point of view is the only logical outcome of the Indian argument for release (mokṣa) as the highest goal of life, which is realization of the soul's own essence of existence, consciousness and bliss. But there are two different sorts of characterizations of the absolute reality. Rāmānuja, for example, finds Śaṅkara's Absolute (Brahman) desolate and dreary, unfit to be an ideal of religious life. If such a pragmatic ground of criticism can be allowed, then the Absolute can be pressed through a humanistic framework in order to make it a fit ideal of life.[2] It is, therefore, possible to conceive of the highest state of man as not necessarily opposed to psycho-physical existence, but as realization or change in outlook which can be achieved in this very life (Śaṅkara's concept of jīvanmukti and Buddhistic Bodhisattva).

Spiritual achievement consists of internal transformation and a change of heart; it may mean union with absolute reality, provided it is itself full of values. The last argument can be valid only on the ground of the complete identity of reality and value, and value and existence.

Existence, Reality and Value

We have seen that a positive account of liberation as the highest aim of life (mokṣa) has been possible on the ground of the vedāntic concept of absolute reality (Brahmavāda). Brahmavādins start from the subject (self) in their attempt to know the nature of absolute reality. The self according to the Vedānta passes through four stages, viz., the bodily self (visva), the vital self (taijasa), the intellectual self (prajñā) and the intuitive self (*turīya*). Broadly speaking, however, different schools of Indian philosophy trace the development of the self through three stages, viz., (i) the psychological self as the observer of objects, (ii) the epistemological self which postulates the categories of subject and object and (iii) the transcendental self which is presupposed in all knowledge. This transcendental self is self-existing, self-revealing, infinite, supra-relational, non-objective and immediate knowledge. It is knowledge, it is existence, for existence is knowledge and knowledge is existence. The reality of self is indefinable and yet undeniable. The transcendental reality is of the essence of consciousness and it steers clear of both substantialism and the view of universal becoming. This account implies two levels of existence, viz., empirical and transcendental. Any value connected with the former is bound to be lower in face of the value belonging to the latter.

The relation between self and self as a principle of individuality has necessitated another concept of the Absolute (Brahman). The Absolute is the universal and absolute reality, the totality of whatever is, the all-pervasive and all-comprehensive existence, and compared to it self (ātman) may be equally transcendental. This raises the problem of relation between self (jīva) and Absolule (Brahman) or as to how identity and difference, universal and particular be conceived. Śaṅkara holds that the absolute is the expression of absolute unity or identity which cannot be differentiated or qualified, and the transcendental nature of the self (ātman) which is also supra-relational and universal, is the same as the Absolute. Hence the self and the Absolute are identical. Rāmānuja sticks to the concept of identity-in-difference; the expression of the whole is universal consisting of particulars as parts. The self (jīva) is a part of the Absolute, which is a unity that preserves the distinctive character of selves. We have found that this position can be logically derived from Śaṅkara's Absolute.

We have also found that Advaitins maintain that the Absolute is in essence both existence and consciousness. It is also the highest reality and totality of all Being. Following the idealistic argument, we conclude that the highest reality must constitute the highest value at the same time. Śaṅkara considers that the valuational approach to reality is relational and therefore, the Absolute reality (Brahman) will have to be supra-valuational. But if existence, consciousness and bliss, which constitute the very essence of the reality, are themselves values, then Śaṅkara's Brahman is both absolute reality and absolute value It has been clearly shown that Śaṅkara's basic stand compels him to accept an identity of axiological and ontological principles. He, therefore, maintains an absolute identity of existence, reality and value; the three are expressions of the self-same essence. This aspect of the unity of existence and value is truly to be called the basis of the indescribability. We have also seen that this tendency to fuse reality and value is present in other schools of thought.

Rāmānuja finds the valuational approach to Absolute reality as the only valid epistemology. He thereby comes to conceive of the Absolute as an embodiment of all values such as truth, beauty, goodness and holiness. Rāmānuja's determinate Brahman is rich in values, it is the fit object of religious devotion and moral and spiritual realization. The Absolute, according to him, is the absolute reality and as such is absolute value which can be differentiated as truth, beauty, goodness and holiness.

Brahmavāda, therefore, faces two alternatives. First, that reality or existence is the only absolute value, whereas definite values such as truth, beauty, goodness and holiness may be absolute in so far they are values, but are descriptions which fall short of the absolute reality. This is the position of Śaṅkara.

Second, that absolute reality embodies absolute values such as truth, beauty, etc., so that the former does not transcend the valuational categories. This is Rāmānuja's line of thinking. There seems to be a fundamental differences in their standpoints which is due to a difference of approach. Rāmānuja's Absolute (Brahman) inspires both religion and philosophy and can serve as the basis of a sound philosophy of value. But logically and metaphysically, the position of Śaṅkara can be regarded as the only sound and perfect explanation of reality on idealistic grounds. The considerations of religion, philosophy, art, etc., being limited will have to be subordinated to the supreme consideration of reality or value. The Absolute of Rāmānuja emerges as absolute unity and identity of reality, existence and value. Hence, Śaṅkara's argument of Absolute reality as absolute value is presupposed here and is final in respect of the Indian concept of metaphysical values.

Absolute Values and the Metaphysical Absolute

The fundamental difference in the approaches of Śaṅkara and Rāmānuja has led to another distinction between the metaphysical Absolute and absolute values like truth, beauty, goodness and holiness. The Absolute as existence, consciousness and bliss is metaphysically the highest and is, therefore, the ultimate metaphysical value. But there are other ultimate values in the fields of normative sciences like logic, aesthetics, ethics and religion. They are ideal norms projected in the value-consciousness such as truth (satyam) in logic, beauty (sundram) in aesthetics, goodness (śivam) in ethics, and holiness in religion. From the value point of view these four values are absolute and ultimate and as such cannot be subordinated to any other values. We can at the most add another absolute value, viz., the metaphysical absolute which seems to be at par with other absolute values ultimately. In such a situation there will be perfect pluralism reigning supreme in the domain of values without any principle of unity.

But every cultural pattern and value-philosophy considers pluralism to be anarchic and chaotic and tries to bring order in the confusion of values. Plato tried it by subordinating ultimate values under the "Idea of the good". Indian philosophy also works towards some sort of monism in absolute values. The concept of the trinity of value (truth, beauty and goodness) is undoubtedly held to be supreme, but human spirit cannot rest contented with it. The discernible absolute values cannot exhaust the possible infinite perfections. The Absolute (Brahman) in essence surpasses all absolute values conceivable by human beings. Metaphysical reality as the metaphysical ideal which constitutes all metaphysical possibilities is, therefore, higher than absolute values such as truth, beauty, goodness and holiness. The Absolute is the ground (ādhāra) of all discernible absolute values. This conclusion is in consonance with Śaṅkara's argument. (Bradley's Absolute also surpasses the highest in normative sciences and religion.)

On the other hand, Rāmānuja likes to put all absolute values at par with the metaphysical ideal. He thinks that the same absolute which is the logical highest as truth, becomes the supreme good, the *summum bonum* on account of its moral excellence and becomes the righteous ruler of the world (niyantṛ) on account of its religious eminence and absolute holiness, while aesthetic consciousness conceives it as the ground of surpassing beauty which resides in the very heart of being and the same Absolute becomes bliss. But Rāmānuja also brings in the unity in these values in as much as he thinks of his Absolute as the harmony of the trinity on the basis of the relation between body and soul (śarīra-śrīrin). The whole must be more than the parts. Indirectly, he accepts that the absolute (the metaphysical ultimate) is higher than the highest values obtainable in the fields of logic, aesthetics, ethics and religion. Brahman as sat, cit, and ānanda is the supreme value. This is the truth which represents the philosophical and spiritual tradition of India.

Hierarchical System of Values

The Indian genius is fascinated with the idea of values forming a sort of harmony (anubandha). During the course of our study, we have found that values of life (puruṣārthas) possess all the characteristics of being welded into a system in which values are interrelated in a hierarchical order. Artha and kāma being biological and psychological values are regarded as lower and dharma and mokṣa being moral and spiritual are rated as higher. The lower values have ontological superiority over the higher values and as such artha-values like money, power and life condition the content of all value-realization, but they lack axiological height without qualitative experience and satisfaction (kāma). Psychological richness and depth of satisfaction are intrinsic, but become undesirable without a moral regulation (dharma). The greater the moral accommodation in kāma, the higher and nobler its manifestations. The *Bhagavad-Gītā* identifies holiness with kāma which is not at strife with dharma. Hence, supremacy of dharma over artha and kāma is thorough though ontologically, economic and psychic values are grounds of moral and spiritual realization.

Sometimes a very pertinent question is asked: 'Is dharma a means or an end?' The Indian attitude is divided on the issue. It is sometimes regarded as a means to the this-wordly welfare and heavenly happiness (abhyudaya niṣveyas). In this context, the *Mahābhārata* clearly enjoins that people want the fruits of dharma but not dharma itself; 'I am crying out with uplifted arms that dharma brings with it both artha and kāma but nobody listens to me.'[4] On the other hand, a life of duty and moral excellence (dharma) has also been regarded as an end in itself. This confusion is due to our tendency to separate end from means. The distinction between them is hard to make. Moreover, values refuse to be graded as merely instrumental, for in that case they are not values at all. All values are absolute. Ends and means form a whole which is absolute. Every action implies some end. Śaṅkara is of the view that no voluntary activity can be carried out without an end in view. Maṇḍaṇa observes, 'Nothing prompts a man to acts of will but what is a means to some desired end.'[5] Thus, dharma is made to subserve mokṣa or Brahman. But at the same time Śaṅkara holds that the final goal lies in the perfection of means to the end.[6] The end is not external to the means, it is means stabilized. The highest life is moral perfection. Mokṣa or Brahman is the highest spiritual state and it is, therefore, axiologically the highest of all values, including the moral, biological and psychological which become its ontological basis.

The concept of four values is the expression of a perfect system of a hierarchical order in which values are graded and ranked according to their ontological and axiological status. The lower is lower axiologically, it is autonomous ontologically and the higher is higher axiologically but it depends on the lower ontologically. The axiological principle of "height" and the ontological principle of "strength" are inversely proportionate. The hierarchical system of values (sopānakrama) faithfully represents the Indian concept of values.

The Principle of Gradation of Values

The idea of the system is a prerequisite of values. Values must form a system. Pluralism is chaotic. Indian culture, like any other historical morality, has systematically worked towards a monism of values which is important on two grounds, viz., the theoretical and the practical. It has been found that values are pointers to reality which is an expression of unity. Knowledge and truth consist in unification, classification and integration. The Absolute (Brahman) is the highest principle of this theoretical unity of values. This theoretical unification is a value-principle which is supreme enough to arbiter the claims of values. On the practical level, values are ideals which affect and influence the conative life of human beings. They are the aims of life, principles of the development and improvement of society and culture. If they are not unified, a conflict of aims, indecision about the value of actions and dissipation in cross purposes result in hesitancy and inaction. The values, therefore, must form a *gestalt*, an organic unity which reconciles and integrates them in a system. But they cannot be coerced into a system unless they themselves admit it. A principle of unity cannot be imposed on values. Any superficial unity will juxtapose values into a loose heap and fail to redefine and transform them into a coordinated system. Hence, values on account of their own nature and interest admit of the principle of unity which cannot rule out or transgress their intrinsic absoluteness and autonomy.

Such a system possessing organic unity has been suggested by Rāmānuja. It is the expression of a whole in which the parts preserve their distinctness like the organs of the body; parts are modes of the whole. But this is only an illustration of a unified system without any principle of unity. Why should diversity be unified into a whole? Organic unity possesses only teleological unity; but perhaps Rāmānuja does not intend to make participation in the purpose of the whole the principle of unity. The whole is higher or superior to its parts; similarly this whole will become a part of a bigger whole and so on till we arrive at the Absolute (Brahman) which is the final whole and is not a part of another whole; comprehensiveness and subsumption is the principle of gradation. We have found that subsumption makes values derivative at the cost of their autonomy. But in keeping with the above, we find an ascending scale of entities in objects (viṣaya), sense-organ (indriya), mind (manas), intellect (buddhi), ego (ahaṁkāra), cosmic will (mahat) and the spiritual self (ātman or Brahman); every entity is considered to be beyond its predecessor. Values connected with them can also be graded accordingly. Hence, the spiritual will be higher than the moral, and the moral higher than the mental and the mental higher than the physical. But the question is why? What is the basis of gradation?

Śaṅkara's principle of sublation of one entity into another or one experience into another makes it higher or more real than that which is sublated. One may object to this principle being adopted as a principle of gradation of values on two grounds. First, it is a metaphysical principle which may not hold good in the domain of values. But we have seen that value and reality cannot be ultimately separated. Different levels of reality constitute the levels of value. Second, the principle of sublation entails the destruction of the lower into the higher so that in face of the highest, nothing lower exists. In such a situation, values cannot retain their autonomy, leave alone forming a system. This misgiving is also, however, baseless because we have seen that the process of sublation implies no destruction of the lower into the higher but a transmutation of its essence in which it gains a new axiological height without losing its ontological core. Dream, for example, is sublated into the waking experience, but the fact of its existence cannot be altered. Hence, the principle of sublation implies two conditions, (i) existential and (ii) axiological which correspond to Hartmann's double norm of "strength" and "height" of values.

We see that Indian culture invariably moves from the gross to the subtle, from the external to the internal and from the material to the spiritual. The eternal, universal, absolute, transcendental and pure is preferred to the perishable, the particular, the instrumental, the empirical and the mixed.[7] If we persist in questioning the ground for such preferences, we are referred to some metaphysical principle like subsumption or sublation. On the axiological level it is the depth and richness of satisfaction which is the ultimate basis of preference of values. Spiritual values are higher than the physical on account of their wealth of experience. But such a gradation must be left to each particular cultural pattern. Freedom to be aware of values and to choose and prefer some of them must be acknowledged, because freedom itself is a supreme value.

Notes

CHAPTER TWO (PP. 8-13)

1. This conception of intrinsic value has been subjected to further analysis by G.E. Moore in *Principia Ethica*, Oxford University Press, London, 1952, pp. 27, 36.
2. *The Mimāṁsā-Sūtra*, I.1. 1-4 'Artham Sukhādhikadukhā—jankatvam '*Subodhini*', quoted by S.K. Maitra in *The Ethics of the Hindus*, University of Calcutta, 1956, pp. 81-2.
3. *General Theory of Value*, Longman Green & Co., New York, 1926, p. 27 ff.
4. *Ibid.*, p. 124.
5. Dr. R.P. Singh regards such definitions as relational and, therefore, circular in as much as they presuppose value. Cf. *The Vedānta of Śaṅkara: A Metaphysics of Value*, Bharat Publishing House, Jaipur, 1949, pp. 21-2.
6. *Principia Ethica*, Oxford University Press, London, 1952, pp. 9-10.
7. *Ibid.*, p. 21.
8. *Ethics*, p. 111.
9. Cf. R.P. Singh: *The Vedānta of Śaṅkara—A Metaphysics of Value*, Vol. 1, Bharat Publishing House, Jaipur, 1949, p. 22.
10. *Ethics* Vol. 1, translated by Stanton Coit, Muirhead Library of Philosophy, George Allen and Unwin Ltd., London, 1951, pp. 184-5.
11. *Ibid.*, p. 185.
12. *Ethics, op. cit.*, Vol. 1, p. 189.
13. *Ibid.*, p. 218.
14. *Ibid.*, p. 221.
15. *Ibid.*, p. 226.
16. *Ibid.*, p. 233.
17. *Ibid.*, p. 235.
18. See *New Ways of Ontology*, translated by Reinhard C. Kuha, Bonn, 1953, Chs. V—XI.
19. "Condanālikṣanaḥ arthaḥ dharmaḥ", Jaimini, 1-1-2. See also *The Ethics of the Hindus*, by S.K. Maitra for analysis of the verity of the moral law (Apūrva). University of Calcutta, 1956, pp. 91-3.

Chapter Two (Pp. 14-22)

20. The Mīmāṁsakas contend that value is dependent on human effort and volition (puruṣavyāpāratantram).
21. 'Ātmanātravṛttiviśeṣagunāḥ'.
22. *Sāṅkhya-Kārīkāḥ*, Īśvara Kṛṣṇa, 43.
23. *The Metaphysics of Value*, pp. 50-51.
24. *Ethics*, Vol. 1, p. 209.
25. *Ibid.*, pp. 213-14.
26. *Ibid.*, pp. 215-16.
27. See John Dewey: *Experience and Nature*, Dover, New York, 1958, p. 21.
28. Hans Reichenbach's article in *The Philosophy of John Dewey*, ed. by Paul A. Schilpp, Evanston, Northwestern University Press, Illinois, 1939, pp. 177-80.
29. *Quest for Certainty*, Houton, Balch and Co., New York, 1929, p. 107.
30. *Principia Ethica*, Oxford University Press, London, 1952, pp. 183-4, also see pp. 27-33.
31. *Ibid.*, p. 8.
32. *Ibid.*, pp. 9-10.
33. *Ibid.*, p. 21 and pp. 27-36.
34. *Ibid.*, p. 30.
35. *Ibid.*, pp. 27-9.
36. *Ibid.*, p. 189.
37. *Mind and its Place in Nature*, p. 488.
38. Sattaiva bodho bodho eva ca satta. SB., 111.2.21. See also R.P. Singh: *The Vedānta of Śaṅkara*: *A Metaphysics of Value*, Vol. 1, pp. 48-50. Bharat Publishing House, Jaipur, 1949. He interprets Śaṅkara's view as existence grounded in value, (*Ibid.*, Ch. IX).
39. His article on 'value' in *Encyclopaedia Brittannica* (14 ed.).
40. *Ibid.*, p. 152. Please also see F.J. Von Rintelen: *Contemporary German Philosophy*, p. 22.
41. *Idealistic Thought of India*, George Allen & Unwin, London, 1953, p. 78.
42. *Ibid.*, p. 90.
43. *Ethics*, Vol. I, Tr. Stanton Coit, George Allen & Unwin, London, 1951, p. 233.
44. Saccidānandam anantanityam ekam yat tadbrahmetya vidhārayet—*Ātmabodhaḥ*-56.
45. R.P. Singh has systematically argued that Śaṅkara's idealism is essentially a metaphysics of value, 'Value and reality being identical in his system'. He observes, 'Śaṅkara's philosophy is based on the idea of value—that it is out and out a value—Philosophy and that his notion of reality itself is that of value.' *The Vedānta of Śaṅkara*, Bharat Publishing House, Jaipur, 1949. p. 12. He writes elsewhere, 'But the truth of Brahman is constituted by its essence which consists in the oneness of the values of Sat, Cit and Ānanda.'

Chapter Two (Pp. 22-30)

46. Rāmānuja's Brahman is not 'Jñānasvarūpa', but 'jñānaguṇāśraya' the substance which supports the attribute of knowledge.
47. *Ethics*, Vol. 1, Tr. Stanton Coit, George Allen & Unwin, London, 1951, p. 258.
48. *Ibid.*, p. 261.
49. *Ibid.*, p. 235.
50. *Ibid.*, p. 248.
51. *Ibid.*, p. 250.
52. *Ibid.*, p. 253.
53. *Ibid.*, p. 254.
54. *Ibid.*, p. 260.
55. *Ibid.*, p. 260.
56. Śaṅkara uses the word 'svārtha' for 'existence-for-itself'. It is self-established (Svataḥsiddha). SB., 11.3.7.
57. G.E. Moore's main contention in *Principia Ethica* rules out the simplicity of intrinsic values. When Sidgwick says that pleasure is an absolute value and simple at the same time, he fails to understand the complex character of pleasure.
58. *Ethics*, Vol. II, Tr. Stanton Coit, George Allen & Unwin, London, 1951, p. 52.
59. *Ibid.*, pp. 52-3.
60. *The Theory of Good and Evil*, Vol. I, Oxford University Press, London, 1948, p. 93.
61. *Ibid.*, p. 220.
62. *Fundamentals of Ethics*, Henry Holt Company, New York, 1949, p. 170.
63. *Ethics*, Vol. II, Stanton Coit, George Allen & Unwin, London, 1951, pp. 56-7.
64. *Ibid.*, pp. 71-2.
65. See SB., 1.1.4.
66. A similar classification has been attempted by Ennismore in his *Values of Life*. He discovers five ultimate values, viz, scientific (truth), aesthetic (appreciation of beauty), practical (pleasure and happiness), moral (goodness) and religious (love of God). He has definitely missed the biological and economic values in his scheme.
67. Consult his article in *Darshan International*, Vol. V, No. 3, and also his widely circulated article *Organicism*.
68. Eng. Translation *Forms of Life*, (Bonn, 1928).
69. *Principia Ethica*, Oxford University Press, London, 1952. p. 188.

Chapter Three (P. 31)

1. Schweitzer resents this approach of blending theory and practice in his *Indian Thought and its Development*. G.R. Malkani also puts the same question in his article, 'Two Different Traditions of Pure Philo-

Chapter Three (Pp. 31-35)

sophy' in *Philosophical Quarterly* (January 1955) and is contented with the two different methods—the theoretical and the practical in pure philosophy. Another Indian writer, Inder Sen, justifies the Indian approach when he writes, 'Philosophy has given mental clarity and conviction to the religious aspirations and practice. Religion and Yoga have given vigour and life to philosophy. 'The New Lead to Philosophy' in *Philosophical Quarterly*, (July 1954).

2. Radhakrishnan writes in a vigorous defence of Indian approach Indian philosophy has its interests in the haunts of men and not in superlunar solitudes. It takes its origin in life and enters back into life after passing through schools. To those who realize the true kinship between life and theory, philosophy becomes a way of life.' *Indian Philosophy*. Vol. I, George Allen & Unwin, London, 1948, pp. 25-6.
3. Naciketas is a small boy (a character in the *Kaṭhopaniṣad*) who prefers an answer to his question about the ultimate nature of Self to the attainment of the wordly things.
4. 'Yena. . . Avijñātam vijñātam bhavati' (*Chhāndogya Up*., 9.1.4). Also 'Kesminnu bhagava Vijñāte sarvamidam vijñātam bhavati', *Muṇḍaka Up*., 1.1.3.
5. 'Yajjñātvā neha bhuyo nyajjñātavyamavaśiṣyate', BG., 7.2.
6. For instance, Śaṅkara in his commentary on BS., 1.1.1. makes practical discipline as an essential precondition of the desire to know reality.
7. It is for the sake of an intensive study of the concept of Brahman that it is accorded a separate treatment from mokṣa; otherwise both of them mean the same for Śaṅkara. For other schools of Indian Philosophy, mokṣa does not necessarily include the quest after Brahman, the absolute reality.
8. 'Brahmāvagatirhi puruṣārthaḥ', SB. 1.1.1.
9. 'Athato Brahmajijñāsā', Brahmasūtra, 1.1.1. Also, 'Atatadbrahma yasyeyam jijñāsā prastutā', SB., 1.1.4.
10. 'Brahmatmaikyāvagatistvapratijñāteti tadartho yuktaḥ śāstrarambhaḥ., SB., 1.1.1.
11. Śānkhya Kārīka, 1. 'dukḥatrayā' bhijijñāsā tadabhighātake heta'.
12. 'Asmindharmo' khilenokto. . .', MS., 1.107.
13. 'Pṛthvyā lābhe palane ca . . . idamarthaśāstrin'. AS., 15.1.
14. 'Brahma veda. . .Brahmaiva bhavati'. F.H. Bradley also subscribes to this when he says, 'Fully to realise the existence of the absolute is for finite beings impossible. In order thus to know, we should have to be and then we should not exist, *Appearance and Reality*, Clarendon Press, Oxford, 1931, p. 159.
15. R.P. Singh observes, 'According to Rāmānuja, the unity of attributes is not an absolute unity, but of inherence, Brahman is the substance in which the qualities of sat, cit and ānanda inhere. *The Vedānta of Śaṅkara, A Metaphysics of Value*, Bharat Publishing House, Jaipur, 1949, p. 82.

Chapter Three (Pp. 35-46)

16. R.P. Singh thinks that sat, cit and ānanda are themselves absolute values and the Absolute is the embodiment of them. The essence of the Absolute is the definition of absolute value. *Ibid.*, pp. 85-6.
17. The four noble truths (catvāri āryasatyam).
18. 'Svayamsiddhatvāt. . . agantukam hi vastu nirākriyate na svarūpam', SB., 11.3.7.
19. *Tatvarthādhigama-Sūtra*, Ch. X.2.
20. Īśvarakṛṣṇa, *Śāṅkhya-Kārīkā*, 1 and 68.
21. 'Caitanyameva tu nirantaramasya svarūpam', SB., 111.2.16.
22. 'Brahmabhāvasca mokṣaḥ'; SB., 1.1.4.
23. 'Brahmātmaikyāvagatiḥ', SB., 1.1.1. Also 'vidyādaikyaṃ mahāvākyair-jīvātinaparamātmanoḥ', *Ātmabhodhaḥ*, 30.
24. MS. 1.117 and 118.
25. 'Caturṇāmapi varnānamacāraścaiva śāśvataḥ', MS., 1.107.
26. '. . . dharmasamūḍhacetaḥ. . . yachhśreyaḥ syāṁniscitaṃ brūhi tanme . . .', BG., II.7.
27. 'Taro me śriyam āvaha'. Also cf. *Ṛg. Veda*, Hymns to Indra, Agni and Uṣas.
28. Cf. S.K. Maitra: *The Ethics of the Hindus*, Calcutta University, Calcutta 1956, pp. 81-2.
29. 'Arthamsukhādhikaduḥkhājanakatvaṃ'.
30. 'Codanālakṣanā' rthaḥ dharmaḥ', Jaimini, 1.1.2.
31. 'Dharmārthavivodhen kāmaṃ seveta. Na nihsukhaḥ syat', AS., III.6.3.
32. 'Sam vā trivargamanyonyanubandham. Eko hyālyasevito dharmārtha-kāmānāmatmanamitarau ca pīdyati', AS., III.6.3
33. 'Marvādām sthāyetācāryanamātyau vā', AS., III.6.5.
34. 'Artha eva pradhāna iti Kautilya: Arthmūlau hi dharmakāmāviti', AS., III 6.5.
35. 'Dharmārthakām-ebhyo nāmaḥ Kāmasūtra'.
36. 'Artho dharmaḥ kāma ityārtha trivargaḥ', KS., G.VI. 6.
37. 'Sukhārthāni dharmārthayoḥ seva'.
38. 'Dharmarthavucyate sveyah kamarthan dharma eva ca, artha eveh vā śreyastrivarga iti tu sthiti', MS., II.224.
39. 'Parityajedartha-kāmau yau syatāṃ dharmavarjitau', MS., IV. 76. Also cf. IV. 3, 5 and 6.
40. *The Mahābhārta Śāntiparva*, 167.6.9.
41. Dharmāvirudhaḥ Kāmosmi, VII.2.
42. Teṣvācaryamā ṇeṣvanyasyāpi nispattiranubandhaḥ', KS., 6.VI.7.
43. *Teachings of Dharmaśāstras*, Motilal Banarsidass, Delhi; 1956, pp. 61-2.

Chapter Four (P. 47)

1. It is better to translate the word "artha" as political economy rather than polity, as its implications comprise both economic and political

Chapter Four (Pp. 47-48)

affairs of man, for otherwise "artha" like "dharma" or "kāma" cannot be translated.

2. The work is dated 321-296 B.C. It is an account of the law and administration of Magdha Empire in India (cf. *Source Book of Indian Philosophy*, Radhakrishanan and Charles A. Moore (ed.), Princeton University Press, Princeton, N.J., 1957, p. 193.
3. 'Sāmargyajurvedastrayiti', AS., I.II.1.
4. 'Atharvavedetihasavedau ca vedaḥ'.
5. 'Ānvīkṣikī trayī Vārtā daṇḍanītiśceti vidyāḥ', AS., I.I.1.
6. 'Ānvīkṣikītrayīvārtānāṃ yogakṣemasādhano daṇḍaḥ', AS., I.III.2.
7. 'Alabdhalābhārthaḥ, lābdhaparirakśani, rakṣitavivardhanī', AS., I.III.2.
8. 'Apranītastu mātsyanyāyamudbhāvayati', AS., I.III.5.
9. 'Pṛthivyāḥ lābhe palane ca yavanlyarthaśāstra. Pūrvācāryai prasthāpitam prayaśāstani samhṛtyai Kamidamarthśāstrani kṛtani'.
10. 'Manuṣyānāṃ vṛttivarthaḥ, manuṣyavati bhūmirtyarthaḥ', AS., 180.1.1.
11. Literally, 'artha' means an object, a thing or a referent or substance. It refers to all objects of senses, desires, volitions, aspirations and actions. It also signifies the object through which pleasure can be achieved. 'Artha connotes attainment of riches, worldly prosperity, advantage, profit, wealth, business-matter, work, price, and in law, plaint, action and petition. With reference to the external world, artha in its widest connotation signifies that which can be perceived, with reference to the interior world of the psyche, end and aim, purpose, object of wish, desire, motive, cause, reason, interest, use, want and concern. . . the term thus bundles together all the meanings of (i) the object of human pursuit, (ii) the means of this persuit and (ii) the needs and desires suggesting this pursuit.' Heinrich Zimmer, *Philosophies of India*, Joseph Campbell, (ed.) Pantheon Books, New York, 1953, pp. 35-6.
12. 'Kṣayasthānāṃ vṛadhirityudayāstsya', AS., 97.II.4.
13. 'Manuṣam nayāpanayau daivamayānāyau', AS., 97.II.5.
14. 'Daivamanusam hi karma lokam yāpayati', AS., 97.II.6.
15. 'Adṛaṣtakāritaṃ daivaṃ. Dṛaṣtakāritaṃ Mānuṣyam', AS., 97.II.6.7.
16. 'Ācintyaṃ daivamiti. . . taccintyam', AS., 97.II.7.
17. The entire discussion in Ch. 7 Books 145 and 146 pertains to the meaning of artha as a positive value ('Arthasyamūlamuthanamanarthasya viprayayaḥ').
18. 'Taśyāḥ pṛthivayā lābhapālanopāyaḥ śāstramarthaśāstramiti', AS., 180.I.1.
19. 'Śaktistrividhā—jñānabalam mantraśaktiḥ, Kosadaṇḍabalam prabhuśaktiḥ, vikrambalamutsāhaśaktiḥ'.
20. 'Arthairarthaḥ prabadhyānte'.

Chapter Four (Pp. 49-52)

21. 'Eṣa Trayīdharṃaśca tūrṇaṃ varnānāmaśramāṇām ca svdharmasthāpanādanpakārikaḥ', AS., 1.II.2.
22. 'Sarveṣāmahiṁsā satyaṃ saucamanasūyaḥ nṛśamsyam kṣamā ca', AS., 1.II.9.
23. *Ibid.*, 1.II.10.
24. *Ibid.*, 1.II.12.
25. 'Tasmātsvadharman bhūtanām rājā na vyabhicāryet', AS., 1.II.11.
26. 'Rājā rājyamiti prakṛtisaṁkṣepaḥ', AS., 128.II.1.
27. 'Svāmyamātyajanapadadurgakoṣadandamitrāṇī prakṛtyaḥ', AS., 96.I.1.
28. Cf. AS., 1.III.
29. Cf. AS., 3.V.
30. Cf. AS., 2.IV.
31. Cf. AS., 96.II.III. IV and V.
32. 'Rājānāmuttiṣṭhamānamanuttiṣṭhante bhṛatyāḥ', AS., 14.XVII.1.
33. Cf. AS., 3.VII.
34. Cf. AS., 11.XV.
35. AS., II.
36. AS., 6.X and XI.
37. AS., 1.III.6.
38. 'Prajāsukhe sukham rājñaḥ prajāṇām ca hite hitam, nātmapriyam hitam rājñaḥ prajāṇām tu prayam hitam', AS., 14.XVIII.10.
39. Janapadaniveśaḥ AS., 17.I.
40. Btrumichhidra-nidhānam. AS., 18.II.
41. Gaudkādhyakṣaḥ AS., 43.XXVII.
42. Upauipātapratīkāraḥ. AS., 98.III.
43. AS., 2.IV.8.
44. 'Dharmaśca vyavaharaśca caritram rājaśāsanam, vivadarthaścatuṣpādaḥ paścimaḥ pūrvabādhakaḥ', AS., 56.57.I.
45. Cf. AS., 56.57.I.23.
46. 'Anuśāsaddhi Dharmaṇa vyavahārena samthayā, nyāyana ca caturthena caturantām mahīm jayet', AS., 56.57.I.
47. 'Śāstram vipratipadyeta dharmanyāyena Kena cit, nyāyastatra pramāṇam syāttra pāṭho hi naśyti', AS., 56.57.I.24.
48. AS., 97.II.8.
49. AS., 97.II.20.
50. 'Upāyaḥ sāmoparadānabhedadaṇḍaḥ', AS., 29.X.22.
51. 'Gūḍhapurusotpatti', AS., V. X and XI.
52. 'Tṛṇakāṣṭham a yojanād dāhayet udakāni ca dyṣayed, avāsrāvayecca', AS., 168-170. X.4.
53. V. J. McGill discusses the relation of ends and means to politics in *The Idea of Happiness*, p. 316. The position of Kautilya can be compared to that of Machievelli who advises tyrants how to preserve their regimes.
54. Cf. *Manusmṛti*, I. 31 and I.87.
55. Cf. *Yājñavalkya-Smṛti*, Ch. I.10.

Chapter Four (Pp. 52-55)

56. *Ibid.*, Ch. I.90-96.
57. Cf. MS., VII.3 and 8.
58. Cf. *The Mahābhārata*, 12-59-5, 13-30, 93-4.
59. Cf. his Smṛti Ch. I. 312-13.
60. Cf. G.C. Field: *The Philosophy of Plato*, Oxford University Press, London, 1949, pp. 18-19. Also Drake: *The People's Plato*, pp. 174-5.
61. Plato thinks that most standards of morality in any society are expressions of the selfish interests of the class which dominates it. 'It follows, then, that the question of the proper organisation of society . . . is inseparably bound up with morality.' Moral standards are determined by the way society is organized. Drake writes, 'where, then is justice? The old principles of the division of labour must be remembered. That principle demands that every man must perform his own most natively appointed labour, whether it be that of a guardian, an auxiliary of an artisan', *The People's Plato*, pp. 203-4.
62. Cf. Drake, "Socrates demonstrates that the individual and state are analogous in their relation to justice. He proves here that just as there are three parts are virtues of the individual soul, just as there are of the State." *The People's Plato*, p. 204.
63. '*Puruṣasūktam*', Janardan Sastri Pandey, (ed.) 1.
64. Cf. Field, "He starts with an analogy between the structure of a community and the structure of the individual personality. But he does not commit the fallacy of supposing that an analogy can provide a proof of anything." *Ibid.*, p. 94.
65. 'Puruṣasūktam', 11. 'Brahmano'asyamukhaṃ āsīdbahu rājannya-kṛtaḥ'.
66. Plato believes that virtue is a natural gift from God. Cf. Drake: *The People's Plato*, pp. 174-5.
67. Cf. G.C. Field: *The Philosophy of Plato*, Oxford University Press, London, 1949, pp. 95-7. Also Cf. Drake: *The People's Plato*, p 204. He observes, 'In individual as in state, reason, the counsellor and courage, the warrior act together with temperance to keep the desires in proper subjugation. This coordination is justice, the quality which makes men and states alike just'. Drake quotes Plato, 'Ought not the rational principle which wise, and has the core of the whole soul, to rule and the spirited part to be the subject and ally?' *Ibid.*, p. 231.
68. *The Philosophy of Plato*, London: Oxford University Press, London, pp. 78-9.
69. Socrates speaks thus in *The Republic*, '. . .we say that philosophers are to rule in the state . . . some men will be discovered who ought to study philosophy and to be leaders in the state, others who are not born to be philosophers are meant to be followers rather than leaders', taken from Drake's *The People's Plato*, p. 259. 'And surely you would not have children and rulers of your ideal state. . .be like posts, having no reason in them. Were this the case, you would not set them in authority over the highest matters. So you will make a law that they shall have

CHAPTER FOUR (PP. 55-59)

such an education as will enable them to attain the skill of dialectic . . . .' Drake: *The People's Plato*, p. 285.

70. Cf. AS., 1.11.2.
71. Drake writes, '. . .when these functions are being harmoniously carried out in the state and each citizen is contributing his appointed labour, then there is justice'. *The People's Plato*, p. 204.
72. Cf. Field: *The Philosophy of Plato*, Oxford University Press, London, 1949, p. 85.
73. 'Svadharma sthāpanādaupakārikāḥ', AS., 1.II.2.
74. AS., I.II.10.
75. Field writes, 'It is one of the cardinal features of the ideal state that in all classes there should be, in Plato's phrase, agreement about who should rule and who should be ruled'. *Ibid.*, pp. 82-3. Kautilya describes it as 'Sarvabhūtahite rataḥ'.
76. Drake, in his book states, 'Besides the perfect state which for Socrates is the aristocratic, there are four significant constitutions of inferior states: timocracy, oligarchy, democracy, and tyranny. . . . As there are five states, there must be five natures in individuals which correspond to them. The royal nature corresponds to the prefect state which Socrates has been constructing, the ambitious nature to the timocratic, the money loving nature to oligarchy and the freedom loving nature to democracy and the power loving nature to the tyrannical state'. *The People's Plato*, p. 289.
77. *The Philosophy of Plato*, Oxford University Press, London, 1949, pp. 87-9.
78. Field believes that there is an essential difference between Plato and Marx. Cf. *Ibid.*, p. 90. Marx thinks that class is an economic category, not a social one. Cf. G.D.H. Cole: *The Meaning of Marxism*, Victor Gollancz, London, 1948, p. 75.
79. Cf. G.C. Field: *The Philosophy of Plato*, Oxford University Press, London, 1949.
80. Cf. Field: *The Philosophy of Plato*, Oxford Ūniversity Press, London, 1949.
81. *Ibid.*, p. 88.
82. 'Maryādām sthāpayedā-cāryānamātyān vā', AS., 3. VI. 5.
83. The dialogue between Bīshma and Yudhistra in the *Mahābhārata*, 12-59.5.
84. Knowledge is identified with virtue. To quote Socrates, 'Wisdom or knowledge alone is the guide of right action. He who has knowledge will always be right. Cf. Drake's *The People's Plato*, p. 174.
85. To the question, 'Do you think that the possession of all other things is of any value if we do not possess knowledge of the Good?' Socrates replies, 'Of no value at all', from Plato's *The Republic*.
86. This is similar to Schweitzer's distinction between principles of life-affirmation and life-negation. The former attitude is lacking in Indian

Chapter Four (Pp. 59-62)

culture, according to him. Cf. *Indian Thought and Its Development*, Ch. I.

87. Cf. P.T. Raju: *Idealistic Thought of India*, George Allen & Unwin, London, 1953, pp. 395-6.
88. 'The life-aim of survival', observes Whitehead, 'is modified into human aim at survival for diversified worthwhile experience.'

Chapter Five (Pp. 63-64)

1. The XIII part of *Atharvaveda* (41 out of 536 hymns) is devoted to this topic of love, magic and charms. Prominent among them are love-spells, to secure a woman's love, to win a man's love, for virility, to obtain a wife, for good relations between husband and wife, and for progeny and the birth of sons. Love and magic are associated to illustrate the truth, viz., magic is the essence of love and love is the essence of magic. Kāma was meant to help men with their marital problems and difficulties; its aim being happiness and success in married life. Cf. *Philosophy of India*, Henry R. Zimmer, Pantheon Books, New York, 1953, pp. 146-8.
2. It is dated approximately 400 A.D.
3. 'Mahādevanucaraśca nandī sahasreṇadhyāyānam pṛthak kāmasūtram provāca'. Kāmasūtra, 1.1.8.
4. KS., 1.I.9-18.
5. 'Saṁkṣipya sarvamarthamalpena granthena Kāmasūtramidam pranītam', KS., 1.I.19.
6. KS., 1.I.1. 'Dharmārthakāmebyo nāmah'.
7. Śatāyurvai puruṣo vibhajya kālamanyonyanubaddham parasparasyā nupaghātakaṁ trivargaṁ seveta', KS., 1.II.1.
8. KS., 1. IV.I.
9. 'Bālye vidyāgrahaṇādīnarthān', KS., 1.II.2. 'Kamam ca youvane', 1.II.3. 'Sthāvire dharmaṁ mokṣaṁ ca', 1.II.4.
10. '. . .Kāmasūtraṁ tadaṅgavidyāśca puruṣo' dhīyīta', KS., 1.III.1.
11. KS., 1.III.2.
12. 'zk. . .iti catuṣaṭirangavidyāḥ kāmasūtrasyā-varyavinyaḥ', KS., 1.III.15.
13. KS., 1.III.24.
14. 'Tiyagyaonisvapi tu svayam provṛttatvāt kāmasya nityatācca na śāstreṇa kṛtyamastītyā cāryaḥ', KS., 1.2.17.
15. 'Sā copayapratipattīḥ kāmasūtraditi vātsyāyanaḥ', KS., 1.II.19. It is sometimes argued that since a person who is not conversant with logic can often argue correctly and a logician can sometimes make mistakes, there is no use in studying logic. But doctors fall ill and a man not knowing the science of medicine may remain healthy, still, we find that the study of the science of medicine is useful.
16. 'Tām śruterdharmajñasamavāyācca pratipadyete', KS., 1.II.8.

Chapter Five (Pp. 64-66)

17. KS., 1.II.9. 'Tamadhyaśapracārādvartasamaya-vidbhyo vaṇighhyaśceti', KS., 1.II.10.
18. 'Teṣām samaveye pūrvaḥ pūrvo grīyān', KS., 1.II.14.
19. 'Arthās-ca rājñaḥ', KS., 1.II.15.
20. 'Tamūlakaivāllokayā trayaḥ', KS., 1.II.15.
21. 'Alaukikat-vādadṛṣṭārthatuādapravṛttānām yajñādīnām śāstratpravartanaṁ, laukikatvād-dṛṣṭarthatvācca pravṛttebhayaśca māmṣabhksanā-de-bhyaḥ śāstrādeva nivāranam, dharmaḥ', KS., 1.II.7.
22. Cf. *Sarvadarsanasaṁgraha*, Ch. I. Also see Dale Riepe: *The Naturalistic Tradition of Indian Thought*, Motilal Banarsidass, Delhi, 1964, p. 59.
23. 'Kāma evaikaḥ puruṣārthaḥ, or paramaḥ puruṣārthaḥ kāmopa-bhogaḥ'. Also 'Aṅganādiganādijnyam sukhameva puruṣārthaḥ'.
24. 'Nitikāmaśāstranusarena arthakāmaeva puruṣārtham manyamānānaḥ pāralaukikam artham apahnuvānās cārvākanatamānu vartamānāḥ'. *Ibid.*, Ch. I. Also see Dale Riepe: *The Naturalistic Tradition of Indian Thought*, Motilal Banarsidass, Delhi, 1964, pp. 74-5.
25. 'Dharmaḥ Bāmāt na paraḥ kāma eva paramo dharmaḥ, tejjanitāmeva paramaṁ sukham', *Ibid.*, Ch.I.
26. Cf. *Manūsmṛti*, II.11. See Dale Riepe: *The Naturalistic Tradition in Indian Thought*, Motilal Banarsidass, 1964, p. 57.
27. KS., 1.II.6-8. Also 1.II.31.
28. 'Nārthamścaret', KS., 1.II.32; 'Prayatnato'pi hyeteanusdhī yamāna naiva kadācitsyuḥ', KS., 1.II.33; and also 'Ananuṣṭhīyamānā api yadrcchayā bhaveyuḥ', KS., 1.II.26.
29. 'Tatsarvam kālakāritamiti', KS., 1.II.35 and 'kāla eva hi puruṣānarthā-narthayorjaya parajayoḥ sukhaduḥkhayaoś-casthā payati', KS., 1.II.36.
30. 'Na niṣkarmano bhadramastīti vātsyāyayanaḥ', KS., 1.II.39.
31. 'Nadharmamścaret', KS., 1.II.25. 'Esyatphalatavt', KS., 1.II.-6. 'Sāmśayi Katuācca', KS., 1.II.27.
32. KS., 1.II.28.29, 30.
33. KS., 1.II.25.
34. 'Na kāmaṅścaret', 1.II.40.
35. KS., 1.II.41.
36. KS., 1.II.42. Also compare with Freudian analysis. (See *The Freudian Ethics* by Richard LaPiere, pp. 62-63).
37. Most arguments against sex advanced by the spiritualists and moralists are based upon the concept of self-control and the control of senses. Passion (lust) is considered to be one of the six enemies of man (ṣaḍripu), the others being anger (krodha), avarice (lobha) infatuation (moha), hauteur (mada) and egotism (ahaṁkāra). Cf. Kautilya's *Arthaśāstra*, 3.VI. Also *Bhagavad-Gītā*, III.37., 39; also V. 23.
38. 'Sarīrasthiti-hetu-tvādāhārasadharmāno hi kāmaḥ', KS., 1.II.37. 'Sri-yante, na hi mṛagaḥ santīti yavaḥ. nopyanta iti vātsyāyanaḥ', KS., 1.II.38.

Chapter Five (Pp. 66-68)

39. 'Sukhasya mūlam dharmaḥ; dharmasya mūlamarthaḥ'.
40. 'Phalabhūtaśca dharmārthyoḥ', KS., 1.II.37.
41. Kant, the greatest advocate of duty for duty's sake, was ultimately led to believe in a concept of complete good which comprises virtue and happiness.
42. This was the chief contention of the Cārvākas. 'Dharmamūlaḥ smṛtaḥ svargastatrapi-paramah striyah, grahasthā-dharmo durvaro narānām dharmayatnajaḥ. hitāścapatyasamtānai striyasviha paratra ca param sampratyayo bhogaprakarṣārthāya vai striyaḥ.' A similar notion of heaven is found in the *Bhagavad-Gītā* (IX.20.21), but it declares such enjoyments as transitory and condemns them in favour of everlasting peace (paramaśānti).
43. KS., 1.II.49.
44. KS., 1.II.50.
45. 'Trivargasādhakam yatsyāddrayo kasya vā punaḥ, karyam tadapi kurvīta na tvekārtham dvibādhakam', KS., 1.II.51. The whole of Ch. VI of Book 5 is devoted to this topic of confusion of values.
46. 'Mrgayākṣu divāsvapnaḥ, parvivādah-striyo madaḥ, tanrytrikaṁ vṛthāṭyā ca kāmajo daśako gaṇāḥ'.
47. Mythologically, kāma is deified as one of the gods known as "the Cupid" (Kāmadeva), accompanied by his glamorous mate (Rati) and equipped with five arrows (Panca-sāyaka). This is quite significant, for Love is personified as the Cupid, sex-delight is his mate (Rati) and five arrows indicate love's operational spells, viz., (i) to rise up (jambha), (ii) to confuse (moha), (iii) to stupify (stambha), (iv) to subdue (vasa) and (v) to capture (pasa). It is often described as bodiless (anaṅga) and heart-churning (manamatha), etc.
48. 'Srotratvakcaksusjihvāghranānāmātmasanyuktena manaśadhisthitānām sveṣu sveṣu viṣyaeṣvanukūlyataḥ pravṛttih kāmaḥ', KS., 1.II.11.
49. By involving the self of man in sexual behaviour, Vātsyāyana is not raising the topic to a higher level of spiritual culture. In the strict terminology of vedānta, self here means only the empirical self (jīva), but Vatsyāyana seems to be concerned with the ego or individuality to which the pleasure can be attributed, for otherwise there can be no valuational achievement in sensual pleasure. Hence Vātsyāyana does not refer to any spiritual content of kāma nor does he mean bliss (ānanda) when he refers to pleasure.
50. *An Outline of Psychology*, Methuen & Co., London, 1949, p. 110.
51. This is comparable to the Feudian pleasure-principle which also works on libidonal motivation based on sex (Eros), but much of Freudianism is based on unconscious motivation in human behaviour. Richard LaPiere writes, "The aboriginal psyche that with which the infant is biologically equipped, is a pleasure-seeking principle and pain avoiding constellation of unconscious drives and urges whose being and striving are thus governed by the pleasure principle.' *The Freudian*

Chapter Five (Pp. 68-71)

Ethics, p. 36. Freud argued on the premise that man is by nature antisocial and individualistic.

52. In the 'Hymn to Creation' in *Ṛgveda* (X.129), kāma is considered to be the sole activating force in the germ of creation. It is the creative force, the fertile power and impulse which became energy. This is a cosmic view of procreative desire.
53. 'Sparśaviśeṣviṣaye tvāsya-bhimāni-kasukānuviddhā phalatyarth pratītiḥ pradhānyātkāmaḥ', KS., 1.II.12.
54. Cf. KS., 2.II and Ch. III. Vātsyāyana's view comes closer to that of Freud, who "recognises sexual intercourse as the most intense pleasure that men can enjoy". Also see *The Idea of Happiness* by McGill, p. 268.
55. KS., 1.II.13.
56. Parmāṇa, kāla, ratibhāva.
57. KS., 2.II, prītibheda.
58. KS., whole of Book 2.
59. KS., Book VII, chapters I-III.
60. 'Gṛhitavidyā pratigrahajaya-krayamveśa-dhigatairartharanvayāgataiu-bhairvā gārhasthyamadhigamya nāgarakavrttam varteta', KS., 1.IV.1.
61. KS., 1.II.9. It is a happy coincidence that both Vātsyāyana and Epicurus have stressed the need of friends in the pursuit of pleasure. "All friendship", says Epicurus, "is desirable in itself, though it starts from the need of help."
62. KS., Book I, Ch. IV.
63. KS., 1.V.1-2.
64. KS., 1.V.3.
65. See KS., 1.IV.16-52. He prescribes a time-table for a voluptuary.
66. 'Śarīrasthitihetu-tvādāhārasadharmāṇo hi kāmaḥ', KS., 1.1.46.
67. 'Daśa tu kāmasya sthānāni', 5.I.4.
68. It is perversion which leads to antisocial behaviour. Cf. KS., 5.I.5.
69. Vātsyāyana seems to think that perversions are due to a lack of social control, but on closer analysis, we find that this is not so. The truth is just the opposite. Also see *The Freudian Ethics*, pp. 62-4; Richard LaPiere writes, 'No society can really be good, for everything social is contrary to the psychic welfare of the individual. Society would and should, however, minimise its disutility to the individual. To this end it should avoid inculcating in him any socially prescribed personality, attributes, motivations, goals, values, sentiments, or feelings of personal obligations. The individual should not be required to submit to social authority whatever its character. . . .' *Ibid.*, pp. 64-5.
70. Vātsyāyana devotes the whole of Book VI of his work to this topic. The account is not to be considered as recommendatory on account of the language; but he admits the over-all necessity for such practices which he recognizes as abnormal and perverted. On the whole he seems to disparage the institution of prostitution.

Chapter Five (Pp. 71-73)

71. He devotes a full chapter to the discussion of this topic. Cf. Chapter 5.1.
72. KS., 5.1.3.
73. 'Ratyarthāḥ puruṣa yena, ratyarthāścaiva yositaḥ, śāstrasyartha pradhārnatvāttena yogoatra yoṣitām', KS., 6.VI.52. "Freud believes that complete freedom of satisfaction would require complete sexual freedom which would conflict outrageously with the reality-principle", *The Freudian Ethics*, p. 268.
74. The concept of happiness is developed in the *Mahābhārata* (Śāntiparva, 177.43.48). Pleasure means gratification of transitory desires, it is both temporary and mixed with pain, but happiness is a durable state of satisfaction with the conditions of life in general including moral and social control. Happiness is the true goal of trivarga. All acts aim at happiness (*ibid.*, 190.6.7). V.J. McGill admits no casual role of pleasure in happiness which is always pleasant in tone (see his *The Idea of Happiness*, p. 270). "If pleasures or a life of pleasure is often condemned, joy or delight or some other variant of pleasure is then made a feature of the highest good." (*Ibid.*, p. 262.)
75. The Absolute (Brahman) is considered to be the embodiment of truth, beauty and goodness and as such he is the fountain-head of all aesthetic delight (rasovai Brahma).
76. Bharata: *Nātya-śāstra*, 6.31. Also cf. *Sources of Indian Tradition* (ed.), p. 263.
77. Bharata lists up eight such sentiments and Mammaṭa mentions nine; see Mammaṭa: *Kāvyaprakāśa*, Ch. 1. Love is an invariable member of these sentiments. Kalidasa, an apostle of love (sṛṅgāra rasa), also refines it in his classic *Śākuntalam*.
78. The word 'ras' is here taken to mean bliss (ānanda) as is implied in the Upaniṣadic expressions.
79. Literally 'hedon' means a pleasant state of mind, and hedonism is a view, according to which pleasure is the only goal of life; pleasure is the supreme value.
80. Consult his lines 1.1.28, 29, 30. "It is better to have pigeon today than a peacock tomorrow; a piece of copper that one gives, is worth more than a piece of gold that one promises."
81. Dale Riepe: *The Naturalistic Tradition in Indian Thought*, Motilal Banarsidass, Delhi, 1964, p. 75.
82. V.J. McGill observes, "The persistent reason for preferring sensuous pleasures is that they are immediate and certain, while all others except death is uncertain and precarious." *The Idea of Happiness*, p. 270.
83. V.J. McGill: *The Idea of Happiness*, p. 122.
84. Epicurus says, "You tell me that the stimulus of flesh makes you too prone to the pleasures of love. Provided that you do not break the laws or good customs and do not distress any of your neighbours or

Chapter Five (Pp. 73-79)

do harm to your body. . . you may indulge your inclination as you please. Yet is impossible not to come up against one or another of these barriers, for the pleasures of love never profit a man and he is lucky if they do him no harm." Epicurus' advice falls in line with the advice of Vātsyāyana to his voluptuary.

85. *The Idea of Happiness*, p. 123: "Provided the quantity of pleasure is the same, pushpin is as good as poetry and the satisfaction of the enlightened statesman has no intrinsic advantage over that of the criminal."
86. Cf. Rashdall: *Theory of Good and Evil*, Vol. 1, Oxford University Press, London, 1948, pp. 58-63.
87. There is a distinction made between what is good (śreyas) and what is pleasant (preyas) in the *Kaṭhopaniṣad* wherein good is preferred to the pleasant in accordance with the spiritual tradition of Indian philosophy.
88. Rashdall: *The Theory of Good and Evil*, Vol. I, Oxford University Press, London, 1948, pp. 71-6.
89. KS., 5.VI.6.
90. The whole of Ch. VI of KS. is devoted to this topic.
91. KS., 5.VI.2. He unfortunately confines this discussion to the life of a prostitute whose only aim is money (artha) but if the topic is removed from its context, we find that it is an independent study of valuational judgment and commensurability of values.
92. V.J. McGill poses a challenge to hedonists to justify murder for utilitarian ends. See his *The Idea of Happiness.*, p. 315.
93. Cf. M.A.R. Tuker: *Past and Future of Ethics*, pp. 155-6.

Chapter Six (P. 80)

1. Cf. J.R. Charpure: *Teachings of Dharmaśāstras*, Motilal Banarsidass, Delhi 1956, pp. 5-6.
2. The word 'dharma' was used fifty-six times in the *Ṛgveda* quite distinctly apart from ṛta. It mostly connoted religious ordinances or rites, cf. P.V. Kane: *History of Dharmaśāstras*, Vol. I, Kalyan Steam Press, Poona, pp. 1-2. Dharma etymologically is derived from the root 'dhṛ' which means that which 'holds', 'integrates' or 'regulates' or 'maintains' a thing (dhāryate iti dharmaḥ).
3. Ṛta literally means 'straight line', 'the course of things' (the cosmic law). MacDonell understands by it order, 'truth' or 'right' in the moral context and 'sacrifice' or 'rite' in the religious context (cf. his *Vedic Mythology*, p. 11). P.V. Kane brings out three senses of the word ṛta: (i) ordered way and cult of gods, (ii) the course of nature and (iii) the moral conduct of man. Cf. *op. cit.*, *History of Dharmaśāstra*,

CHAPTER SIX (PP. 80-84)

Vol. IV, p. 2. Anṛta, the opposite of ṛta was also used. Also see J.R. Charpure's *The Teachings of Dharmaśāstras*, Motilal Banarsidass, Delhi, 1956, p. 11.

4. *A Source Book of Indian Philosophy*, (ed.) Radhakrishnan and Charles A. Moore, Princeton University Press, Princeton, N.J., 1957, p. 27.
5. Cf. *The Concept of Man*, London, 1969, p. 222. Dr. P.T. Raju explains the historical transition from ṛta to dharma on mythological grounds which signifies the replacement of 'the right' (ṛta) by 'the good' (dharma). Śaṅkara also gives to dharma the implication of 'duty' as against 'value', 'ṛtam yathāsastram yathākartavyam buddhau suparini-ścitam'. *Taittiriya Up.*, S.B.I.1.
6. He bases his observations mainly on Vasubandhu's work which is a systematic exposition of Abhidharma-vibhaṣāśāstra, a commentary on Abhidharma.
7. Cf. *The Central Conception of Buddhism and the Meaning of the Word 'Dharma'*, Royal Asiatic Society, London, 1923, p. 60.
8. Cf. *Mahavagga*, i.23 as quoted in Stcherbatsky: *The Central Conception of Buddhism*, Royal Asiatic Society, London, 1923, p. 2.
9. Cf. Radhakrishnan, *The Dhammapada* (tr.), p. 41.
10. Mrs. Rhys Davids interprets the meaning of dharma, as used in Buddhistic philosophy, as a regulating force (cf. *Buddhism* p. 235).
11. This is the conclusion arrived at by Prof. Stcherbatsky in his book *The Central Conception of Buddhism*, Royal Asiatic Society, London, 1923, pp. 60-61.
12. Cf. Stcherbatsky: *The Central Conception of Buddhism*, Royal Asiatic Society, London 1923, pp. 26-7.
13. Cf. Stcherbatsky: *The Central Conception of Buddhism*, Royal Asiatic Society, London, 1923, p. 41.
14. This ultimate goal of the world process, according to the Buddhists, resembles the concept of Sarvamukti of the Sāṁkhya.
15. Cf. P.T. Raju: *Idealistic Thought of India*, George Allen & Unwin, London, 1953, p. 285.
16. Cf. N.K. Devaraja: *The Mind and Spirit of India*, Motilal Banarsi Dass, Delhi, 1967, p. 168. He writes: "Among the metrical smṛiti the Manu-smṛiti is universally considered to be the most authoritative." Yājña-valkya's is another. Manu's treatise on dharma is a faithful exposition of the character and sanction of dharma (law). Smṛitis are a systematic treatment of dharma based on memory of Vedic knowledge (śruti).
17. 'Ācāraḥ paramo dharmaḥ śrutyuktah smārtta evaca', MS., I.108.
18. 'Asmindharmoakhilenokto guṇadoṣau ca karmanaram, caturṇāmapi varṅānāmś-caraścai-va śāśvataḥ', MS., I.107.
19. 'Vidvadbhi sevitaḥ. hidāyenābhyanujnāto yo dharmaḥ tam nibodhata', **MS., II.1.**

CHAPTER SIX (PP. 84-86)

20. 'Vedaḥ smṛtiḥ sadācāraḥ svasya ca priyamātmanaḥ', MS., 11-12. Also 'vedo aknilo dharmamūlam smṛtiśile ca tadvidām, ācāraśceva sadhunām-ātmanstuṣṭireva ca', MS., II.6.
21. MS., XII.105-106.
22. 'Prāmaṇam paramam śrutiḥ', MS., II; 13. P.V. Kane observes, 'It is clear that the later rules contained in the dharmaśāstras had their roots deep down in the most ancient vedic tradition and the authors of dharmaśāstras were quite justified in looking up to the vedas as the source of dharma.' *History of Dharmaśāstras*, Vol. 1, Kalyan Steam Press, Poona, p. 7.
23. Mimānsikas focus their research on this point and define dharma as that good (arthaḥ) which is prescribed by the Vedas ('Codanālakṣanaḥ arthaḥ dharmaḥ').
24. 'Sankalpamūlaḥ Kāmo. . . akāmasya kriyā kācidṛaśyate na', MS., II. pp. 3, 4.
25. 'Kāmātmatā na praśastā na caivāhostyākāmatā', MS., II.2.
26. 'Tesu samyagvarthamano gacchatyamaralokamamyatha Sankalpritanśce hai sarvān kāmān sama-śnute'. MS., II.5.
27. This is more systematically expounded in the Bhagavad-Gītā.
28. 'Dhṛtiḥ kṣamā damosteyam śaucamindṛyanigraha, dhirvidyā satyamakrodho dhaśakam dharma-lakṣaṅam', MS., VI. 92.
29. 'Lokanam tu vivṛddhyartham mukhabāhūrūpa-dataḥ, brahmanām kstriyam vaiśyam śūdram-śca nirvaṛttayam', MS., I.31.
30. MS., I.87.
31. MS., X.67., Also cf. Charpure: *Teachings of Dharmaśāstras*, Motilal Banarsidass, Delni, 1956, pp. 55-7.
32. MS., X.67.
33. MS., X.45.
34. 'Caste was the Hindu answer to the challenge of a society in which different races had to live together without merging into one'. *The Eastern Religion and Western Thought*, Oxford University Press, London, 1946, p. 373.
35. MS., VI. 87.
36. MS., II, III and VI.
37. Cf. MS., II. 27-44. Also cf. Charpure: *Teachings of Dharmaśāstras*, pp. 63, 65.
38. MS., XII.88.
39. Yugadharma is determined by the place (deśa) and time (kāla) to which the person belongs. Dharma is, therefore, not rigid. It is subject to change.
40. 'Yathokiakarinam vipram nayanti paramam gatim', MS., VI. 88. Also MS., VI. 93 and 96. Also cf. *The Mind and Spirit of India*, by N.K. Devaraja, p. 169, and *Teachings of Dharmaśāstras*, pp. 101, 102.
41. 'Dhyānayogena sampaśyedgatimasyāntaratmanaḥ', MS., VI. 73.

Chapter Six (Pp. 86-91)

42. MS., XII. 125. 'Ihaiva loke tiṣṭhansa brahmabhūyāya kalpate', MS., XII. 102. Also *ibid.*, VI. 81.
43. 'Śreyastrivarga iti tu sthiti', MS., II.224.
44. Parityajedarthakāmau yau syātām dharma varjitau', MS., IV.76.
45. 'Pṛchāmi tvām dharmasamūdhacetaḥ, yachhṛeyaḥ syānniśchitam bhrūhī tanme', BG., II.7.
46. 'Dharmyāddhiyaddhāchhreyo anyat kśatriyasya na vidyate', BG., II.31.
47. 'Chaturvarṇyam mayā sṛṣṭam guṇa karma vibhāgasaḥ', BG., IV.13.
48. *Ibid.*, XVIII.41. Also 'Svabhāvajena kaunteya nibaddhaḥ svena karmaṇā Karttunecchasiyan mohatkarisyasyavśo'apitet', BG., XVIII.61.
49. 'Kim karma kimakarmeti Kavayo'pyatra mobitaḥ', BG., IV.16. Also BG., 17 (gahanā karmano gati).
50. 'Karmanyevādhikāraste mā phaleṣu kadācina, mā karma-phalahetur bhūrmā te saṅgo'astvā-karmani', BG., II.47. Also cf. BG., XVIII.6, also III.9 and 51.VI.20.
51. 'Viṣayā viniyarttante nirāhārasya dehinaḥ, rasavarja raso' apyasya paramam dṛstvā nivartate', BG., II.59.
52. 'Sukhadukhe same kṛtva lābhālābhau jayājayau, tato yuddhāya yujyasva', BG., II.38. Also IV. 22.
53. 'Tānī sarvānī samyamyayukta āsīta matparaḥ, vase hi yasyendriyāṇī tsya prajñā pratiśḍhitā', BG., II.61. Also IV.26-30.
54. 'Yogasamnyastakarmānam jñānsamchinna-samśayam, ātmavantam na karmāni nibadhnanti dhanajaya', BG., IV.41.
55. BG., IX.32; VIII.21 and VII.29. Also VI.3.
56. Cf. C.D. Broad: *Five Types of Ethical Theory*, Routledge & Kegan Paul Ltd., London, 1950. Kant himself has given expression to this idea when he writes, 'Thus the moral worth of an action does not lie in the effect expected from it, nor in any principle of action which requires to borrow its motive from this expected effect.' *Fundamental Principles of the Metaphysics of Ethics* (Tr. T.K. Abbot), Longman Green & Co., London, 1949, p. 20.
57. Cf. Immanuel Kant: *Fundamental Principles of the Metaphysics of Ethics* (Tr. T.K. Abbot), Longman Green & Co., London, 1949, pp. 14-16.
58. *Ibid.*, pp. 18-19.
59. *Ibid.*, p. 19.
60. Cf. C.D. Broad: *Five Types of Ethical Theory* (Chapter on Kant), Routledge Kegan Paul Ltd., London, 1950.
61. *Op. cit.*, 'The conception of an objective principle in so far it is obligatory for a will, is called a command and the formula of a command is called an imperative (p. 35).
62. *Op. cit.*, p. 48.
63. *Op. cit.*, pp. 46, 47.
64. *Op. cit.*, p. 13. Kant writes, 'The moral culture of man must begin not with the improvement in morals, but with the transformation of the mind'. Both Kant and the Gītā favour the suppression of desires.

Chapter Six (Pp. 91-95)

65. *Op. cit.*, p. 14.
66. *The Concept of Perfection in the Teachings of Kant and the Gītā*, Motilal Banarsidass, Delhi, 1967, p. 146.
67. *Ibid.*, p. 148.
68. Cf. *ibid.*, pp. 165, 166. Also *Bhagavad-Gītā*, IX.22. (anayāścintayanto mām ye janah paryupāsate teṣām nityābhiyuktānām yogakṣemam vahāmyaham).
69. F.H. Bradley: *Ethical Studies*, Clarendon Press, Oxford, 1935, p. 159.
70. *Ibid.*, p. 159.
71. *Ibid.*, p. 150.
72. *Ibid.*, p. 156.
73. *Op. cit.*, p. 161.
74. *Ibid.*, p. 154.
75. *Op. cit.*, p. 174.
76. *Ibid.*, p. 163.
77. *Ibid.*, p. 163.
78. *Ibid.*, 173.
79. *Op. cit.*, p. 163.
80. *The Bhagavad-Gītā*, II. 31-32. Similarly, F.H. Bradley writes 'common social morality is the basis of human life. It is specialized in particular functions of society and upon its foundations are erected the ideals of a higher social perfection'. *Op. cit.*, p. 227.
81. *Op. cit.*, p. 199.
82. *Op. cit.*, p. 187.
83. *Ibid.*, p. 154.
84. *Ibid.*, p. 196.
85. The whole of Chapter XIII is devoted to distinction between jiva and ātman in the form of kṣetra and kṣetrajña (cf. XIII.1-13).
86. *The Bhagavad Gītā*, XIII.30
87. Cf. *ibid.*, V.26.
88. 'Brahmaiva tenagantavyam brahmakarma-samādhina', BG., IV 24; also XIII.13, 18; V.26-4.
89. *Op. cit.*, p. 205.
90. *Op. cit.*, p. 234.
91. Cf. S.N.L. Shrivastava: *Śaṅkara and Bradley*, Motilal Banarsidass, Delhi, 1968, p. 40.

Chapter Seven (P. 96)

1. Mokṣa is derived from a verbal root 'muc' which means to give up, to get rid of, to leave or to be free from. It means liberation, emancipation, and freedom. Mukti has the same connotation.

Chapter Seven (Pp. 96-103)

2. S.N. Dasgupta observes in this connection that mokṣa is the pivot on which all the systems of Indian philosophy revolve. Cf. his *Yoga Philosophy in Relation to Other Systems of Indian Thought*, p. 316.
3. A.K. Lad writes, 'Thus Mokṣa is the highest value on realising which nothing remains to be realized.' *A Comparative Study of the Concept of Liberation in Indian Philosophy*, Rewa, 1967, p. 2.
4. Cf. N.K. Devaraja: *The Mind and Spirit of India*, Motilal Banarsi Dass, Delhi, 1967, p. 223. The problem of self has been initiated by the Upaniṣads in Indian philosophy and it has continued to dominate the mind of all Indian philosophers till today. All mokṣa-śāstras are, as a matter of fact, mere interpretations of the true meaning of the vedic texts.
5. Cf. Stcherbatsky: *The Central Conception of Buddhism*, Royal Asiatic Society, London, 1923, pp. 2, 40.
6. *Ibid*., p. 60.
7. 'Get up (rouse yourself), do not be thoughtless', *The Dammapada*.
8. 'It is asking too much about that which it is not necessary to know'.
9. Cf. Radhakrishnan: *Indian Philosophy*, Vol. I, George Allen & Unwin Ltd., London, p. 447.
10. Cf. Stcherbatsky: *The Central Conception of Buddhism*, Royal Asiatic Society, London, 1923, p. 30.
11. *Ibid*., p. 41.
12. *Op. cit*., pp. 40, 44.
13. Cf., *Majjhina-Nikāya*, 1.483-8. *Buddhism in Translations* by H.C. Warren, pp. 123-8.
14. For example, Mrs. Rhys David, Bigandot, Oldenberg and Dahlke are inclined to believe that Nirvāṇa is total extinction.
15. Cf. *A Comparative Study of the Conception of Liberation*, pp. 83-5. Dept. of Philo, T.R.S. College, Rewa, 1967, pp. 83-5.
16. *Indian Philosophy*, Vol. I, George Allen & Unwin Ltd., London, 1948, p. 453.
17. *The Central Philosophy of Buddhism*, George Allen & Unwin Ltd., London, 1960, pp. 272-3.
18. Cf. Coomaraswamy: *Hinduism and Buddhism*, Philosophical Society, New York, 1946.
19. *The Central Philosophy of Buddhism*, George Allen & Unwin Ltd., London, 1960, pp. 274, 275.
20. The doctrine of the Sāṁkhya is originally attributed to some ancient sage, Kapil, but the text is available in the form of *Kārikās* expounded by Iśvarakṛsṇa, cf. *Kārikās*, LXXI.
21. Kārīkās, 1.
22. 'Sryānvyakta-vyakta-jña-vijñānāt', *Kārīkās*, 2.
23. Kārīkās, 10.
24. 'Vikāro na prakṛitiv-na vikṛtih Puruṣaḥ', SK., 3.
25. SK., 18.

Chapter Seven (Pp. 103-107)

26. 'Siddhim sākṣitvam asya puruṣasya. Kāivalyam, mādhyasthyam, draṣṭṛtvam, akartṛbhāvaś-ca', Kārīkās, 19.
27. SK., 21.
28. SK., 63.
29. 'Tasmān-na bādhyate-ddhānamucyate nā'pi samsarati kaścit, SK., 62.
30. 'Dharmena-gamanam-Ūrdhvam. . .jñānena ca' pavaigo', SK., 44; also SK., 45-6.
31. SK., 63.
32. 'Nā'-smi na me nā-'ham-iti-apariśeṣam', SK., 64.
33. SK., 59, 61.
34. SK., 65.
35. Ai Kāntikam-atyantikam-ubhayam Kaivahyam-āpnoti' SK., 68. The Sāṁkhya believes that there are two stages in liberation, viz., the embodied, wherein the accumulated disposition continues to function, and the disembodied which is final after death. Cf. SK., 67 and 68.
36. Max Muller attributes a blissful condition to the liberated soul which is not warranted by any text. Cf. *Samkhya and Yoga*, Sushil Gupta (India) Ltd., 1952, p. 81.
37. Cf SK., 19. The incidence of birth and death, of difference in taste and inclination, etc., cannot be true of the puruṣa, for it is neither bound in the cycle of the world nor released.
38. Cf. *A Comparative Study of the Concept of Liberation*, Dept. of Phil., T.R.S. College, Rewa, 1967, pp. 109-10.
39. *Ibid.*, p. 111.
40. *The-Vedānta Sūtra,-Śaṅkara-Bhāṣya*, 1.1.4., 'Nityaḥ sarvajñāḥ-vijñānam ānandam brahma iti', SB., III, 2.16, 'caitanyameva tunirantaramasya svarūpam'.
41. SB., I.iii.19 and also SB., 1.1.1. 'Ātmanameva nirviśeṣam brahma viddhi', *Kena. Up.*, SB., 1.4. 'Abhedena ātma eva brahma brahmaivātmā'. Also 'Ātmā ca brahma'.
42. SB., 1.IV.3.
43. SB., I.1.19.
44. 'Brahma veda brahmaiva bhavati', SB., 1.1.4.
45. 'Brahmaiva hi muktyavasthā', SB., III.4.52. Also 'Brahmabhāvaśca Mokṣa', SB., 1.1.4.
46. SB., 3.IV.1.
47. SB., 3.IV.26.
48. SB., 3.IV.27.
49. SB., 4.1.15.
50. SB., 4.1.19.
51. SB., 1.II.8.
52. SB., 1.I.17.
53. Cf. *Vedāntapribhāṣā*.
54. 'Akāryam ca brahma tasmātkālato' syānantam'.
55. 'Anustheyakarma phalavilaksanam'; also 'Nityaśca Mokṣa', SB., 1.1.4.

Chapter Seven (Pp. 107-126)

56. *The Vedānta of Śaṅkara: A Metaphysics af Value*' Vol. 1, Bharat Publishing House, Jaipur, 1949, p. 87.
57. Cf. F.H. Bradley: *Ethical Studies*, Clarendon Press, Oxford, 1935, Chs. I-IV.
58. C.E.M. Joad, for example, observes, 'For a condition in which I shall cease to exist, to feel as an individual or indeed to be an individual is a condition in which I shall cease to be at all. Why should I hope or seek to realize such a condition unless my individual personality is of no account? But if it is of no account why am I to take trouble with it?' *Hibbert Journal*, October 1952.
59. *The Vedānta of Śaṅkara: A Metaphysics of Value*, Vol. I, Bharat Publishing House, Jaipur, 1949, p. 91.
60. B.G., XVIII.6.
61. B.G., X.10-11.
62. 'Tadasya trividhasya bandhasya atyantikaḥ vilayaḥ Mokṣaḥ'.
63. *The Vedānta-Sūtra: Rāmānuja-Bhāṣya*, 1.I.1.
64. *A Comparative Study of the Concept of Liberation* Rewa, 1967, p. 1.
65. *The Chief Works of Benedict De Spinoza* (Tr. R.H.M. Elwes) 2 vols., George Bell & Sons, London, 1898.
66. 'Self-realization has always impressed me as a conumdrum rather than its solution', Adamson: *Development of Modern Philosophy*, Vol. II, p. 109, quoted in *The Theory of Good and Evil*, By Hastings Rashdall, Vol. 1, Oxford University Press, London, 1948, p. 62.
67. Rashdall derives the idea of self-realization when he writes, 'To realize means to make real. You cannot make real what is real already, and the self must be certainly regarded as real before we are invited to set about realizing it.' *Theory of Good and Evil*, Vol. II, Oxford University Press, London, 1948, p. 62.
68. 'This double effort of the mind to enlarge by all means its domain to widen in every way both the world of knowledge and the realm of practice, shows us merely two sides of that single impulse to self-realization.' *The Principles of Logic*, p. 452.
69. 'If myself which I aim at is the realization in me of a moral world which is a system of selves, an organism in which I am a member, and in whose life I live, then I cannot aim at my own well-being without aiming at that of others. The others are not mere means to me, but are involved in my essence.' *Ethical Studies*, Clarendon Press, Oxford, 1935, p. 105.

Chapter Eight (Pp. 128-129)

1. *Brahmasūtra*, 1.1.1, 'Athāto Brahmajijñāsā'.
2. 'Pratipādanaprakriyā tvesā' yato vaco nivartante aprāpyamansā saha', SB., III.2.22.

Chapter Eight (Pp. 129-138)

3. 'Sarvasambandhākhyasparśavarjitatvat asparśayogaḥ'.
4. 'Viścṣanirakaraṇarūpa Brahma', SB., III.3.33.
5. 'Guros tu maunaṁ vyākhānam'.
6. 'Caitanyameva ta nirantaramasya svarūpam', SB., 1.1.4.
7. 'Abhedena ātmā eva brahma brahmaivātma', SB., 1.III.19.
8. 'Śūnyam eva tarhi tat, na, mithyavikalpasya nirnimittatvānūpapatteḥ', SB., *Gaudapada-Kārīkā*.
9. 'Brahma mandabuddhīnām asad iva pratibhāti'.
10. 'Brahmno rūpaprapancam pratisedhati praiśinaṣṭi Brahma'.
11. 'Sanmatram hi Brahma', SB., II.3.9. 'Tattvamasi iti', SB., I.1.4.
12. 'Brahmaveda brahmaiva bhavati', SB., 1.1.4.
13. *Appearance and Reality*, Clarendon Press, Oxford, 1931, p. 159.
14. 'Brahmavagatirhi puruṣārthaḥ'. Also 'Tathā brahmajñānatapi param-purṣārtham darśayati', SB., I.1.1.
15. Cf. his *Advaita Vedānta*, Motilal Banarsi Dass, Delhi, p. 63.
16. *Ibid.*, p. 58.
17. *The Cultural Heritage of India*, p. 234.
18. Cf. *Advaita Vedānta*, p. 205.
19. 'Dharmādharmau saha kāryeṇa Kālatryaṁ ca nopāvartate tad etat'.
20. *Op. cit.*, p. 205.
21. *Ibid.*, pp. 21-2.
22. *The Vedānta of Śaṅkara, A Metaphysics of Value*, Vol. 1, Bharat Publishing House, Jaipur, 1949, pp. 10-11.
23. Cf. *Ibid.*, pp. 239-49.
24. *Ibid.*, p. 17.
25. *Ibid.*, p. 12.
26. *Ibid.*, p. 289.
27. *Ibid.*, p. 292.
28. *Ibid.*, p. 91.
29. *Ibid.*, p. 85.
30. *Ibid.*, p. 87.
31. *Ibid.*, p. 92.
32. *Ibid.*, p. 92.
33. *Op. cit.*, p. 92.
34. *Ibid.*, p. 352.
35. *Ramanuja's Bhāṣya*, BS., 1.1.1.
36. 'Saviśeṣavastūviśayatvat sarvapramāṇām', RB., 1.1.1.
37. Radhakrishnan: *Indian Philosophy*, Vol. II, p. 684.
38. *Appearance and Reality*, p. 403.
39. 'Dvirūpam hi bhahamāvagamyate', S.B., 1.1.11. The distinction is commonly maintained in concepts of saguṇa and nirguṇa Brahman.
40. *Op. cit.*, p. 394.
41. *OP. cit.*, p. 396.
42. *Ibid.*, p. 336.
43. *Ibid.*, pp. 362-363.

Chapter Eight (Pp. 138-144)

44. *Op. cit.*, p. 404.
45. Cf. *Śaṅkara and Bradley*, p. 49.
46. *Ibid.*, p. 8.
47. *Ibid.*, p. 140.
48. *Appearance and Reality*, pp. 143-47.
49. *Śaṅkara and Bradley*, pp. 8-9.
50. Cf. *Appearance and Reality*, p. 393. Also, pp. 3-9.
51. *Ibid.*, pp. 380-81.
52. *Ibid.*, p. 366
53. *Ibid.*, p. 380.
54. *Op. cit.*, pp. 139-44.
55. *Śaṅkara and Bradley*, p. 40. Cf. *Bṛahad* Up. SB., 1.4.7.
56. *Collected Essays*, p. 9.
57. *Appearance and Reality*, p. 415.
58. 'Sarvo hi ātmastitvam pratyeti Tadviśeṣaṁ prāti vipratipatteḥ', SB., 1.1.1.
59. Cf. A.C. Mukerji: *The Cultural Heritage of India*, Vol. III, pp, 477-80.
60. 'Ātma hi nāma svarūpam', SB., 1.1.6.
61. 'Satta eva jñānameva satta'.
62. *Ethics*, Vol. III. pp. 66-8.
63. 'Brahmabhāva mokṣa', SB., 1.1.4.

Chapter Nine (Pp. 147-163)

1. *Presuppositions of India's Philosophy*, pp. 9-10.
2. P.T. Raju argues for the humanization of the concept of the Absolute when he writes, "Man can take interest in the Absolute only if it is humanized.' *Idealistic Thought of India*. George Allen & Unwin Ltd., London, 1953, p. 324.
3. Nicolai Hartmann: *Ethics*, Vol. II, pp. 71.72.
4. *The Mahābhārata* , XVIII.5.62.
5. *Vidhiviveka*, p. 243.
6. *Śāṅkara-Bhāṣya on Bhagavad-Gītā*, II, 55.
7. These values correspond closely to the five-fold criterion mentioned by Hartmann in his book *Ethics*. These are indivisibility, independence, depth of satisfaction, eternity and autonomy.

Bibliography

Sanskrit Texts and Translations

The Arthaśāstra of Kautilya and The Cāṇakya Sūtra, Śrivachaspati Gairola (ed.), The Chowkhamba Vidya Bhavan, Varanasi.

The Kāmasūtram of Vātsyāyana, Yashodhar (2 Vols.), Laxmi Venkateshwar Steam Press, Kalyan, Bombay.

The Manusmṛti (with Hindi translation), Keshav Parshad, Laxmi Venkateshwar Steam Press, Kalyan, Bombay.

The Bhagavad-Gītā (with Hindi translation), Geeta Press, Gorakhpur.

The Bhagavad-Gītā-Śāṅkara-Bhāsya, Motilal Banarsidass, Delhi.

The Sāṅkhya-Kārīkā of Īśvarakṛṣṇa, Jagannath Sastry, (ed.), Motilal Banarsidass, Delhi.

The Brahma-Sūtra: Śāṅkara-Bhāṣya, Motilal Banarsidass, Delhi.

The Brahma-Sūtra: Rāmānuja-Bhāṣya, Motilal Banarsidass, Delhi.

Buddhism in Translations by Henry Clarke Warren (Harvard Oriental Series Vol. III) Cambridge; Mass., Harvard University Press. 6th issue, 1915.

Brahmasūtra with *Śāṅkara-Bhāṣya*, (English Translation) 2 Vols. by George Thibaut, the Sacred Books of the East: Oxford, Clarendon Press, 1896.

The Dhammapada, (Eng. Translation) by S. Radhakrishnan; London, Oxford University Press, 1954.

Catussūtrī, English translation by Hardutt Sharma.

OTHER BOOKS

Bradley, F.H.: *Appearance and Reality*, Oxford: Clarendon Press, (1931).

Bradley, F.H.: *Ethical Studies*, Oxford: Clarendon Press, (1935).

Bhattacharya, H. (Ed.): *The Cultural Heritage of India*, (3 Vols.), Calcutta: Belur Math, (1937).

Broad, C.D.: *Five Types of Ethical Theories*, London: Routledge and Kegan Paul Ltd., (1950).

Charpure, J.R.: *Teachings of Dharmaśāstras*, Delhi: Motilal Banarsidass, (1956).

Coomaraswamy, A.K.: *Hinduism and Buddhism*, New York: Philosophical Library, (1945).

Dasgupta, S.N.: *A History of Indian Philosophy*, Cambridge University Press, (1932).

Dewey, John: *Experience and Nature*, New York: Dover, (1958).

Devraja, N.K.: *The Mind and Spirit of India*, Delhi: Motilal Banarsidass, (1967).

Field, G.C.: *The Philosophy of Plato*, London: Oxford University Press, (1949).

Ganchhwal, B.S.: *The Concept of Perfection in the Teachings of Kant and The Gita*, Delhi: Motilal Banarsidass, (1967).

Ghoshal, Upendranath: *A History of Hindu Political Theories*, London: Oxford University Press, (1923).

Hartmann, Nicolai: *Ethics* (3 Vols.) (Tr. Stanton Coit), Muirhead Library of Philosophy, London: George Allen & Unwin Ltd., (1951).

———*New Ways of Ontology* (Tr. Reinbard c. Kulm), Bonn.

Hiriyana, Mysore: *Outlines of Indian Philosophy*, London: George Allen and Unwin Ltd., (1951).

———*The Quest after Perfection*, Mysore: Karyalaya Publishers, (1952).

Iyer, Venkatarama: *Advaita Vedānta*, Delhi: Motilal Banarsidass.

Iyengar, Srinivasa: *The Metaphysics of Value* (2 Vols.).

Kant, Immanuel: *Fundamental Principles of the Metaphysics of Ethics* (tr.) Abbot, London: Longman Green & Co., (1949).

Kane, Pandurang Varman: *History of Dharmaśāstras* (Vols. I & II) Poona: Kalyan Steam Press.

Lad, A.K.: *A Comparative Study of the Concept of Liberation in Indian Philosophy*, Rewa Deptt. of Philosophy, T.R.S. College (1967).

Maitra, S.K.: *The Ethics of the Hindus*, Calcutta: University of Calcutta, (1956).

Murti, T.R.V.: *The Central Philosophy of Buddhism*, London: George Allen & Unwin Ltd., (1960).

Moore, Charles A. (Ed.): *Philosophy—East and West*, Princeton, N.J.: Princeton University Press, (1946).

Moore, G.E.: *Principia Ethica*, London: Oxford University Press, (1952).

Radhakrishnan, S.: *Indian Philosophy* (2 Vols.), London: George Allen & Unwin Ltd., (1948).

———*Eastern Religions and Western Thought*, London: Oxford University Press, (1940).

———*Idealistic View of Life*, London: George Allen & Unwin Ltd., (1947).

———*Hindu View of Life*, London: George Allen & Unwin Ltd., (1951).

Radhakrishnan, S. and Raju, P.T. (Ed.): *The Concept of Man*, London: George Allen & Unwin Ltd., (1960).

Raju, P.T.: *Idealistic Thought of India*, London: George Allen & Unwin Ltd. (1953).

Rashdall, Hastings: *The Theory of Good and Evil* (2 Vols.), London: Oxford University Press, (1948).

Riepe, Dale: *The Naturalistic Traditions in Indian Thought*, Delhi: Motilal Banarsidass, (1964).

Singh, Ram Pratap: *The Vedānta of Śaṅkara, A Metaphysics of Value* (Vol. I), Jaipur: Bharat Publishing House, (1949).

Shastri, D. Ranjan: '*Cārvāka Philosophy*,' *The Humanist Way*, Calcutta, (1950).

Spinoza, Benedict: *The Ethics, The Chief Works of Benedict De Spinoza* (2 Vols.) (Tr.) R.H.M. Elwes, London: George Bell and Sons, (1898).

Stcherbatsky, Ph.: *The Central Conception of Buddhism and The Meaning of the Word 'Dharma'*. London: Royal Asiatic Society, (1923).

Spranger, Edward: *Lebens Formen* (Eng. Tr.) *Forms of Life*, Bonn.

Tagore, Rabindranath: *The Religion of Man*, London: George Allen & Unwin Ltd., (1949).

Urban, W.M.: *Fundamental of Ethics*, New York: Henry Holt and Company, (1949).

Zimmer, Henry R.: *Philosophy of India*, (ed. Joseph Campbell), New York: Pantheon Books, (1953).

Index